"THE GIANTS WIN THE PENNANT! THE GIANTS WIN THE PENNANT!"

"THE GIANTS WIN THE PENNANT! THE GIANTS WIN THE PENNANT!"

CITADEL PRESS
KENSINGTON PUBLISHING CORP.
www.kensingtonbooks.com

CITADEL PRESS books are published by

Kensington Publishing Corp.
850 Third Avenue
New York, NY 10022

All Kensington titles, imprints, and distributed lines are available at special quantity discounts for bulk purchases for sales promotions, premiums, fundraising, educational, or institutional use. Special book excerpts or customized printings can also be created to fit specific needs. For details, write or phone the office of the Kensington special sales manager: Kensington Publishing Corp., 850 Third Avenue, New York, NY 10022, attn: Special Sales Department, phone 1-800-221-2647.

Citadel Press logo Reg. U.S. Patent and Trademark Office
Citadel Press is a trademark of Kensington Publishing Corp.

First Citadel printing: April 2001

10   9   8   7   6   5   4   3   2   1

Printed in the United States of America

Library of Congress Catalog Card Number: 91-061500

ISBN 0-8065-2300-X

I would like to dedicate this book to Winkie, who was always there to encourage me and support me through the good times and occasionally the not-so-good times. Also to my Mom and Dad, who endured much hardship to bring me to America, and to my sisters and brother, Jim, who were always my greatest fans and were there to root for me.

B.T.

To my wife, Roberta, who exhibited nothing but good cheer and tolerance, and uttered nary a negative word during the many months I was totally immersed in the spirit and drama of the 1951 National League pennant race. And most of all, to those marvelous men who played all-out baseball 40 years ago and gave us a vivid portrayal of what the game was like back then.

L.H.

For my wife, Cathy. Thanks again for your patience, support, understanding and your help.

B.G.

It's just something about baseball. People remember an important hit, a special occasion, a World Series game, a pennant clinching. It's amazing the way these things stay with baseball fans. They remember as if it were yesterday.

—Stan Musial

A thing that I hate with a passion came from a man I liked. I remember hearing Russ Hodges' call—*The Giants win the pennant! The Giants win the pennant!*—over and over again. I just hate it with all my heart. But, oh, would it have been wonderful to have been in their shoes, to come back and do such a thing. That's what sports is all about.

—Clem Labine

The greatest thrill in the world is to end the game with a home run and watch everybody else walk off the field while you're running the bases on air.

—Al Rosen

Contents

Acknowledgments

In retracing and recreating the many details and circumstances of the historic 1951 pennant race, we found it necessary to examine many sources, some going back more than half a century. We also wanted to speak to as many people as possible who participated, both directly and indirectly, in one of baseball's greatest dramas. The research and subsequent assembling of a large amount of material would not have been possible without the generous help of the following people, all of whom donated their time, knowledge, and recollections, allowing us to bring this project to its completion.

The authors would like to thank Harvey Garbar, whose knowledge of both baseball and the law were invaluable; Larry Mandel, who was at the third game of the Giant-Dodger playoff and whose keen memory was a rich source of leads and information; Dr. Ted Saretsky, whose insights helped clarify the psychological aspects of the 1951 pennant race; Phil Berger and Dave Weiner, who helped provide leads to additional sources of information; Larry Petterson of the New York Public Library, who allowed us to open dusty old files at both the New York and Brooklyn library systems; Sal Morriello of the Freeport High School Library, who went to great pains to furnish us with old materials from the 1930s, '40s and '50s, including access to his own fine collection; Bill Deane of the Baseball Hall of Fame, who provided valuable material from the archives at Cooperstown; and Jay Behrke, whose time and effort enabled us to have detailed accounts of each and every game the Giants and Dodgers played during 1951.

Also thanks to Roberta Heiman, who put in countless hours typing and proofreading, as well as making helpful editorial suggestions; and Celeste Giandalone, Kathleen Stymacks, and Cathy Gutman, who performed the arduous task of transcribing hours and hours of taped interviews.

We would also like to thank those people who were willing to search through four decades of memories and speak candidly about the pennant race, its origins, and its aftermath. They include former newspapermen Charlie Feeney and Jack Lang, current secretary of the Baseball Writers Association of America; broadcasters Ernie Harwell and Red Barber; publicist Irving Rudd; writer Donald Honig; statistician Allan Roth; Mrs. Jean Thomson Hicks; Mrs. Elaine "Winkie" Thomson; and Al Corbin.

Also, thanks to former ball players and coaches Bill Rigney, Carl Erskine, Whitey Lockman, Rube Walker, Pee Wee Reese, Sam Jethroe, Walker Cooper, Andy Pafko, Clem Labine, Alvin Dark, Willard Marshall, Duke Snider, Wes Westrum, Don Newcombe, Stan Musial, Warren Spahn, Larry Jansen, Clyde Sukeforth, Herman Franks, Monte Irvin, Don Mueller, Dick Williams, and Jim Hearn.

And a very special thanks to Leo Durocher and Ralph Branca, not only for talking freely about an event that has meant so much to their lives, but also for consenting to write a foreword and an afterword which shed additional light on "The Shot Heard Round the World."

Thank you again, one and all.

Bobby Thomson
Lee Heiman
Bill Gutman
March 1991

Authors' Notes

When a home run that was hit 40 years ago is still talked about today, perhaps it's not unusual that a book covering the event would follow. Unless, of course, the author of the home run has the name Bobby Thomson. I didn't feel at all comfortable with the idea since I'm basically a private person. I also wondered how many people would be interested in a book about a guy who had a fairly good, but inconsistent baseball career. With a bit of prodding, I finally decided to go ahead and do the book.

I have always felt that I received more attention than I deserved for hitting one home run. There can be little doubt that the Pittsburgh fans consider Bill Mazeroski's home run against the Yankees in the 1960 World Series a bigger event than my '51 shot. Yankee fans probably feel that Don Larsen's perfect game in the 1956 World Series was more memorable. In Boston, Red Sox rooters are likely to talk more about Carlton Fisk's dramatic homer in the 1975 Series than mine.

But we have done a book and I would like to express my sincere appreciation to my teammates and former opponents (especially the Dodgers) for their willingness to share their time and recollections from 40 years ago in helping us to complete the book. Certainly, it was Leo, the coaches and 25 ballplayers who won the 1951 pennant.

There are many other people, including a number of good friends, who have been part of my life both in and out of baseball and who could have contributed to my story. I wish it was possible to include all of them.

Not to mention a word here about my immediate family would be like hitting an inside the park home run and having it nullified for failing to touch first base. My daughter Nancy Mitchell and son-in-law Chuck have blessed us with two wonderful grandchildren, Megan and Coley, son Bob is a recent graduate of Rutgers University and my daughter Megan is presently working in Bethesda, Maryland. They are all a major reason I decided to do this book.

It would be nice to think that in the years ahead my grandchildren and those who follow will find enjoyment in reading about my career and about the 1951 Giants.

B.T.

I now find it hard to believe, but 40 years ago the big love in my life, my reason for living, was a baseball team called the Brooklyn Dodgers. If it sounds crazy consider this; I wasn't alone. There were tens of thousands of Brooklynites who felt the same way. Nowhere on the face of this earth was there ever a group of fans whose loyalty ran as deep and all-giving as Brooklyn fans.

Then on October 3, 1951, the first major heartbreak of my life occurred when Bobby Thomson hit the "Shot Heard Round the World." Brooklyn that night was a city in mourning.

But now, 40 years later, it has become evident to me that within that excruciatingly painful defeat for the Dodgers and their fans lies an exquisite truth. This is what baseball, and indeed life, is all about. Everything is possible. Take nothing for granted.

Leo Durocher and his New York Giants scratched and fought against unbelievable odds to force an unscheduled playoff against the Dodgers. What began as the story of Bobby Thomson's life and career, and a recreation of the 1951 pennant race soon became much more, a story with many strange twists and turns, a great deal of controversy as well as racial overtones. I am proud to be part of the telling of the complete story.

L.H.

I can remember rushing into the house from school on October 3, 1951, and charging upstairs where my mother had the Giant-Dodger playoff game on television. Like most young Yankee fans, I hated the Dodgers. Yet here it was the ninth inning and Brooklyn had a 4-1 lead. Within seconds of my arrival, the score was 4-2 and the Giants had two runners on base with Bobby Thomson at the plate.

Although I was not quite nine years old, I sized up the situation immediately and told my mother, "Only a home run will save the Giants now."

Seconds later, they were saved. Thomson slammed Branca's second pitch into the leftfield seats and I leaped into the air with glee. Though I would revert to being a Yankee fan the very next day, Bobby's home run filled me with jubilation. It was truly a moment I have never forgotten.

That memory has made this project even more enjoyable. Talking to Bobby and so many others from a bygone era has been both pleasurable and informative. The 1951 pennant race contained many contrasting elements and complex personalities that provided us with numerous surprises. Yet, at the same time, baseball was more of a game back then and its great moments should not be forgotten.

B.G.

Foreword

by Leo Durocher

It's no secret that I always played to win. Hell, it was the only way I knew, especially since losing left me with a rotten feeling. It was that way from the day I first came to the big leagues as a player in 1925 until the day I retired as a manager in 1973. When you played with teams like the New York Yankees of Murderers Row fame of the late 1920s and the St. Louis Cardinals' Gas House Gang of the middle 1930s, you had to play that way to survive. Those guys fought and scrapped to win, something I had been doing all my life, as far back as I can remember.

My first manager in the big leagues was Miller Huggins with the Yankees. His philosophy was simple—I come to play and I come to win. That was the way Huggins broke me in and that's the way it's always been with me ever since. I loved that little guy. Then at St. Louis I played alongside guys like Frankie Frisch, Dizzy Dean, Joe Medwick, and Pepper Martin. Fighters, each and every one of them. They fought with the opposition and sometimes even among themselves.

But looking back now, I would have undoubtedly played that same way even if I hadn't made it to the big leagues. It wouldn't have mattered whether it was in the minors, on the sandlots, or wherever I could find a game. The overwhelming need to win was always there, the thing that drove me and made me drive others. As a manager, I

1

used to say, give me some scratching, diving, hungry ball players who come to kill you. That was always the kind of team I wanted to play on, and the kind of team I had to manage.

When I took over the New York Giants in 1948 the team's owner, Horace Stoneham, asked me to evaluate the ball club. My answer to him was short and sweet. I said, "Horace, back up the truck." Even though the Giants had set a major league record with 221 home runs in 1947, they were a ball club that couldn't win, a team of sluggers with very little speed or defensive ability. They lived and died by the long ball, and to be successful, I knew I had to make major changes.

By 1950 I was beginning to feel I almost had the team I wanted. Building the ball club wasn't always easy. There were times when Horace and I really went at it over player moves. But once I started putting together my kind of team, I didn't want to stop until the job was done. And if that meant butting heads with the owner, then we butted heads.

I had traded for Al Dark and Eddie Stanky, two guys who would do anything to win and were natural leaders on the ball field. And I was able to work young players like Whitey Lockman, Don Mueller, and Wes Westrum into the lineup. Monte Irvin, who didn't reach the majors until the age of 30 because of the color of his skin, was also ready to make his mark. Sal Maglie, back from the Mexican League, and Larry Jansen were my two best pitchers, both capable of beating anyone.

The only leftover starter from that power-hitting 1947 team was Bobby Thomson. Bobby was a rookie in '47 and had it not been for Jackie Robinson, he or his teammate Larry Jansen, who was 21–5, might well have been the Rookie of the Year. Though Bobby contributed 29 homers to that ball club, he was definitely more than just a slugger. He may also have been the fastest man in the league. I don't think there was anyone who could go from first to home as quickly as Bobby or anyone who could beat him in a hundred-yard dash.

He was still my center fielder in 1950 and a solid all-around player. Of course, I had no way of knowing then the role Bobby would play for all of us—for all of baseball—the very next year. I do know that in the spring of 1951 I told everyone that my ball club would win. We had finished a strong third in 1950 and there could be no more excuses in '51. We had to win. Sure, that was a lot of pressure to put on myself and on the team. But like I said, you play to win, and I wanted everyone on the team thinking that way, thinking pennant. Second place was nothing. It just wasn't good enough.

I've always felt that a manager has to have confidence, both in himself and in the men he puts out on the field. Back in 1951, there was still room for only 16 men in all of America to manage a big league ball club. That's a rather small fraternity and there were always guys knocking on the door. So you had to have the confidence you could do the job and that meant being able to handle your players. Besides having a consummate knowledge of the game, a manager also had to be a master psychologist.

Each player was different. Some, like Dark and Stanky, never needed a wake-up call. They were ready every day. Hell, those two were ready every minute. But others needed an occasional kick in the pants, a few had to be babied a bit, and some had to be angry at someone to play well, even if it was the manager. And it was the manager's job to make sure they were.

I never had a complaint with a guy who came to play every day. In fact, if a guy gave me everything he had on the field, I'd back him 100 percent off the field. If I felt he deserved a raise, I'd go to bat for him with management. And believe me, I got in hot water on more than one occasion for doing that. But if a guy won for me, he was my man, because he was helping to put money in all our pockets.

Despite everything I've just said, the Giants of 1951 got off to a terrible start. Before the season was a week old we were in the midst of an 11-game losing streak and people were beginning to write us off. We weren't hitting and weren't playing well defensively. I knew right then and there that I couldn't stand pat, that I'd have to make even more changes.

I made a number of moves, but the biggest was bringing Willie Mays up from the minors in May. Willie was just 20 years old then and his natural talent was unbelievable. He was hitting .477 and playing a great center field for Minneapolis in the American Association. It took a while to convince Mr. Stoneham that I needed Willie and he wasn't an overnight sensation when I finally got him. Time and patience proved to be the necessary ingredients on my part before he began to produce. But then things began to happen, because Willie's arrival necessitated other changes that turned out to be just as important to the success of the club. In a sense, Willie was the final piece to the puzzle, because all of the changes I made worked, and that's what made us a championship ball club.

Willie, of course, took over in center. I also moved Whitey Lockman from the outfield to first base, where he quickly became a very solid first sacker. Monte Irvin, who was floundering at first, returned to left. Not only did Monte play an outstanding left field, but he was invaluable in helping Willie to play the hitters and learn about the league. Of course, once the ball was in the air, Willie didn't need help from anyone.

The other change involved the man I'm really writing about— Bobby Thomson. Bobby had been my center fielder since 1949 and he did a good job for me. He could run with anyone and make all the plays. But center had to be Willie's position. He had all the instincts of a great center fielder, plus a rocket for a throwing arm. And if you remember the old Polo Grounds, center field seemed to go on forever.

So Bobby eventually became my third baseman. To his credit, he accepted the change without complaint because he knew it was for the good of the team. Back then, most players thought about the team first and themselves second. And that's the way it should be.

Anyway, Bobby did a fine job at third. Like everyone else, he made a few mistakes, but he was also capable of making the big play for us. Even more importantly, though, he didn't let the change affect his hitting. In fact, Bobby may have been our best hitter during the stretch drive, and he wound up leading the team with 32 home runs and finishing second in RBIs with 101.

I don't think there's a baseball fan anywhere in America who doesn't know how things ended in 1951. In the final weeks of August we won 16 straight games to get back in the race, then chased down the Dodgers until we finally caught them the next to last day of the season. And brother, was it exciting. It was the kind of excitement that could only be created by the most intense, heated rivalry in all of sports. Every time we met there was electricity in the air, helped by the media crush and the enthusiasm of the fans for both teams. It was the same on the ball field. Whenever the Dodgers and Giants played each other, hitters could expect to be picking themselves up out of the dirt. Knockdown pitches were part of the game and both teams were going to protect their players.

There was even more to it than that. Since I had managed the Dodgers from 1939 through 1946, I had a hand in building that ball club, as well. Then in 1947 I was out of baseball for a year after being suspended by Commissioner Happy Chandler. He never elaborated on the reasons at the time and while I never claimed to be a goody two-shoes, to this day I could not tell you why I was suspended. Hell, you can even ask the sportswriters who covered the story at the time. They didn't know, either.

But I returned to the Dodgers in 1948 only to move across the river to the hated Giants after just 75 games. Yet, as soon as I joined the Giants, the Dodgers became my mortal enemies and I wanted to beat them as badly as anyone else. It's funny how things happen. I still wonder whether I would have left the Dodgers if I hadn't been suspended the year before. And if I hadn't switched from the Dodgers to the Giants in '48 I doubt very much if we would have had the pennant race of 1951. Things surely would have been somehow different, especially with the Giants.

None of that really matters now. What matters is that we were losing the third and final playoff game, 4–1, in the last of the ninth inning. Yet we didn't quit. We rallied and then Bobby Thomson hit perhaps the most famous home run in baseball history. They still call it the Shot Heard Round the World. But no matter what name it's given, the bottom line was that it won a pennant for me and the Giants, and earned Bobby a permanent place in baseball history. I know it was a moment I'll never forget, one of the most exciting single moments I experienced in all my years in baseball.

They say that for great things to happen, the right person has to be in the right place at the right time. On October 3, 1951, Bobby Thomson was that guy. But besides being there, he came through royally in one of the most pressure-packed situations I can imagine. Looking back now, I'm glad Bobby was the one who did it. He was one of the greatest guys to ever play for me and I really don't know anyone who has ever said a bad word about him . . . not counting the old Brooklyn Dodger fans, of course. That's one reason why I was happy to help out when I learned that Bobby was telling his story and the story of the 1951 pennant race.

I can't tell you what old-time baseball fans think about when they hear the name Leo Durocher today. I'd like to think they remember me as a winner, because that was the one thing I always strived to achieve. Many, I'm sure, also remember a line of mine that has been quoted and repeated quite often over the years.

Nice guys finish last!
Yeah, I said it, all right. In fact, it was the title of my autobiography and in many instances I believe it to be true. But let's face it, there are exceptions to every rule. An exception to that one has got to be Bobby Thomson. He's a nice guy who has never finished last, and knowing Bobby all these years, I'm sure he never will.

Prologue

The date was October 3, 1951. The place: the Polo Grounds in New York City. More than 34,000 fans had come to watch the New York Giants and the Brooklyn Dodgers go at each other for one final time. It was the third and deciding game of just the second best-of-three pennant playoffs in National League history—winner take all between two teams that had the fiercest rivalry in the world of sports. Yet, by all rights there should never have even been a baseball game played in that ancient ballyard at the foot of Coogan's Bluff on that early October afternoon.

For most of the preceding five months, there was no question which team would be the National League champion. The Dodgers were on target for a nearly wire-to-wire run, ready to justify their growing reputation as one of the great teams of recent years. While the Giants had clawed their way into second place, it didn't appear that they could go any further. As late as August 11, they trailed their Brooklyn rivals by a seemingly insurmountable 13½ games.

It was only then that the real story of the 1951 season began to unfold. The Giants parlayed a 16-game winning streak into an incredible 37–7 finish. The result was a season-ending tie, necessitating a playoff that would hold the entire baseball world hostage to its energy and drama. Yet, even with the unfolding, sudden-death scenario, no one would have dared to predict the outcome of the deciding game. It was the stuff from which legends are made.

The words that have been written about that overcast October afternoon, depicting the ball game and its once-in-a-lifetime ending, are too numerous to count. Writer after writer has described in his own way the wonder of an event that wasn't supposed to happen. It was a game with a crescendo of a finish so unbelievably dramatic that it almost defies description. It was a game that has been analyzed and dissected, second-guessed and what-if'd more than any game played in recent baseball history. Its closing moment has been replayed incessantly over the years, especially in today's nostalgia-filled baseball world, in which the past often occupies the same lofty position of importance as the present.

There isn't a diehard baseball fan anywhere who can't relate to the late Russ Hodges's delirious voice, exalting in a frenzy of emotion: *The Giants win the pennant! The Giants win the pennant!*

Hodges would repeat those words four consecutive times to his radio audience before even remotely describing what had happened on the field. But he didn't have to. Everyone listening knew immediately. New York Giants third baseman Bobby Thomson had hit a three-run, last-of-the-ninth-inning homer that brought his team from the brink of defeat to a 5–4, pennant-winning victory. The game ended with such swift and shocking suddenness that even some of the participants couldn't believe it was over.

"I was in shock," Dodger shortstop and captain Pee Wee Reese said recently. "To this day I honestly can't remember how I got to our clubhouse, which was in dead center field in the old Polo Grounds. I don't remember whether I ran there or whether I walked there, or whether I talked to anyone on the way out. I couldn't stop thinking that it wasn't really over, that we had another chance, another time at bat or *something*. It was some kind of time out and we were going to go back out and play some more. They just couldn't do this to us. They just couldn't beat us with one swing of the bat, not after we were ahead like that all year!"

Bobby Thomson's home run, of course, became known as "The Shot Heard Round the World" and it is still considered one of the single most dramatic moments in baseball history. It is a home run that has grown to Bunyanesque proportions, transcending by a large margin the encyclopedic facts and figures, strategies and statistics so dear to the hearts of baseball buffs everywhere.

There have been exciting pennant races before and since, as well as dramatic, game-ending hits and home runs: Gabby Hartnett's "Homer in the Gloamin' " in 1938, Bill Mazeroski's World Series–winning shot in 1960, Chris Chambliss's pennant-winning poke in 1976, and Bucky Dent's drive over Fenway Park's Green Monster in 1978 are all well-remembered four-baggers that surely rank right up there with Thomson's blast. But Thomson's homer always had a special, almost surreal quality about it. And as if the game and the ending weren't enough, the players on the two teams also added to the drama. They were as diverse a group of competing personalities as ever captured the imagination of their fans and the baseball world at large. It began with the managers, Leo Durocher of the Giants and Charley Dressen of the Dodgers. Durocher had started out as the Brooklyn skipper with Dressen not only as one of his coaches, but also his oft-described right hand man as well. Leo's move to the Giants in 1948 sent shock waves through the baseball world. But it did something else, as well. It also set up the eventual confrontation with Dressen, a man who was driven to prove he was more than the equal of his former boss as a field leader. Thus, each meeting between the two teams had the potential for a myriad of managerial moves and decisions that would be more conducive to a tactical chess match than a baseball game. And when these failed, the pitchers simply knocked the hitters down.

Even apart from the managers, a Giant-Dodger game was a knock-down, drag-out battle. Both teams were loaded with individuals whose names are still highly recognizable today. Each game was a show in itself, starring Robinson, Reese, Irvin, Maglie, Newcombe, Roe, Mays, Thomson, Hodges, Snider, Dark, Stanky, Furillo, Campanella, Lockman, Jansen, Erskine, Cox, Mueller, and Westrum. These were the players who would eventually produce a script that would make storytellers from New York to Hollywood green with envy.

But it was even more than the players that made the event so remarkable. It was the very nature of the game itself. In the early 1950s, baseball was entering a period of growth and change. By 1951, four years had passed since Branch Rickey and Jackie Robinson had combined forces to break baseball's infamous "gentleman's agreement" that prevented any black man from participating in the national pastime. Yet, there had still been no stampede to sign black players. Aside from the Dodgers and Giants, only one other team in the National League had a black player in 1951. He was Sam Jethroe, the center fielder for the Boston Braves. The presence of the black players on the two New York ball clubs, however, would figure prominently in the pennant race in several ways.

All of these factors combined to make the National League pennant race the main show, the featured performance in 1951. Even the World Series that year was something of an anticlimax. Baseball had already reached the pinnacle and the fall classic was clearly played on the back side of the mountain, on the way down.

While Leo Durocher had brashly predicted victory for his Giants even before the season began, the immediate scenario had the loquacious Lip running for cover. After the first three games, his team plunged into the tailspin of an 11-game losing streak, a disaster most experts felt had sealed the Giants' fate even before the grass at Ebbets Field and the Polo Grounds had started its late spring surge of growth.

By midseason, the Dodgers' fanatical but also prudent fans dared to peek into the future, and began wondering if this was the year their beloved team would finally become world champions, maybe even beating that "other" New York team, the one that occupied the high-rent district of the Big Apple's diamond hierarchy, the nearly invincible Yankees.

But all that changed in late season when the Giants got hot and Bobby Thomson had his final chance to swing the bat. For the Dodgers, it was a disaster of still-lingering proportions. For the Giants, it was a victory whose sweetness would whet the taste buds of the memory for generations. And for Bobby Thomson, it was a moment that would change his life forever.

Ancient Greek dramatists created a device to solve the difficulties of a wayward plot in need of a dramatic ending. The deus ex machina usually took the form of a godlike figure that would descend to the stage at a moment of near defeat and achieve, with a mighty blow, battlefield success. Though a mere mortal, Bobby Thomson became the Giants' deus ex machina for one glorious day.

His is a story of almost fairy-tale, once-upon-a-time proportions—an immigrant youngster from Scotland who is a baseball star in his adopted land and with one swing of the bat becomes an American legend. Though Bobby didn't immediately recognize the enormity of his heroics, others did. The eloquent sportswriter Red Smith knew that Bobby's home run was a larger-than-life achievement. "Now it is done," he wrote. "Now the story ends. And there is no way to tell it. The art of fiction is dead. Reality has strangled invention. Only the utterly impossible, the inexpressibly fantastic, can ever be plausible again."

A second man also achieved a certain immortality that day. There's hardly a baseball fan alive who doesn't know that Ralph Branca was on the mound for Brooklyn when Bobby Thomson connected. The two men would become eternally and inexorably linked. Thomson and Branca. Branca and Thomson. It's hard to mention one without the other. The remarkable fact is that the two men have become genuine friends who often appear together at golf tournaments, old-timer's days, card shows, and other baseball gatherings. But don't think for a minute that the old competitive fires have burned out. Branca has said time and again: "I would give back every dime I have made from that pitch if I could go back in time and strike Bobby out."

Similarly, Thomson can't forget a base-running gaffe he made earlier in the game—steaming into second with teammate Whitey Lockman already there—and a couple of questionable plays he didn't make at third. He candidly admits, "If I didn't hit the home run I may well have been the goat."

But, in reality, this is more than a simple story of a hero and a goat, a perception that has been too easily accepted over the years. The events that created the 1951 season began much earlier, even before Leo Durocher managed the Dodgers and Branch Rickey was his boss. The old "what if?" adage certainly applies, because the extenuating circumstances are so many. If only one of these occurrences had changed or if the sequence of events had somehow broken, there would have been no real pennant race in 1951, no playoff, and no chance for Bobby Thomson to create baseball's greatest moment.

Rocky Bridges, a rookie utility infielder on the '51 Dodgers, once told Ralph Branca: "You didn't lose the pennant. We lost it because we were beaten on opening day."

Simple, but true. One more Dodger victory, one additional Giant loss—that's all it would have taken. Yet, as Bobby himself remarked to a teammate before the ninth inning of the third and final playoff game: "Can you imagine? We've played almost 157 games and nothing is resolved." Shortly after making his comment, Bobby would resolve it all.

This is Bobby Thomson's story, told fully and completely for the first time in 40 years. It's a testament to his greatest moment, and also the story of his life before, during, and after the one swing of the bat that has made him an everlasting legend.

It is also the story of two great baseball teams, bitter rivals, who once staged a pennant race unlike any before or since. There might be some that are statistically comparable, but none would have the personal undercurrents, the intensity, the near hatreds so often tempered by profound respect. None involved two major league teams in such close proximity geographically. And because both the Giants and Dodgers decided to seek their fortunes 3,000 miles away, it can never happen again.

 **BOBBY**

A Home Run on the Shelf

I remember reading a clipping about a Scotsman who won, I
think, the Nobel Prize. The article described the man's personality, but it might have well been Bob's. He hated pretentious-
ness, was completely turned off by any kind of ostentation,
played himself down, was humble to a point where it was a
fault. I sometimes think this has been the monkey on Bob's
back, his thing to handle in life. He's sensitive and humble to a
fault with a tendency to play himself down.

—Elaine "Winkie" Thomson

What do you do when your whole life has been wrapped up in the
game of baseball and suddenly it's over? It's something all big
leaguers have to face. When I played, the guys didn't have the built-in
financial security players have now. And many of them—myself included—really didn't give life after baseball a second thought until it
was right there, staring them in the face. But I sensed it was coming.

The 1960 season was by far the most frustrating of my career. Sure,
I had all the memories, good friends, good years, and good teams. And
the 1951 season. But by 1960 that was ancient history, a glorious
moment that suddenly seemed irrelevant. In fact, when it was time to
answer the big question—Hey, Bobby, what are you going to do with
the rest of your life?—my entire career seemed irrelevant.

If I had been smarter at the time I'd have seen it coming. I spent the
1959 season with the Cubs and as soon as it ended I made a point to
talk with the ball club about the next year. When they offered me a
contract for 1960 I figured, heck, I'm all set. What I didn't remember
was that baseball is always changing. The Cubs needed pitching and
Thomson was the bait. On December 1, I was traded to Boston for a
righthander named Al Schroll.

When you're 36 years old and going to your fourth team in four
years, you should begin getting the message, the one that labels you
a bounced-around ball player. But because I felt I could still play, I

said, "Oh well, let's go to Boston." But a strange thing happened the following March. Wink and I had just bought our home in Watchung, New Jersey, and were having a good time during the off-season fixing it up. One day Wink reminded me that spring training was just around the corner. For the first time in my baseball life I didn't want to go, and I'd been around long enough to know that ball players weren't supposed to think that way.

We had bought our home in 1958 when I was playing in Chicago. But both of us were easterners and Wink was brought up in New Jersey, so we decided to settle there. It had nothing to do with my future, whether it was in baseball or not. I always felt your home is completely separate from baseball, so the decision was simply based on where we wanted to live. By 1960, we were at the point where the house was in pretty good shape. And there I was, with no real enthusiasm for spring training. In a nutshell, baseball wasn't much fun anymore.

Maybe I wouldn't have felt the same if I stayed with the Cubs, but now it was a kind of here-we-go-again feeling, getting bounced around. I wasn't happy with my performance. Throw in my age, 36, and I guess it should have been clear what was coming. But that didn't make it any easier. The other side of me kept saying, "Bobby, you can still play this game."

But the spring training thing was a definite tip-off. Most ball players love spring training and I had been no exception. It's a fun time and I had a wife who looked forward to it as much as I did. We were always raring to go . . . until 1960. Even though I wasn't earning as much as I had in the early and middle 1950s, my salary was a good one. There was never really a question of not going to spring training that year. I just didn't go with the same attitude.

Playing in Boston would be a new experience, my introduction to the American League, and I went there not knowing what my role with the ball club would be. When I got there, no one told me anything. That isn't easy for a guy who was used to playing regularly. I sat some at Milwaukee, but had started 152 games with Chicago just two years earlier. With Boston, I was *really* sitting and things can become pretty clear when that happens. For one thing, you feel like you've been kicked in the ass because management thinks someone else can do the job better than you. But I was a pragmatic guy. I sat on the bench and waited.

There were the other signs, as well. I still played the outfield, but there was one game when Vic Wertz, the regular Red Sox first baseman, got hurt and they asked me to fill in for him. I was certainly willing to try it, since I had played some second as a rookie back in 1947, and quite a few games at third. We were playing Cleveland at Fenway Park and early in the game Harvey Kuenn bunted, undoubtedly trying to take advantage of a guy playing first for the first time. I ran in to field it and literally booted it, kicked the ball with my damn foot.

Then they tried a pickoff play at first. The pitcher threw the hell out of the ball, right across the runner, and I had to lunge for it. It went off my glove and that's when the fans started getting on me. I'll never forget it. Late in the game I came up and got into a good battle with the pitcher. I fouled a bunch of balls off and finally got a hit off the wall in left, but overall that certainly wasn't one of my better days on the field.

I didn't consciously try to pull the ball at Fenway because of the short wall. I had heard enough stories about that. Walt Dropo supposedly used the wall as an excuse, claiming it screwed up his batting style. I always believed in hitting naturally and taking your chances. But I also remember thinking, Hey, if I can't play here I ought to quit.

Because I was new to the team I was more of a loner than ever before. When we went out on the road I didn't have any real buddies to hang around with. I don't even remember who my roommate was. So another fun part of the game was gone. I guess the most enjoyable part of the whole experience was being around Ted Williams. It was Ted's last year, too, and I got a kick out of playing alongside him. Ted was a unique individual and he talked hitting all the time. Hitting, hitting, hitting. It was an obsession with him. But it wasn't until one afternoon in Boston that I realized guys like me didn't think like Ted Williams. Ted would watch other guys take batting practice whenever he could. I remember taking my five swings that day and then going to the outfield to shag. All of a sudden Ted is standing beside me.

"Which one of your five swings did you like the best?" he asked.

He took me by surprise, kind of woke me up, and I had to think a little bit. Finally, I said, "Well, I hit that second pitch off the left field wall. I guess that was the best one."

"No," he said, without hesitating for a second. "That third pitch. It was outside, but you went out and got it, and hit it right through the middle. Base hit up the middle."

That was his thinking, his philosophy. You don't try to pull the outside pitch, just go up the middle with it. Otherwise, it's a ground ball to the shortstop. But that was the difference between Ted and a lot of the rest of us. He thought about his hitting constantly. Most of us just went up, looked for the ball, and swung at it. If we were thinking at all it was: "I'm not gonna swing at a pitch until I get one right where I want it or until I get two strikes." With two strikes, you've got to protect yourself.

On the other hand, I can remember a night in St. Louis years before. I wasn't hitting well and Al Dark started shouting at me.

"Come on, Hoot Mon, pull the ball. Go up there and tell yourself you're gonna pull the ball."

The pitcher threw me an outside pitch and I just let my wrists go and pulled it off the wall in left. Williams's philosophy worked for him, but how many of us are Ted Williams?

Other than enjoying Ted, my stint in Boston didn't go well. I began to feel like I was just hanging on. No one even mentioned the home run anymore. It was like it never happened. In a sense, I had forgotten about it, too. It wasn't about to help me get more at bats.

The funny part—or maybe the sad part—of the Boston experience was that it ended just as Winkie and I were starting to get used to being there. After spending the whole spring in hotels we finally found a home to rent for the summer. It must have been close to midseason and I remember Wink and I and our daughter had just sat down to dinner our first night there when the phone call came. It said, So long, Bob. I had been released.

As difficult as it was to take, I still considered myself a ball player. By that time any sensible guy would be looking ahead, but I didn't. My first instinct was to find a way to finish out the season. Wink and I still didn't sit down and try to figure out what the future might hold for us although looking back now, it's hard to know why we didn't. Of course, if I hooked up with another ball club and finished the season, I'd still get paid. My baseball salary still represented more money than I thought I could make elsewhere.

Two teams contacted me, the Orioles and the Indians. None from the National League. I thought it over and chose Baltimore, simply because it was an East Coast team and closer to home. I had to sit around a week or two until they could make room for me on their roster, then I was activated. Again, I didn't analyze the situation. All I knew then was that if a team signed you, they wanted you to put the suit on and win some ball games for them. They didn't pick you up because they liked the way you combed your hair.

Talk about going from bad to worse. Maybe I should have gotten a clue when we flew down from Boston to join the team. When we landed in Baltimore one of the first guys I saw was Jim Gentile, the big first baseman. Jim shook hands with me and said, "Welcome to Donkeyville." Apparently the Baltimore fans had a reputation for booing their players.

Paul Richards was the Oriole manager and he had a reputation for being a fine baseball man. But all he said to me when I got there was "hello" and that was it. The first week I wasn't playing because I was waiting for the roster spot to open. But I was with the team. One day, just after the game ended, one of the coaches said that Paul wanted me to come out and take some batting practice. I thought, gee, the guy has some interest in me after all. I even made the mistake of being flattered by it.

So I got dressed, grabbed a bat, and rushed out to the cage. Standing out on the mound was a young left-hander, Steve Barber. He was a rookie with great stuff, but he was leading the league in walks and was trying to find his control. And that's why Richards wanted someone out there. He needed a body. Barber got one pitch in five over the plate and I'm up there trying to take batting practice. I should have seen it for the insult it was. Here I was looking to get my timing back and he's got a wild kid out there firing all over the place.

I should have said to Richards right there, "You've got a helluva nerve calling this batting practice." But I didn't. I took it. And that pretty much defined my role with the Orioles. The only guy I knew on the ball club was Hoyt Wilhelm, who had come up with the Giants in '52. Hoyt used to kid around with me, trying to set me up racing against young guys, like I used to do with the Giants. But those days were gone, too.

I was in only a handful of games and it didn't go well. I was playing left field one day at Comiskey Park and I let a fly ball drop behind me, a ball I could have caught in my hip pocket a few years earlier. And for the first time a very scary thought went through my mind: Bob, you don't belong here anymore.

Looking back, I don't think the problem was physical. It had become a mental thing. I remember talking to Bob Lemon, the great Cleveland pitcher, some years later. He told me a story about Al Rosen, who was a heck of a good slugging third baseman in his time. Rosen reached a point were he began feeling he couldn't get around on the ball anymore. Lemon said the guys on the team all talked to him, tried to snap him out of it, telling him he could still do it. But Al had it in his mind that he just couldn't get around on the ball and retired when he was 32 years old.

I think that's how it was with me. I know I began losing confidence. All I could do was take it one day at a time, but I didn't feel good about it. I wasn't producing and began feeling I was on shaky ground. I remember hitting against Whitey Ford of the Yanks one day. I struck out swinging at bad balls and as I walked back to the bench the fans booed the hell out of me. Gentile was right.

So I knew it was coming. It took about a month and they released me. Good-bye. I grabbed my stuff, tipped the locker room guy, and said so long. It was in early August. I received 30 days' severance pay and that was it. And you know something? I was relieved to get home. Now, it was time for Wink and me to talk.

There were no more major league offers, but I did receive a feeler from Japan. They said they would offer me more money than I ever made in my life. There was another feeler from the Pacific Coast League. The PCL also paid well, so I probably could have equaled or topped my last big league salary. But this time Wink and I really thought it through. The conclusion we both reached was: Why put off the inevitable? Wink was ready to go to Japan. She was always ready to go anyplace. But we both realized that we had to think about the long-term future. It was time to get out, cut the cord for good. But it wasn't an easy decision to make.

I thought about Yogi Berra. Yogi got out about the same time I did and I remember that his wonderful wife, Carmen, said, "Well, Yogi, what else do you know? Why leave baseball?" And she was right. Yogi belonged in baseball. But I didn't feel that way. Neither did Winkie. "Why don't we try to find out what else is going on in the world?" She said. "There's been nothing but baseball in our lives."

To be honest about it, we had never really been part of society outside of baseball. I hate to admit it, but there was probably a time when, if you asked me, I would have had trouble telling you who the vice-president was. The world of professional baseball is a strange world. As a ball player, you can become self-centered because you are the center of attention. You're wrapped up in the game, in how you're doing and how your team is going. You're a baseball player and treated like one, by the fans and by the media. You don't even have to be grown up.

It's not that ball players aren't in the real world. There's a very real world for ball players, but it's a totally different place than the world most other people live in. While we're in a real world, we're not in the *whole* world. I began to feel it was time for me to become part of the whole world. And in 1960, that meant I had to become Robert Thomson. Bobby Thomson the ball player, the guy who had hit a big home run just nine years earlier, would have to put that and the rest of his baseball career on the shelf. For how long, I didn't know.

Putting the Pieces in Place

The 1951 pennant race didn't just happen. The fortunes of the Giants and Dodgers had been shaped and guided by events that began years earlier. Ironically, the majority of these events centered around the Dodgers, and in 1951 the Giants would become the unwitting beneficiary of a Dodger power struggle among a number of individual and powerful personalities that began more than three decades before.

The story begins in 1919, the year Wesley Branch Rickey became the manager of the St. Louis Cardinals. Born in 1881 in Lucasville, Ohio, Rickey had a brief playing career that lasted for just 119 games over four seasons. But despite his mediocrity on the playing field, the young man was developing what would be a lifelong love of the game and formulating the ideas that would allow him eventually to excel in yet another capacity.

By 1913, at the age of 31, Rickey became the manager of the St. Louis Browns. He stayed on the field through 1915, then went upstairs as vice-president and business manager. Two years later he moved crosstown and became president of the National League St. Louis Cardinals. In 1918, Rickey enlisted in the army, quickly becoming a major in the new Chemical Warfare Service. After the armistice, he returned to the Cards to do double duty as field manager. He stayed on the field through the early part of 1925, then turned the managerial reins over to his star second sacker, Rogers Hornsby. Once again,

Rickey became vice-president and business manager. He might have had a losing record on the field, but as an executive, he soon had no peer.

While still serving as manager, Rickey began gathering minor league teams to be associated with the Cardinals, eventually giving the ball club an unending source for young players. Though his first farm system was ridiculed as "Rickey's Chain Gang," the idea worked and would eventually be copied by virtually every other big league team. Rickey became known as the father of the modern farm system and along the way made the Cards into a winner.

Besides being an excellent organizer, Rickey was also a shrewd businessman, making sure both the ball club and its frugal business manager turned a nifty profit. He squabbled with players looking for raises and in doing so perfected a negotiating stance that would serve him well the rest of his career. He became known as a tough man to beat out of a dollar.

In 1933, Rickey had difficulty in signing a cocky young shortstop acquired in a trade with Cincinnati. The kid was a buzzsaw, but Rickey eventually signed Leo Durocher on Rickey's terms, then watched Leo and the rest of the rowdy, talented Cardinals—the Dizzy Dean, Ducky Medwick, Pepper Martin–led ball club that in 1934 became known as the Gas House Gang—make themselves into a championship team.

After the 1937 season, Rickey was forced into making a surprising move. Frankie Frisch, the Cards manager, who had ended a Hall of Fame playing career that same year, demanded that the brash and outspoken Durocher go. It seems that Leo was constantly drawing attention to Frisch's waning skills as a second baseman, complaining to Rickey that Frankie was no longer quick enough to turn the double play. "It's either him or me," Frisch said to his boss. As a result, Leo was sent packing to the Brooklyn Dodgers, where he was the regular shortstop in 1938 and then appointed playing manager a year later.

By 1941, Leo, who had imparted his aggressive style of baseball to an already talented ball club, persuaded club president Larry Mac-Phail to make some key trades and managed his team to a 100-win season and a pennant, the Brooks' first since 1920. Leo the Lip had not only become a hero in Brooklyn, but his team had beaten out Rickey's second-place Cardinals by 2½ games.

Now the plot thickens. In 1942, Rickey's young Cardinals, many of them the by-products of that farm system, hit their stride at midseason and came on strong to win 37 of their final 43 games, edging out Durocher and the Dodgers at the wire. The Cards won 106 games; the Dodgers, 104. Shortly after the season ended, Rickey learned he was fired. The reason was financial. Rickey had both a large salary and a profit-sharing arrangement that was putting too big a drain on the Cardinal coffers. The Cards fired him to save money.

Not one to sit on his laurels, Rickey was prepared. Almost immediately after leaving the Cards, he signed a five-year deal at a reported $85,000 salary to become president and general manager of the Dodgers. Rickey and Durocher were together again. At first, Durocher was overjoyed. It had been Leo's feeling all along that Rickey had let him go to the Dodgers because he knew there would be a managerial opening. So when he learned Rickey would once again be his boss, Leo's first reaction was short and sweet. "Oh, boy. I'm in," he said.

The question would become: In for what? There had always been fundamental differences in the characters of the two men. While Leo was just a player under Rickey, the situation was livable. But now that Durocher was the manager and had to work closely with his boss, answer to him, and live up to Rickey's preconceived image of a major league manager, things began taking another turn.

Branch Rickey was a lay preacher, a religious man brought up in the strict Wesleyan discipline. He didn't drink, use profanity, or work on Sundays. The closest he came to the profane was his oft-used exclamation, "Judas Priest!" And his only outward venture to the common side of life was his addiction to cigars. He was seldom without one smoldering in his mouth or hand. His critics were also quick to point out that Mr. Rickey, as he was almost universally called, might not have worked on Sundays, but always called in to check the size of the gate. No one would deny that Rickey's devotion to the dollar for both the club and himself—and not necessarily in that order—seemed to dominate his life.

Durocher, on the other hand, liked life in the fast lane. Easy come, easy go. He loved to play cards and gamble on the horses. He was an impeccable dresser, and enjoyed hobnobbing with those often referred to today as the "beautiful people." One of his best friends was actor George Raft, a man often associated with known gamblers, and his second wife was the glamorous movie star, Laraine Day. Put it this way—Rickey and Durocher would definitely not make the same plans for a Saturday night.

It wasn't long after Rickey arrived that Leo realized it wasn't a matter of, Oh, boy. I'm in. In fact, soon after Rickey arrived, there were rumors that Leo might have to go. Too many shenanigans around the clubhouse and on the field. But after making Leo crawl a bit for his job, Rickey took out his wrath on coach Charley Dressen, who was bumped in mid-November of 1942 for allegedly having a problem with betting on the horses. Durocher objected immediately, telling Rickey that Dressen was an invaluable aid, a great baseball man, and his "right arm." In July of the following year Rickey relented and rehired Dressen, who had professed to have reformed. But the message was clearly intended for Durocher.

As *Look* magazine reported a year after Rickey came to Brooklyn, the man who was soon to be known as the "Mahatma" had "ironed out many a Dodger wrinkle—umpire-baiting, beanballs, and high-stake card games have been replaced by seriousness and esprit de corps."

Yet, there were still accusations of head-hunting and beanballs, high-stakes card games in the clubhouse and guys who loved to play the horses. And wherever the highly competitive, incredibly aggressive Durocher went, there was umpire baiting. No man ever wanted to win more than Leo Durocher and his style was to do it any way he could. Rickey had to know that. After all, he was widely regarded as one of the shrewdest judges of baseball talent ever. Judging his managers was simply another part of the job. Harold Parrott, the Dodgers' traveling secretary and a one-time Rickey confidant, recalled Rickey's answer when once asked why he rated Durocher so highly as a manager.

"Because," said Rickey, "he can steal a pennant for you with a third-place team, if he puts his mind to it."

But Rickey also said that Durocher was "a man with an infinite capacity to take a bad situation and make it worse." The two men had a strange and complex relationship. There was obviously mutual respect, though Rickey often referred to Leo as his favorite reclamation project. But Rickey also knew that no one would ever change Leo Durocher. It was just a matter of how long the two could get along, keep the Dodgers winning, and avoid any incidents that would be embarrassing to Rickey and the ball club.

Pee Wee Reese, who came up with the Dodgers in 1940, was in a position to observe Durocher on several levels. For one thing, Pee

Wee was the heir apparent at short, and Durocher the player gladly turned over the position to the youngster without having to battle that recalcitrant demon of aging ball players—an unrealistic ego.

"I originally signed with the Red Sox," Reese said. "Joe Cronin, like Leo, was both the shortstop and manager. But unlike Leo, Cronin thought he could play a couple more years and wasn't ready to give up his job to a kid. So they sold me to Brooklyn.

"Leo, on the other hand, accepted me immediately. He wanted me to take over the job and helped me. I remember him as a player then. He didn't have great range anymore, but he had great hands and compensated for a so-so arm by getting rid of the ball faster than anyone I ever saw in my life. He watched every move I made when I first came up and gave me a hard time once in a while. He also told me to quit trying to play like him and to just be myself. When I look back at it now, I have no doubt that Leo was very good for me.

"He also drove the ball club and was tough on younger players. But the team was made up mostly of veterans in 1941 and '42, and Leo worked well with them. He had some problems with Bobo Newsom and Arky Vaughan, but that was all. We had a veteran team then. Pete Reiser and I were really the only young guys. The older players like Dolf Camilli, Dixie Walker, Mickey Owen, Joe Medwick, and Billy Herman all came in trades. The Dodgers had almost no farm system at all."

That was the key. Obviously, Branch Rickey could not exist without a farm system, and as soon as World War II began depleting the rosters, Rickey began building something the Dodgers never had. Once again, his all-encompassing baseball genius showed through. While the team faded on the field after 1942, Rickey worked feverishly to build up a network of minor league teams and to bring as many ball players under the Dodger banner as he could. It was during this period that Rickey conceived of a plan that would forever change the face of baseball.

The story, by now, is well known. In October of 1945, the Mahatma shocked the baseball world by signing Jackie Robinson to a contract to play for the Dodgers' International League farm team at Montreal. It was the first time a black man had ever been signed to play in modern organized baseball. Rickey had masked his plan by telling people he was thinking about starting a new Negro League. That gave him the excuse to have his scouts search far and wide for black talent.

No one doubted that the talent existed. Some of the finest players in the country had toiled in the Negro Leagues for years. Now Rickey was out to right what he called a terrible wrong. Others said he did it for purely business reasons, to be the first to grab from a huge pool of untapped talent that would help bring the Dodgers back to the top. It would be difficult to deny either reason. There is little doubt that it was a combination of both. Mounted on the wall over the desk in his office, Rickey had a framed saying, which read:

He that will not reason is a bigot
He that cannot reason is a fool, and
He that dares not reason is a slave.

The reasoning man would know that black players belonged in the big leagues and that their abilities could turn a major league team around. Branch Rickey was both a man with honorable intentions and a businessman. He had the ability to look into the future and see that the longtime "gentleman's agreement" that kept blacks out of baseball was destined to crumble. He just made it happen sooner.

Another testament to Rickey's genius was his choice of Jackie Robinson to pave the way. In Robinson, Rickey had chosen a great all-around athlete, a highly intelligent, competitive man ready to fight for what he believed in. Robinson had proved that many times over before Rickey even met him. The story of their initial confrontation is well known, Rickey shouting racial epithets in Robinson's face to show him the kind of things he would hear in the big leagues, then telling him he had to have the guts to turn the other cheek, not to fight back, at least during his first few years.

Robinson went to Montreal for the 1946 season, where he would lead the International League in hitting and get plenty of practice taking the vicious racial jabs from fans up and down the East Coast as well as from other ball players, many of whom came out of the Deep South. At the same time, a young outfielder named Bobby Thomson was playing his first full year of professional ball for the Giants' top farm club at Jersey City, where he learned firsthand what a fine ball player Jackie Robinson was.

And back in the majors, events were escalating that would eventually put all the pieces in place for 1951.

The Dodgers under Durocher were in another dogfight with the

Cardinals for the National League crown. The club had Pee Wee Reese ensconced at short and a scrappy second baseman named Eddie Stanky. Young Carl Furillo was the center fielder for much of the year. Dixie Walker was the club's best hitter and the only player aside from utility man Augie Galan to hit over .300. It's a tribute to Durocher's managing skills that he piloted the club to a regular season deadlock with the Cards. Each team finished at 96–58, prompting the first unscheduled, best-of-three pennant playoff in league history.

On paper, St. Louis seemed to have the superior team, with the likes of Stan Musial, Red Schoendienst, Enos Slaughter, Whitey Kurowski, Marty Marion, and the league's best pitcher in young Howie Pollet. But it took a pair of playoff wins for the Cardinals to finally dispense with Brooklyn. Many blamed the fact that the Dodgers chose to play the first game in St. Louis and the next two in Brooklyn. That meant a long, 22-hour train ride to the Midwest, where the tired Dodgers were beaten, then another exhausting train ride back to Brooklyn, where they were beaten again.

So the season was over and the sniping began. By signing Robinson, Rickey had opened himself up to criticism from those who didn't want to see the color line fall. There were many, though not all had the courage to speak up. The Mahatma also came under fire from the local press that had picked up on his monetary practices, his penchant for filling his own pockets while paying his players as little as possible.

Outfielder Willard Marshall, who was a teammate of catcher Walker Cooper with the Giants, remembers Cooper telling a story of his negotiations with Rickey when Coop was still with the Cardinals.

"Rickey told Coop what he wanted to give him to sign," Marshall said, "and Coop shook his head, said he wasn't going to sign for that amount. When he got up to leave, Rickey coolly told him, 'Walker, when you come back it will be less.' Coop must have known he meant it, because he signed."

Sportswriter Jimmy Powers coined the phrase "El Cheapo" in describing Rickey, and many of the fans at Ebbets Field picked up on it. Rickey's five-year contract with the Dodgers was up in 1947, and there were some rumors that he might not be asked to return. In addition, another power was emerging at the Dodgers' headquarters at 215 Montague Street. He was Walter O'Malley, a corporation lawyer who was now the Dodgers' attorney and a stockholder. O'Malley's influence with the club was growing, and some said that the soft-spoken, cigar-smoking lawyer had a long-range plan to gain control of the ball club. If that happened, the team wouldn't be big enough to hold both O'Malley and Rickey. So the practice of Rickey-bashing by Powers and other sportswriters provoked no objection from O'Malley.

Durocher, too, was not without problems. Leo's associations with the likes of George Raft and his crowd were under constant scrutiny. When it was learned that Leo was dating Laraine Day late in 1946, the gossip columnists had a field day, pointing out that she was still married, and that her estranged husband was accusing Leo of breaking up their relationship. Even the Catholic Church voiced its disapproval. All was not happy in Flatbush.

It all came to a head just before the start of the 1947 season, when the Dodgers announced they had purchased the contract of Jackie Robinson from Montreal. Rickey was going to do it. He knew Robinson would go through hell his first year, and would need all the support he could get. With the combative Durocher running interference, Robby might not have it so bad. But by the time Robinson reported to the Dodgers on April 10, Leo Durocher was gone, suspended from baseball for one year by Commissioner A. B. "Happy" Chandler.

The suspension was a complex matter. To some it smacked of a feud between former Dodger boss Larry MacPhail and Rickey. To others it had to do with known gamblers attending a Dodger exhibition game in Cuba. Complaints from many quarters about Durocher, his friends, and his life-style began piling up in the new commissioner's office. There was even a phantom letter from an alleged high official in Washington, D. C., asking for Durocher's ouster. But there was no single "smoking gun" event that precipitated a judgment that came as a total shock to everyone, the verdict couched in the all-encompassing, no burden-of-proof phrase: "conduct detrimental to baseball." One-year suspension. Leo was gone.

There was immediate fallout. According to one story, Branch Rickey cried when he heard the news. Other rumors said Rickey did nothing to challenge the suspension. What he did do was immediately bring his old friend, Burt Shotton, back to manage the ball club. The 62-year-old Shotton, the antithesis of Durocher, was a laissez-faire manager who sat and watched, and let the chips fall where they may.

Since there was no middle ground with Leo, those who loved him deplored the move; those who hated him applauded it. Ralph Branca, who would be one of the major players in 1951, was a 21-year-old righthander in 1947, a young pitcher who would produce a 21-win season for Shotton and the Dodgers. Though just a youngster, Branca felt Leo's suspension was a crime and he still thinks that way today.

"I always felt that Rickey didn't like Leo's connection with George Raft and gambling," Branca said. "Chandler threw him out wrongfully. Wrongfully and probably illegally. There was a vendetta against him. His suspension allowed Rickey to bring in his buddy Burt Shotton for a lot less money. Shotton was a doddering old man with a stubborn streak. The game had passed him by and we won in spite of him in 1947."

The Dodgers indeed won the pennant by five games over the Cardinals. Robinson, despite going through a personal hell unequaled in modern baseball annals, was named the National League Rookie of the Year. The team also got solid seasons from Reese and Stanky, Dixie Walker, Furillo, and several others. And while Shotton himself was quoted as saying, "You fellas can win the pennant in spite of me," Dodger coach Clyde Sukeforth was one who gave the veteran skipper credit.

"We got along very well without Durocher in '47," the 89-year-old Sukeforth recently said as he looked back more than 40 years with an amazingly clear memory. "I had a lot of respect for Burt Shotton as a manager. In fact, he's the only manager I know who won a pennant without a veteran starting pitcher."

That part was true. Branca and 22-year-old Joe Hatten won 38 games between them. And because Robinson was an island of color in a white league, his teammates, notably Reese and Stanky, rallied around him, prompting Rickey to boast that he knew Jackie's ordeal would bring the team closer together. Maybe it did, for in just a few short years, the Dodgers would become one of the closest teams ever.

"I get a lot of credit for helping Jackie," Pee Wee Reese said. "But Jackie also got a pretty good reception from a lot of the players on our ball club. There were a few, like Dixie Walker, who were from the Deep South and couldn't accept him. And I'm sure Dixie took it to the grave that he played it wrong and was very sorry he did. Basically, Dixie was a fair man, but that was the way he was brought up.

"I always liked Jackie. I enjoyed being around him, being with him. He liked a lot of the same things I did. He was a good bridge player, liked poker, was a good golfer and a hell of a tennis player. In fact, he was the best all-around athlete I ever saw. Besides that, he was a very,

very intelligent individual who didn't beat around the bush. He always called things just as he saw them."

So the Dodgers survived and they won. They would win again in 1949 with Shotton at the helm. But in between there would be the final chapter with Leo Durocher, the one that sent him to the Giants and made him more determined than ever to win. To this day, Leo feels the suspension was unfair, and most who were there at the time agree with him.

"I got suspended over nothing, over nothing," he said recently. "That's the one thing that still bothers me today. Every owner knew what happened. Yet when I was reinstated, they never took the mark off my record."

So Leo Durocher had to watch his team win without him. He would marry Laraine Day, and after she met Branch Rickey for the first time, she turned to her husband and said, "This man is not your friend."

So things promised to heat up again as soon as Leo returned to the team in 1948.

Jersey City, Jackie, and the Giants

> The thing I noticed about Bobby more than anything else when
> I first played against him in 1948 was his tremendous running
> ability. I was impressed with his stride and thought he was one
> of the greatest runners from first to home that I had ever seen.
> —Alvin Dark

My first full year in organized ball was 1946. I had actually signed with the Giants the day after I graduated from high school in 1942, but after playing just part of the season with two clubs in the low minors I went into the service. I didn't come home until Christmas of 1945 and I went back to living at home on Staten Island with my mother and brother, Jim.

The following spring, the Giants took all returning servicemen to their Triple-A training base in Florida. It seemed like a million guys were down there that year. It wasn't a normal spring training and I felt kind of lost. My brother Jim was my biggest booster then and was always eager to hear from me, but with everything going on I just didn't write. Finally, he couldn't stand it anymore so he went to Jersey City and began going through all the back stories about spring training in the *Jersey City Journal*.

Mom told me later that she'd never forget the look in Jim's eyes when he came home. He had cut out an article about me saying that I was the hotshot of the training camp, a $100,000 gem. I guess I was too naive to let it go to my head, although I knew no rookie was about to make $100,000. But after high school I'd only played in 34 professional ball games before going into the service, so I had virtually no experience to judge myself by or others. I honestly didn't know how well I was doing and it came as a surprise when I made the Jersey City Giants.

I'll never forget opening day in Jersey City. The game was big news because we were playing Montreal and they had Jackie Robinson. That made it a historical occasion for baseball. I guess most of the talk was about Jackie, but I honestly don't remember thinking too much about him or the significance of what he was about to do. Bobby Thomson was the big news to me. I had made the team, found out I was starting in center field, and was one nervous rookie. Just making it through that first game was what was really on my mind.

My first problem that day was getting to the game. I didn't own a car, and to reach Jersey City from Staten Island I had to take two buses to get to the Bayonne Ferry. From Bayonne I took the Hudson Boulevard bus and then still had a mile to walk to the ballpark. The trip took more than two and a half hours and I hadn't planned my time well. When I finally walked in the clubhouse everyone else was already there, dressed in spanking new white uniforms and in the middle of a team meeting. Everyone stopped and just stared at me. That didn't help my nerves, either.

I had been moved from third base to the outfield in Florida because of my speed, so I was playing a relatively new position. When I finally stepped out of the dugout I was amazed by the size of the crowd. The place was packed with some 25,000 fans, and there was only one word to describe how I felt: intimidated, to say the least.

It showed, too. There was one fly ball hit in the gap that I should have caught easily, but I shied away because I was hoping the other guy was going to catch it. As tough a day as it was, I still managed to get a couple of hits.

But you had to give Jackie a lot of credit. He was under tremendous pressure and he played well. Montreal always did well against us that year, beat us by some big scores, and Jackie usually ran wild. There was one game in Montreal when I was playing third that I remember well. Jackie was on second and the batter hit a grounder to me. I grabbed it and we had Jackie in a rundown. I was determined to run right up his back and tag him hard because I knew I could catch him. But it turned into a typical Robinson play. He was so quick that just as I was about to tag him he dropped to the ground. I fell over him and went sprawling in the dirt like a jerk while he scampered to third. He'd really suckered me on that one.

Like everyone else, I realized what Jackie had to go through those first years, but I never became a real Robinson fan. In fact, when I became a Giant I wasn't a fan of any of the Dodgers. That's how deep the feelings ran. Jackie was a pretty cocky guy and I think in the long run he dished out a lot more than he he took. One time when we were playing the Dodgers, Jackie walked in front of our dugout before the game. I was sitting with Sal Yvars and Sal said something to him, nothing out of the ordinary. Well, Jackie jumped right on him verbally, cut him right down to size for no reason.

But there's no disputing the fact that he was a great ball player. He hit about .350 that first year at Montreal and led the International League in hitting. I settled down, too, once I got over my case of the nerves, and had a solid season. When the Jersey City schedule ended the Giants called me up and I hit .315 with a couple of home runs in 18 games. Now that I had some confidence I figured I had a good chance to make the club in 1947. So did my brother. I remember him saying sometime during the 1946 season, "Bob, there's no doubt in my mind that you're going to make it to the big leagues." And I can recall assuming that was my next stop, only maybe not as quickly as it happened.

The Giants did not have a good team in 1946. While the Dodgers were battling the Cardinals for the pennant, the Giants were finishing in last place. Mel Ott was the manager then, and Mel was one of the all-time Giant greats, having been with the club since 1926 when he was 17 years old. He had become manager in 1942 and was still a part-time player in 1946. He ended up pinch hitting a couple of times in '47, then took himself off the active list.

But Mel was a real Giant hero and one of the most popular guys ever to play there. He had taken over the managerial job from Bill Terry, another Giant legend, but never really had a good team to work with. The 1946 team had some power, but little speed or pitching. The next spring, however, we had some good young players in camp. Whitey Lockman was there and so was Larry Jansen.

I came to camp as a third baseman and Mel had me splitting time with Jack Lohrke, another rookie, and Sid Gordon, a power-hitting vet. The way it was set up the three of us alternated during the exhibition games, so I got to play every third day. We were training in Arizona that year as were the Cleveland Indians. The Giants were in Phoenix, the Indians in Tucson. When we broke camp we boarded a private train with the Indians and on the two-week trip east we played each other in a different city every day.

I was concentrating so hard playing third that I never realized that Ott and the coaches weren't happy with Buddy Blattner, our second baseman. Then someone hit a grounder to him one day and the ball took a bad hop and smacked off his shin. Buddy didn't bother to go after it and maybe that was the last straw. Not long afterward I was sitting on an embankment alongside the railroad station with some other guys, waiting for the train to take off, when Mel came up.

"Bobby, how would you like to take a crack at second base?" he asked.

You can imagine my surprise. I had never played second in my life. Plus I'm a little over six feet, two inches, and you don't usually see second sackers that tall. But I was also a kid who wanted to make the ball club and I felt I had all the equipment to play second. So I said, "Sure, anything you want."

Because we were traveling with the Indians, I had a built-in tutor. Joe Gordon was the Cleveland second baseman then, and one of the best in the game. Mel told me to watch Joe and work with him. Joe was a big help and would work with me before ball games. That kind of thing wasn't uncommon then. The two ballclubs were traveling together, sharing the same lounge car, so you couldn't help but get friendly. Plus we were in two different leagues.

Looking back, I think I know why Ott asked me to try second. Call it the enthusiasm of youth. I couldn't wait to get out to the ballpark and put on my suit in those days. I remember one day when I came out early and Mel and the coaches were working with the shortstop and second baseman, Buddy Kerr and Blattner. Bill Rigney, who was the backup shortstop, was also there, and I filled in at second to work with Rig. Mel was hitting ground balls all over the place and I was scooping up everything—I had good speed back then—and I guess I was impressing them without realizing it. I remember hearing Mel say, "Hey, this kid can really move around and he's got the hands to pick up a ball."

All this occurred with opening day just a week away. We had quite a few rookies on the team that year and I opened at second. Whitey would have been there, too, but he had broken his leg in spring training. Larry Jansen moved right into the starting rotation and became our best pitcher.

I'll never forget the first chance I had to turn a double play. It was in the opener against the Dodgers. With a runner on first there was a grounder hit to Kerr at short. I was playing so deep I felt like I was in right field. So I started running like hell to beat the runner to second and then I had to stop and get the ball. There wasn't enough time to complete the play, especially having had to run so far, and I blew the whole thing. Fortunately, I hit a home run that day and we beat the Dodgers by a big score.

I was at second for about two or three weeks to the point where I was starting to relax and feel somewhat comfortable and learning to play the position. Then, we started having problems in the outfield. Mel had a couple of rookies out there—Lloyd Gearhart and Joe Lafata—and some fly balls were dropping in. Maybe it was the windy spring we were having, but one day Mel asked me to go to the outfield and try to catch some of those balls. And that was the end of second base.

I didn't become the regular center fielder right away. In fact, I played all over the place. But I knew I could hit. And I was on the ball club. That was the most important thing. To stay in the lineup I'd have played anywhere.

While I was glad when the move to center became final, there was one drawback I hadn't anticipated.

I had a lanky build and a long stride and—wouldn't you know it?—a few sportswriters began comparing me with Joe DiMaggio. I even had a batting stance and swing that was similar to Joe's and one article suggested I was copying him. That was nonsense, of course, but it made for good copy. And pretty soon reporters were coming around and asking Mel about it.

"I know Bob can run faster than DiMaggio," Mel told them, "and he can hit with as much power. He can also throw as hard and has got great instincts in the outfield."

Just what I needed! The Giants had experienced some recent rookie busts. There was a kid named Johnny Rucker who came up in 1940 and was going to be the new phenom. He played a few years, but never did live up to his press clippings. There were others, too, and now here was this Giant rookie being compared with DiMaggio, one of the all-time greats and a guy also playing in New York.

The comparisons didn't really put any extra pressure on me and I think the reason was that I was just an immature kid and didn't realize what that kind of comparison meant. I knew Joe was a great player with a lot of desire, but I honestly didn't know what the hell I had then.

Here I was, a young kid in the big leagues, doing the stuff I loved to do. That was the only thing that mattered.

The Giants, of course, had a pure power team in 1947. This was the club that set a new major league home run record with 221. On the downside, we were slow as a team and except for Jansen and Dave Koslo, the pitching wasn't very deep. But we finished fourth and with a winning record, so I guess everyone considered the season to be fairly successful, especially since the ball club had been last the year before.

We sure had a bunch of free-swinging guys on the club. Johnny Mize had 51 homers, Willard Marshall 36, Walker Cooper 35, and I had 29.

I was always impressed by Johnny Mize as a hitter. He had a great eye and whenever he took a 3-2 pitch, it was almost always called ball four. The umpires knew the kind of hitter he was and he got the benefit of the doubt where others wouldn't. A young kid like me would have no right to take a close pitch on a 3-2 count. I would be called out. And just about anyone else would. In that respect, Mize was a lot like Ted Williams.

It was a fun team to be on as a rookie because we could explode with power at any time, make all kinds of wild comebacks to win ball games. It wasn't unusual for us to hit three home runs in a row. Boom! Boom! Boom! We weren't a pennant contender, but I don't think the other teams liked playing us because you never knew what was going to happen.

Once I settled in the outfield I felt comfortable and just did my thing. It helped that I played well from the beginning, didn't experience any early-season slumps, so I felt as if I was part of the team in a relatively short period of time. There was the usual "rookie razzing" from other teams, but nothing earth-shattering except for the Cards, who razzed the hell out of me at the beginning, making all kinds of distracting noises when I came up to bat. One night in St. Louis, Harry "The Cat" Brecheen was pitching. He threw me his famous screwball and I ripped the heck out of it off the right field screen for an extra base hit. That quieted them down. As soon as a rookie shows he can play it's back to business.

Verbal razzing wasn't the only way to get on a rookie. We went into Ebbets Field for a series early in the season when I was still playing second. In those days, we used to throw our gloves down at the end of the inning, leave them right out on the field. Whenever I came back onto the field that day I couldn't find my glove. It was never where I left it and I'd always spot it way out in right field. This went on for a couple of innings and I began to wonder what was going on. The next time we got them out I ran like hell to the dugout and then turned around real fast. There was Eddie Stanky, the Dodgers' second baseman, kicking my glove all the way to the right field bullpen. It was a typical Stanky ploy, showing his contempt for a rookie. It was also my introduction to the Brat, a guy who would be an important teammate of mine a few years later.

Stanky was the complete opposite from Mel Ott. Mel wasn't an aggressive person or an aggressive manager. He was simply a nice guy and a well-respected individual, a real hero to Giant fans from his playing days. He used to tell us to just go out there and swing the bat.

I remember one conversation we had in spring training that really surprised me. As usual, we were waiting for a train, and Mel turned to me and said, "Bobby, I'd like to see you go out there and create a little excitement. I was the type of guy who just went out and played ball. But John McGraw would want me to go out and cause excitement. He thought I had the ability to do a lot of things other guys couldn't. And we'd like you to go a little beyond that, too."

But right after telling me this he admitted that he could never bring himself to do it, even though McGraw was always after him. But the advice had stuck in his head and now he was giving it to me. Don't get me wrong. Mel could still be a tough manager and he did get mad occasionally. We had a pitcher named Bill Voiselle who got beat a couple of times when he had 0-2 counts on the batter and then boom, home run! The first time Mel fined Voiselle. When it happened again they made a trade and Voiselle was gone.

The one problem I had as a rookie was sliding. I just didn't know how to slide then. I started out sliding headfirst. But early in '47 I banged up my knee with all the headfirst sliding and finally developed a bone spur on the kneecap that had to be shaved off after the season. It really started to bother me in August, but because the club wanted to finish in the first division, I kept playing. There were times I couldn't go the whole game and other times when they would shoot me full of novocaine. Toward the end of the season we even took a doctor on the road with us to take care of my knee. After the bone spur operation the knee didn't bother me again. I also stopped sliding headfirst.

But my poor sliding ability would come back to haunt me later in my career and I had no one to blame but myself.

All in all, it was a good rookie year. Jackie, of course, was Rookie of the Year, but our numbers weren't all that different. He hit a few points higher, but I topped him in homers and RBIs. But the guy I think really had the superior stats was Larry Jansen. Larry was 21–5 as a rookie and that's outstanding. I think he finished second to Jackie and I was third.

Of course, Jackie had to endure a hell of a lot more than we did. It's funny, but I don't recall any special feeling about Jackie that year. Maybe if I had been a veteran then, I would have noticed it more. But to me he was just another ball player. Maybe it was my Staten Island upbringing. Years before my dad used to bring a big basket of food every Christmas to a black family we knew and I interacted with black people all the while I was growing up. So Jackie was no big deal to me. I knew later there were guys who didn't want to play with and against him, but I don't recall any talk on the Giants about it then. I remember Walker Cooper getting into it with Jackie a few times, but that was because of Jackie's aggressive nature. He had a habit of throwing his bat when he connected and it would often bounce off Coop's shin-guards. Finally Coop said, "If you hit me again, I'll stick this bat right up your butt." Jackie turned around and said, "You can't talk to me that way." But nothing really came of it.

One thing I did feel was the special kind of rivalry whenever we played the Dodgers. You couldn't be a Giant without feeling it. And I suppose you couldn't be a Dodger without the same feelings about the Giants. Little did I know then that a year later it would heat up another notch or two. And that's because we were about to get their manager in 1948.

Leo's Big Switch

The problems between Durocher and Branch Rickey began soon after Leo was re-signed to manage the Dodgers in 1948. Because the team had won with the aging Burt Shotton at the helm during Leo's suspension, there were those who thought that perhaps Rickey would have liked to keep the situation status quo. But there was an undeniable moral obligation to give Durocher his job back. Once Rickey got clearance from Commissioner Chandler, he offered his manager a new pact.

Only this time there was a kicker. In his autobiography, *Nice Guys Finish Last,* Durocher says his contract for 1948 contained a new twist, a little clause typed across the top that gave both parties the right to terminate the agreement at any time. Leo signed it immediately, but when his wife read it, Laraine Day Durocher just shook her head. "After all that procrastinating, he puts that little ticking bomb in there," she told her husband. "The first chance he gets, my boy, you're going to get the old heave-ho."

At first, Durocher didn't see it that way. His respect and admiration for Rickey were deep. He continued to think of the Mahatma as the best pure baseball man he had ever known and also as his friend. But it didn't take long for the dauntless manager to realize their relationship had changed.

The first problem came when second baseman Eddie Stanky tried to hit Rickey for a $5,000 raise. Living up to his "El Cheapo" reputation, Rickey said he would only go another $2,500 for a ball player he himself had once characterized as a guy who "can't hit, run, field, or throw. All he can do for you is win." And indeed, Stanky had put together a solid 1947 season. Besides acting as a buffer for Robinson (The Brat had once challenged the Philadelphia Phillies to pick on someone who could fight back when they rode Robinson mercilessly), Stanky hit .252, drew 103 walks (he had led the league the two previous years) and had a career best 53 runs batted in. He also led all second sackers in fielding percentage and in double plays—all for the then average sum of $10,000.

Rickey, however, was playing hardball with Stanky for another reason. He had already decided that Robinson, who played first base as a rookie, was ready to take over at second, the position he had played so well at Montreal. That made Stanky expendable. Durocher didn't know this and, as he had done so often in the past, went to bat for his player. Finally, when the three men had a meeting, Rickey asked Leo point-blank if he felt Stanky deserved $15,000, which meant a $5,000 raise. When Leo said yes, the Mahatma wrote the figure on Stanky's contract. He then rose and looked at the two other men. "I won't forget this," he said, unsmiling and fingering his cigar.

A short time later, at the beginning of March, the word got out that Stanky was going to be sold to the Boston Braves. The Brat was always Leo's kind of ball player and the manager didn't want to see him go. Stanky didn't want to leave, either. He loved playing for the Dodgers, especially with Durocher coming back. But Rickey was insistent on making the deal. Even today, Durocher remembers the scene vividly. He and Rickey went to Stanky's room to tell the player he was going to Boston.

"I had fought for four days to keep Stanky," Durocher recalls, "but he sold him to Boston anyway for a couple of players and cash. When we went to see Eddie he was sick in bed and once he heard the news he got mad. 'Are you telling me that this man here wants to trade me off this ball club?' he asked Rickey, pointing at me. And Rickey said, 'We make no deals on this ball club without the full consent of the manager.'

"Well, that just wasn't true. And then when Stanky asked me to confirm it I just stared at him, hoping he would get my message. Evidently, he didn't. When we finally left Eddie and went outside,

Rickey put his hand on my shoulder and said, 'You embarrassed me in there!' I looked right back at him and said, 'And you embarrassed me.' Then I called him a hypocrite. That was the start of it. Stanky thought I had stabbed him in the back and Rickey and I were now at odds. I guess I knew right then and there that I was gone."

But it didn't happen immediately. Rickey needed grounds, and maybe a subtle, backstage push from Walter O'Malley. He didn't have long to wait before he could start making a case. There were more problems as soon as spring training opened. They began when Jackie Robinson reported to camp some 20 pounds overweight after a winter on the banquet circuit.

"Jackie weighed about 216 pounds when he came in," Durocher remembers. "My remark to him was that he couldn't play second weighing 216. I told him he had to get down to 195. He answered by saying he didn't come to play second, but would be playing first. That's when I asked when they made him the manager. And after that the two of us didn't really get along, either.

"Later, when I was with the Giants, I always had a little trouble with Jackie. I once left the third base coaching box to go after him. I wanted to fight. But as I got near shortstop at Ebbets Field, Pee Wee stopped me. He just said, 'Leo, Leo,' and I said, 'Yeah, I know.' I knew Robinson would have licked me, but I didn't like what he was hollering. It sometimes got personal, away from the game. Stay in the realm of baseball and you can call me anything you want. But don't make any remarks about my wife or family. That was something I never did.

"But let me say this about Jackie. Despite our problems over the years, if I went to war, I'd want Jackie Robinson on my side. If I'm a manager, I'd want him playing for me."

Robinson's weight wasn't the only problem in 1948. Before long, Rickey and Durocher were clashing on personnel moves at several positions, as well as about a couple of minor leaguers that Leo wanted brought up to the parent club. It didn't help, either, when the ball club got off to such a bad start that they touched ground in the basement briefly.

For openers, the club needed a first baseman. Rickey wanted to move Pistol Pete Reiser in from the outfield. That made sense, in a way, because Reiser was always running into outfield walls and injuring himself. But many thought that by 1948 Reiser was already a shot ball player.

"I told Rickey he was crazy when he told me about moving Reiser," Leo says. "We began arguing and when he asked me what I had in mind I said one word. Hodges. Gil had been our third-string catcher, but I asked him to try fooling around with a first baseman's mitt. In three days he looked better than any first sacker this side of Dolf Camilli."

Then there was Roy Campanella. Campy was a 26-year-old rookie in 1948, but a player who had already been an outstanding catcher in the Negro Leagues for years. Leo recalls coach Clyde Sukeforth telling him before the season began, "Don't let Campanella get away." But once again Rickey had other plans. After fooling around with Campy in the outfield during a few exhibition games, the Mahatma announced that he wanted his erstwhile catcher to break the color line in the American Association and immediately dispatched him to St. Paul, where Campy proceeded to tear up the league. By the time he returned, Leo's fate was just about sealed. Roy wound up playing just 83 games for the Brooks in '48.

Then there was Carl Erskine. Leo says even today that he wanted the young right-hander all along because the club needed pitching. "I saw Erskine pitch when we played an exhibition game against Fort Worth and I kept telling Rickey to give me that guy. He wouldn't do it. It was like he was covering him up."

This story is confirmed by Carl Erskine, who also remembers the incident very clearly. "Leo had tried to get me up all season from Fort Worth, where I was having a real good year," Ersk recalls. "And I knew the Dodgers needed pitching real bad. Burt Shotton, the manager in '47, had become the troubleshooter for the Dodgers in '48, traveling the minor leagues. It was Burt who told me how Leo was trying to convince Mr. Rickey that I was ready and how Mr. Rickey kept saying I hadn't had enough time in the minors.

"But by midseason, mid-July, Burt Shotton came to me in Oklahoma City and said *he* had finally convinced the Dodgers that I was ready and that they were gonna bring me up. But before that could take place, Leo was gone and Burt Shotton was the interim manager, so I never got to play under Leo directly."

Erskine would go 6–3, completing 9 of 17 second-half starts after he finally arrived. Interestingly enough, the moves Durocher claims he fought for at the outset of the season (Hodges to first, Campy behind the plate, Erskine on the hill) were all implemented before the year was over and each player involved became a star. Stanky, incidentally, went to Boston, where he played his usual major role in the Braves winning the 1948 National League pennant, further solidifying his reputation as a winner.

Carl Erskine always considered Leo Durocher his first real booster in the big leagues, and he remembers vividly his reaction when he first pitched against the Giants after Leo took over their helm.

"It was at the Polo Grounds," Erskine recalls, "and Leo was coaching third. I considered him my friend because he had been so encouraging to me. Now, all of a sudden, he's getting on me, I mean *really* getting on me. All I kept thinking was, 'Why is he being so nasty to me? He was my friend. What's wrong with Leo?' I was just a young kid then and he upset me so much, nearly broke my heart, that I balked in a run. But that was Leo. When I balked in the run he had done his job."

But what about Leo's job with the Dodgers? With several positions still unsettled and Jackie Robinson not playing well because of his excess weight, the team got off badly. The proud Dodgers plunged into the second division. On one western trip, Durocher only had six healthy pitchers, a situation he likened to "heading into the desert with half a canteen of water."

By early July the team finally had Campanella, but the pitching was still thin. In a July 4 game against the Giants at Ebbets Field, Leo got into it with an umpire and was ejected. While he was in the locker room shaving, Harold Parrott, the Dodgers' traveling secretary, came into the clubhouse looking for the manager.

"Harold said flat out that Mr. Rickey wanted me to resign, just like that," Leo recalls. "And I turned to him and said, 'You tell that man if he wants me to resign to come down and look me in the eye. Eyeball to eyeball. Don't send someone else to do it or do it over the telephone. Eyeball to eyeball.' "

Leo wasn't about to be fired by a messenger. And while all this scenario was playing out deep in the bowels of Ebbets Field, Campanella clubbed a homer to win the game, something Durocher recalls as turning the season around. He remembers the Dodgers going on the road and winning five of the next six games. The ever-battling, ever-optimistic manager really believed his team could make a run of it in the second half. The club was just a game under .500.

Because Shotton was no longer there, Leo managed the National League All-Stars that year. The next day there was a charity exhibition game in Cleveland, and from there Leo was told to head up to Canada to scout the Montreal farm team. Shotton was supposed to be scouting St. Paul and the purpose was to try to find some extra pitching, the commodity Leo felt the team needed the most. But when he reached Montreal, Leo learned that Branch Rickey wanted him back in New York immediately.

That's when the ax dropped. A very strange ax, indeed. The story told to Leo was that Horace Stoneham, the owner of the New York Giants, had called to ask for permission to talk to Burt Shotton about managing the Giants. Dipping into the same bag of tricks that he always used when making a trade, Rickey asked Stoneham the 64-dollar question.

"You can have your choice, Horace," he said. "Shotton or Durocher."

When Rickey gave an owner a choice while negotiating a trade, he was always 99 percent certain which of the players would be taken. Could it have been any different with the managers? Shotton or Durocher? A man who would be 64 years old that October, ready for retirement, or a man a few weeks away from his 43rd birthday? A man who sat and watched and rarely interfered, or a saber-rattling fighter who pushed, prodded, fought, scrapped, and argued, and would do anything to win? Which one? The Giants were managed by Mel Ott, a relaxed let-'em-play skipper, and the team was going nowhere. In fact, it was Ott and the Giants who inspired Durocher's much-quoted phrase, the one that became his byword: *Nice guys finish last!*

Ott and the Giants were the nice guys. So was Shotton. If Stoneham was serious about winning, about challenging the rival Dodgers for National League supremacy in New York, he had only one choice. And he made it quickly.

"I'll take Durocher," he said.

Of course, Rickey, being Rickey, also gave Leo a choice. "You don't have to go," he said, slowly. But when Leo asked his boss if he could guarantee that he would still be the manager of the Dodgers the next day, the next week, and the next month, Rickey just puffed on his cigar and said nothing. Leo had his answer. He would go where he was wanted. On July 16, 1948, Leo Durocher, the man Giants fans loved to hate, crossed over the loyalty line and became manager of the Brooklyn Dodgers' most hated rivals.

Shock and disbelief were probably the two words that cropped up most consistently once the news got out. But there was still another word, a one-word question that had to be asked. Why? One of the most steadfastly adhered-to maxims in sports is that you do nothing to strengthen your biggest rival, not through trades or deals of any kind. Why, then, would Branch Rickey allow Leo Durocher to go over to the archrival New York Giants while the Dodgers got absolutely nothing in return? Rickey obviously knew all about Leo's fighting spirit. In fact, he voiced it to Arthur Mann, one of his valued assistants. In his 1951 book, *Baseball Confidential,* Mann said he asked Rickey shortly after Leo left what would happen to his former manager and his new team.

"Oh, Leo," Rickey said. "Why he'll fight back, he always does. Yes, he'll fight back, right to the top."

Was that the prophecy of a baseball genius or a drowning man? Could Branch Rickey have seen the handwriting on the wall? Could he have known that the cunning and powerful Walter O'Malley was gathering power in his quest to control the Dodgers and that his—Rickey's—days were numbered? It's certainly a possibility, since the Mahatma would be forced out by O'Malley just a little over two years from the day he gave Leo to the Giants.

There is also evidence that Rickey's health was beginning to deteriorate. He was suffering from Ménière's syndrome, an inner-ear disorder that caused him frequent and sometimes disabling dizzy spells. At the same time, his only son, Branch, Jr., had become diabetic and was prone to frightening comas. It could be that the Mahatma was just operating a shade below his usual, think-of-everything, keep-the-edge efficiency. He certainly was arming the enemy and part of him had to know it.

Harold Parrott, admittedly not one of Walter O'Malley's biggest fans (Parrott felt O'Malley was ruthless in his drive to control the Dodgers), wrote in his book, *The Lords of Baseball,* that O'Malley had embarked on a carefully orchestrated plan to wrest control of the team from Rickey. Parrott also felt O'Malley wanted Durocher out, and said that at one point early in 1948, O'Malley made Rickey promise that if the team dipped to last, Durocher would be fired. And, indeed, the Dodgers did touch last place, though ever so briefly.

Perhaps the final indictment of this seemingly irrational action comes from a player, Ralph Branca. Branca had won 21 games for replacement skipper Burt Shotton in 1947, but always admired Durocher's managerial skills. With Leo gone, Branca and the rest of the Dodgers would have to deal with Shotton again.

"If you look at the record, sure, we started terribly that year," Branca remembers. "Robinson was overweight, Leo got on his case, and Jackie didn't like it. But after the terrible start we began winning games. I'm not sure of the exact date, maybe late May or June—it was a long time ago—but we started to win. We were making our move and we were going to continue to come on. And what does Rickey do? He gets rid of Leo. The team had just started to jell and he got rid of the best manager in baseball. I had to think it was coming ever since the suspension and the reasons were Leo's off-field friends, his connections with the Hollywood crowd, and money."

Of course, Leo's move to the Giants was filled with all kinds of ironies. But it's interesting to remember that Branch Rickey had rid himself of Leo Durocher once before, back in 1938, when he was running the Cardinals. Rickey sent Leo packing to the Dodgers, probably knowing Durocher would soon be the Brooklyn manager. Three years later, in 1941, Rickey had to chew extra hard on his cigar when Durocher piloted the Dodgers to a pennant over his Cardinals.

Now, just ten years later, it had happened again. Three years up the road would be 1951. While Rickey would no longer be with the Dodgers then, Leo would do to the Dodgers what he had done to the Cardinals ten years earlier; only this time he would stand the whole baseball world on its ear in the process.

 **BOBBY**

Journey to the Big Leagues

The six of us were a very, very close knit family and my father had each one of us trained to excel in something. When I went to music school—I'm a vocalist—my father kept saying, "Stay in the background. Stay in the background." But eventually I noticed that all these other kids were getting solos and I wasn't. So I changed. And remember, Bob was brought up the same way.

—Mrs. Jean Thomson Hicks

If things had worked out differently I might have been a soccer player. There wouldn't have been any takers if someone had set odds on Bobby Thomson becoming a rookie center fielder for the New York Giants in 1947. Not if the odds were being set in 1923 in my home town. When my mother announced she was expecting me, her sixth child, our family lived in Glasgow, Scotland.

My father, James Hay Thomson, was a cabinetmaker in Glasgow but he was finding it increasingly difficult to support his growing family. He'd been looking to America as the land of opportunity ever since the end of the First World War, in which he had fought along with his two younger brothers. Robert Brown, the youngest of the three, whom I was named after, was killed at the Dardanelles. The decision to emigrate was difficult for both my parents but there was no other choice. In those days you got a visa number, then waited for about a year for the number to come up. It was shortly after my father got his number that my mother became pregnant with me and that presented a problem. If my father left when his number came up, my mother would be left with five children and one on the way. But if he stayed, he would have to get another number, and that would delay the whole process by another year or more.

They finally decided he would go when the number came up. My sister Jean has always called our parents pioneers because of what

46

they did. I was born five days after my dad left, on October 25, 1923, when he was still at sea. Jean has told me that my mother became ill shortly after I was born, but we had a wonderful grandmother who came and stayed with us and we just had to make do until my dad could send for us.

He didn't have it easy, either. First he had to get a job and make enough just to live on. Then he had to find enough to send back to Scotland to help support us and finally he had to save enough money to bring us all over. From what I understand, there were a few times when he came close to giving up and heading back to Scotland because things weren't going as well as he hoped.

But he continued to pursue his trade, doing various types of carpentry work. He finally got a job with a large company, the Rhinestein Construction Company, and soon had the money to send for us.

We landed on July 1, 1926. You can imagine how my dad felt seeing us after such a long absence—and seeing me for the first time. While we didn't have any family members who came over before us, we did have friends who had and we moved close to them in the New Dorp section of Staten Island. We were right next to the New Dorp Moravian Church and on our first Sunday we went to church together there.

The early years weren't easy. My dad still had a tough time of it. A loyal and honest man, he elected to stay with Rhinestein Company even when things slowed down and he would be temporarily laid off. Things were fine when he was working, but when he wasn't we had a problem. And for some reason it seemed to me he was out of work more at Christmas than any other time of the year. That made it doubly rough for us as kids, especially an impatient five-year-old like me who dreamed of owning a two-wheeler bike. I remember coming downstairs in the semidarkness that Christmas morning and seeing what I thought was a bike standing against the wall. I let out a yell! "I got my bike! I got my bike!" But it was only something that in the shadows *looked* like a bike. That was a pretty rough Christmas for me.

But once we were old enough to understand the situation we came to understand the kind of people our parents were. A few years later, when we lived in the Midland Beach section of Staten Island, my father used to take a basket of food to a nearby family every Christmas. He also found ways to do things for us. We didn't have a car when we were young, but somehow he managed to find a piano and was able to scrounge up two bucks a week so my sister Betty could take lessons. It soon became a Sunday night ritual for us to stand around the piano while Betty played and everyone sang. Except me. My sisters and my brother all sang in the church choir and knew how to harmonize with each other. I just didn't have the voice or the talent. Those were big moments for my dad and it certainly brought us all closer together.

It wasn't long before sports entered the picture, especially for me. Dad had always been a big soccer fan on the other side, but soccer wasn't a very big sport over here and it wasn't long before my dad transferred his loyalties to baseball. Believe it or not, he soon became a Dodger fan and we began going to Ebbets Field occasionally to see them play. Dolf Camilli, the Dodger first baseman, was my dad's favorite. I remember one game when Dolf smacked a home run and my dad stood up and really cheered. That was something for him, because he was always such a nondemonstrative person. I never forgot that. Years later I met Dolf at an old-timers' game and it was really exciting for me. Dolf was in his seventies then, but he looked about fifty, and was just as strong as always. I told him my dad had been his biggest fan, and because Dolf turned out to be the solid person I'd heard he was, he seemed very pleased to hear it.

Dad was a proud man and very big on principle. That meant he wanted his kids to do what was right. And he always put us before himself. A good deal of our family's early life centered around the church. We always went to Sunday school. There were times when Dad was out of work, but every extra penny went to make sure we had good clothes to wear to church. As usual, he neglected himself, and because he didn't feel his clothes were good enough to wear, he stayed home. That's the kind of man he was.

The thing that eventually put an end to the Sunday routine for me was baseball. I was growing faster than most kids my age and as soon as we'd get back from Sunday school I'd head out to find a game. One day, when I was 14, Dad and I went to Clove Lake to watch a game between some older guys when all of a sudden they needed another player. They looked around and I guess I was all there was. So young Thomson got into the game. And got a hit. It wasn't much of a hit, just a bouncing ball between first and second, but the first one I remember getting in a real game. It was exciting for me because most of the other guys were maybe 20 and up and it sure made my dad very proud.

It also made me want to play more. Most of the games on the Island were played Sunday mornings and that presented a problem, because my mother felt very bad when I stopped going to Sunday school because of baseball. By this time my dad had a car. He also became my ally. He never said much about it, just waited for me in the car on Sunday morning, and knew my mother was very unhappy. One Sunday when I already had my baseball suit on, Mom walked into the room.

"You're not going to church, Bob?" she said, in her quiet way. I can remember saying, very sheepishly, "No, Mom." My dad was even more sheepish about it. But he loved the whole scene, taking the guys to the games and home again.

By the time I reached high school age it was baseball, baseball, baseball. I started playing for every team I could find. When we lived in the Thompkinsville section, I played for the Thompkinsville Blue Jays. A guy named Moe Cohen ran the team. He was a great guy who did a lot for the kids, a real institution on the Island.

Another team I played for was sponsored by two fellows named Gugliuccio and Petrangello. I remember their names were stitched on the jerseys and I used to tell my mom I hoped she didn't mind strangers' names hanging on the line after they were washed.

When I began playing Sunday morning ball I didn't own a pair of spikes. But my brother Jim did. He was a first baseman and played in the afternoon with the older guys. One morning I just grabbed his shoes, figuring my game would end in time for me to bring the spikes back for him to use; but it didn't work out that way. Jim came looking for me. He took his spikes back right in the middle of the game, leaving me to finish the game in my stocking feet. But I guess I deserved it.

I played at Curtis High School under Harry O'Brien, who was both the baseball and basketball coach and another institution on Staten Island. I played shortstop and Coach O'Brien would always come over to me before a game and say, "Son, just go out there and relax. I'll give you two errors, so don't worry about fouling up." Even then I was a guy who could make a good play as well as a guy who could botch it up. I never changed.

Things started to get interesting my last two years in high school. While I was playing for Curtis High I was also playing in a semipro league with a team called the Gulf Oilers on Sunday afternoons. That was when a Giant scout named George Mack saw me for the first time. He was scouting another outfielder, and invited him to work out with the Giants at the Polo Grounds. He also said, "Bring that kid Thomson with you."

So I worked out at the Polo Grounds. It now was my introduction to professional baseball. They allowed us five swings each before the game. But when I got up to take my cuts I was so excited I forgot to count. Dick Bartell, a veteran infielder they called Rowdy Richard, was standing nearby and hollered, "Get the hell out of there, kid!"

It was a thrill to work out at the Polo Grounds and I was beginning to become a Giants fan. By this time I was listening to the major league games on the radio at night.

I remember one game that really got me excited. The Giants were losing by three runs in the last of the ninth inning. I figured it was over when they suddenly got two home runs to win it. I don't remember who hit the first one, but a guy named Harry Danning hit the one that ended the game. I couldn't believe it. I was thrilled and I imagined how great Danning must have felt. Shades of things to come.

Even though I had worked out with the Giants, the Dodgers were showing interest in me. There wasn't a draft then, so the local teams checked out the local kids. The Dodgers had an amateur team called the Dodger Rookies. If you played for them you got a chance to work out with the big club and play games against other amateur teams in the area. It was a good system. They gave us uniforms and we played in some of the parks around the city. I was primarily a shortstop then. The Dodgers asked me not to sign any contract before talking to them. They said they would better any contract the Giants offered me. But it didn't mean that much to me then. Besides, I was a Giant fan. Mel Ott was already my idol.

My senior year at Curtis High was one of mixed emotions. My father died that December of 1941 and that cast a pall over everything. That was the same month the Japanese attacked Pearl Harbor. With those two things happening it was really pretty tough to think about anything else, let alone a baseball career. There was never any thought of college.

In the spring I played out my senior year with the Curtis High team. I also continued to play with the Dodger Rookies, and—would you believe it—the day I graduated from Curtis in June of 1942 George Mack made an offer on behalf of the Giants. There was no response from the Dodgers, no topping the Giants' offer, so I signed with the Giants the next day. I met George Mack in New York City and signed

for $100 a month. Things weren't very formal then, no press confer-
ences, no big announcements. I signed on the stone windowsill of a
building while we were standing on the street.

I remember my sister Betty telling me a story later on. When I was
a freshman in high school, Dad got sick and ended up in the hospital.
One of his friends came to visit him and my dad started telling him
how I was going out for the Curtis High School baseball team as a
freshman. Well, I guess the guy must have said something like, "Oh,
sure, and someday he'll be playing for the Giants."

Betty said my father looked right at the man and said, "And don't
you bet that he won't." It always made me feel that maybe he had seen
something or felt something, or just had a premonition. Betty didn't
tell me about that until years later and naturally my one regret is that
he didn't live long enough to see me play in the big leagues.

It's difficult to think back nearly half a century and know why the
Giants signed me. The image I have of myself then is of a young kid
having fun but just going through the motions. I guess I still don't
realize how good I was.

The Giants wanted me to get some games under my belt that
season, and told me to report to the Bristol Twins in Bristol, Virginia,
in the Appalachian League. My mother and my sister Marion saw me
off on the bus to Bristol. Talk about being wet behind the ears. This
was my first trip away from home and I didn't have a clue what to
expect. Hal Gruber was the Twins' manager and they had a winning
ball club, so I didn't break into the lineup right away. But I remember
going out to third for a workout and being so scared that the first
ground ball they hit to me slammed into my leg. I never got my glove
on it. Nice way to start things off. And that was just the beginning.

The Bristol team had a big pitcher, a good-looking kid who could
throw hard. Next to him, I must have seemed like a tall string bean.
He was pitching one day and I was playing third. When we ran out on
the field one inning I figured I'd be a nice guy. So I picked his glove up
and handed it to him. He almost tore my head off. "Don't you ever
touch that glove!" he hollered, so everyone could hear. That was my
first exposure to a ball player's superstitions. Don't touch another
guy's glove. But how was I, Thomson, the green kid from Staten Island,
supposed to know that?

I only played five games at Bristol. The rest of the time I sat and it
wasn't an easy experience. My brother wrote encouraging letters,

trying to pump me up. "When things aren't going well," he said, "don't get mad at the coach. Get mad at yourself. Let them know you're out there."

Finally, word came that they needed a third baseman at Rocky Mount in the Bi-State League. Bill Terry, the former Giants star and later manager, was in the front office then, and word came down from him to get me into the lineup. The first night I joined the team I got into the game but didn't get a hit. On the way home, the bus stopped at a roadside stand and I went out back to the men's room. When I came back, the bus was gone. A man was standing there who just laughed and said, "I thought they were missing a guy." So he offered to drive me in his car to catch the bus, which we did. I really must have made a big impression, because no one even missed me.

By the time I got to Rocky Mount there wasn't much left of the season, maybe about a month. I played in 29 games and didn't do too well. I hit a couple of home runs, but my batting average was under .250. When the season ended, I was 19 years old and, with the war going on, didn't have any plans for the future.

I came home to Staten Island and began working at the same defense plant in Jersey where my brother worked. But I knew it was just a matter of time before Uncle Sam called. In fact, my brother Jim finally said, "Bob, they're gonna draft you anyway, so why not take your pick." He was right. I checked around, picked the air corps, and enlisted late in 1942. Baseball was now on hold.

Though I came close several times, I never made it overseas. Whenever I was about to go, something would happen to change the orders. I started out in radio operator's and mechanic's school, but a while later I became inspired and put in for the air cadets, took a test, and passed it.

Now I had a chance to be a pilot, a bombardier or navigator, but I had to start all over from scratch, even go through basic training again. I reached the point where I was flying in Piper Cubs. There was the usual Thomsonlike introduction to flying. One day the pilot pulled the nose up and we went into a stall. That's when I said, "What in the world am I doing up here?" And for a few seconds it didn't look as if I would be there for long. But it didn't take long to get used to that kind of stuff. I finally soloed and took my final tests in Santa Ana, California. The result was that I would become a bombardier.

That was in 1944 and there was a baseball team on the base back then. They put up a notice that tryouts would be held and that none other than Joe DiMaggio would be watching. Joe lived in San Francisco and must have been there during the off-season. Anyway, I didn't go out. I was plain scared and didn't think I was good enough to make the team. Maybe I just didn't want to go out and mess up in front of Joe D.

By the time I reached the final phase of combat training and was ready to go overseas, our orders were canceled. By that time they had too much of everything. That's when I finally joined the baseball team at the base and from that point on began playing a lot of ball. I also played for an outside team with professional connections and for the first time in my life had a lot of scouts watching me. My brother even saw me play one night and after the game he had a surprised look on his face.

"Bob," he said, "you've really improved. You look like you've really matured out there."

I took my discharge in California so I could keep playing ball. Now I was 22 and wanted to give the game a real shot. Oddly enough, I had no idea whether I still belonged to the Giants or not, but I found out when the San Francisco Seals of the Pacific Coast League tried to sign me. They did some checking and learned I was still officially the property of the Giants. But I stayed on a little longer, worked in a steel factory, and played more ball.

I came home at Christmastime in 1945 and learned that the Giants were going to take all the returning servicemen to early spring training in Florida for the 1946 season. I didn't have a whole lot of self-confidence and figured I'd be going back to Class D to start all over again. But I had to do it. There could be no fooling around. It was time to find out whether I had what it takes or not.

Back Up the Truck

Leo Durocher wasn't the kind of guy to let the grass grow under his feet. It's never easy for a manager to switch teams in the middle of the season, but to go over to your bitterest rival in the space of a single day has got to be a major managerial culture shock. Yet Leo cut the cord to the Dodgers quickly and emphatically. One day he was a Dodger; the next a Giant. Just like that. There was no middle ground with the Lip.

In fact, with the help of his wife Laraine, never a Branch Rickey fan, the Durochers made their feelings clear in a picturesque way. Using a woman's touch and sense of style, Laraine had furnished her husband's office at Ebbets Field in a magnificent manner. What was normally a dingy office in an ancient clubhouse was now a splendid room: carpeted, adorned with many pictures on the walls, with a coordinated desk and chair, and more subtle lighting, all obviously done with loving care and at great expense. When Leo got the gate, she wanted everything out of there quickly, and personally saw that the office was stripped clean. Only one thing was left behind.

It was an autographed photo of Branch Rickey that Leo had hanging on the office wall. Before she left, Laraine Day Durocher moved Rickey's photo. It could now be found hanging in the bathroom off Leo's office, directly over the toilet.

The symbolic repositioning of a photo notwithstanding, the news of

Leo's sudden departure for the Giants came as a complete surprise to the Dodgers. Pee Wee Reese, who began his career by taking over at short for Leo the player, was quick to realize the bizarre quality of the sudden move.

"It came as a real shock to all of us when Leo left," said Pee Wee. "Not only were we surprised to see him leave the Dodgers, but the real shock was that he was going to the Giants. As Dodgers, all of us—from Leo, coaches like Charley Dressen, and the ball players— learned to hate the Giants. That was part of being a Dodger. It wasn't that we didn't have respect for them, but we always seemed to end up in some kind of little fracas when we played them. So for Leo to go and manage the Giants after managing the Dodgers, well, that was just unheard of.

"I remember almost laughing about it, saying, 'My God, I can't believe Durocher would go to work for the Giants.' But, hey, the man needed a job and they had a pretty good ball club over there, so I guess it really wasn't a bad move for him."

Reese also acknowledged that Leo's forced defection caused an immediate increase in the intensity of the Giants-Dodgers rivalry.

"When Leo went over it jumped the rivalry up a couple of notches right away, and it was because of some of the players on our ball club. Leo was just not a big favorite of some players. So when the guys who didn't like him had a chance to beat him, well then things got pretty hot."

The news wasn't received with universal approval on the Giants' side of the street, either. Leo Durocher may have stirred the emotions, but he also frightened them. With Mel Ott, the Giants players always knew what to expect. Leo brought with him the element of the unexpected, the unknown. Larry Jansen was a second-year pitcher with the Giants in 1948 and he remembers the news of Leo's pending arrival being met with mixed feelings.

"I think we were in Pittsburgh at the time," Jansen remembers. "Most of us couldn't believe it had happened. I thought the world of Mel Ott and just didn't think he would be let go and Durocher, of all people, would take over the ball club.

"We all realized that something was going to happen, that under Leo we would be playing a different kind of baseball for sure. But exactly what that would be, none of us really knew."

There were a couple of veteran players on the team who saw the coming of Durocher quite differently. In the case of Willard Marshall and Walker Cooper, Leo was perceived as the man who would orchestrate the end of their Giant careers. Marshall, a slugging left fielder, remembers his first reaction when he heard the team was getting a new manager.

"I knew once Durocher came over that the chances were good I would be traded," he said. "I realized that players like Johnny Mize and myself were a little slower than average and didn't fit Leo's concept. But in those days you played your whole career expecting to be traded."

For Walker Cooper, the hard-hitting, gutsy catcher, it was a more personal thing. He had been a bitter rival of Durocher's since coming into the league in 1940, and didn't feel he could adjust to life under Leo.

"I wasn't a Leo Durocher fan," Cooper admits. "When I heard Leo was coming to manage the Giants in mid-1948, I knew I wouldn't be there long. It went back years. Leo and I just didn't get along. No matter what team I was on, we would always get on Leo pretty good. We would let him have it about the company he kept. We would always yell at him about his wife. We asked him where Laraine hid her jewelry at night."

Leo hated it when the riding became personal. But it's doubtful he would have traded a player for reasons other than pure baseball. If a man produced on the field, Leo loved him, at least between the white lines. Even Willard Marshall remembers Leo's philosophy when it came to gathering his kind of ball player.

"There were times when some people didn't think Leo would go after a certain ball player," Marshall said. "But I heard Leo say on more than one occasion, 'I can hate you like a snake, but if you can play good ball for me, I'll take you.' I really think Leo meant that."

Either way, Durocher's arrival made a lot of Giant players nervous. Ott had been easygoing, an idolized former hero, a guy everyone loved to play for. Suddenly, he was gone and here comes Durocher. Leo wasn't exactly perceived as riding in on a white horse. No knight was he. In fact, he was still considered a Dodger, the enemy, the man they loved to hate—and beat.

Even Mrs. John McGraw, the widow of the greatest manager the Giants ever had, cried unabashedly when she heard that Durocher would replace Ott. She was comforted by a friend who commented sagely, "He's got G-I-A-N-T-S written across his chest now, and until he does something to disgrace it . . ." It would take nearly three years, but Leo Durocher would prove to Mrs. John McGraw and everyone else that he would, indeed, not disgrace the Giants uniform and that he was probably closer in spirit to John McGraw than any Giants manager who preceded him.

When Leo met with his new team for the first time, the air was so thick it could stop a Bob Feller fastball. No one knew what to expect from this often loudmouthed firebrand. But the manager just looked at his new team and then did something that is remembered to this day, something that echoed the prophecy of Mrs. McGraw's friend. The new manager ran his hand across the front of his chest and said one word: "Giants!"

Then, for emphasis, he did it again, telling the players that no matter what had gone before, all that mattered from this moment on was the Giants. And they believed him, because that's the way Leo Durocher was. He was a loyal man, though his greatest loyalty was to winning. And that presented the new manager with a problem.

With the Giants team he was taking over in 1948, winning was something Leo didn't feel he could do often enough. But he had promised owner Horace Stoneham that he would work with the ball club until the end of the year, then evaluate the situation.

While Durocher was sitting out his suspension in 1947 and *his* team was winning a pennant under Burt Shotton, the New York Giants under Mel Ott were finishing in fourth place despite fielding one of the great slugging teams in baseball history. In a year when the champion Dodgers had just 83 home runs as a team and only two other National League clubs hit over 100, the New York Giants set a major league record by belting 221 balls out of the park.

Three veteran sluggers and a surprising rookie did the bulk of the four-base damage. Big Johnny Mize, the first sacker, led the National League with 51 homers and 138 runs batted in. The aforementioned Willard Marshall had 36 homers and 107 RBIs. Catcher Cooper slammed 35 and drove home 122. Yet these three men, who hit 122 home runs among them, expected to be traded once Leo arrived.

The rookie, of course, was Bobby Thomson, who slammed 29 homers his first season. But there was a difference between Bobby and the other three, and it wasn't only age. Bobby could run. In fact, in a straight, 100-yard race, he may well have been the fastest man in the entire National League. The other three were slow, almost lumbering players, and if there was one thing Leo Durocher liked in a baseball team it was speed. Speed to play defense. Speed to leg out an infield hit. Speed to break up the double play. Speed to work a suicide squeeze. Speed to take the extra base. Speed to hit and run.

And speed, or the lack of it, was the main reason Leo gave his now classic answer when owner Horace Stoneham asked for his feeling about the ball club.

"Horace, back up the truck," Leo growled.

The team Leo inherited in 1948 again led the league in homers, this time with 164. But they were barely a .500 club, finishing fifth at 78–76, just 41–38 under Durocher. Mize had another big year, leading in homers with 40 and driving home 125. Third sacker Sid Gordon improved to 30 homers and 107 RBIs. But Marshall, Cooper, and Thomson all saw their production fall off, each failing to reach the 20–home run mark. It was obvious Durocher couldn't continue like this. But the changes didn't come overnight. At first he encountered some resistance from owner Stoneham, who felt an allegiance to his longtime slugging stars.

At the outset of the 1949 season, things did not go well for Leo Durocher or the Giants. The club simply wasn't playing winning baseball. To make matters worse, Leo was still trying to convince a reluctant Stoneham that changes had to be made, and it came to a point when Stoneham began to feel bringing in Leo was a mistake. At the same time, Durocher found himself beleaguered at not one, but two ballparks—Ebbets Field and the Polo Grounds.

Despite a succession of mediocre teams, Giant fans loved Mel Ott and in the early going hated the man who took his place. Leo was booed mercilessly, and admitted, "They hated the sight of me, hated my guts." Even some sportswriters jumped on the bandwagon. Kenny Smith of the *Mirror*, a personal friend of Leo's, was so upset at Ott's leaving that he told the new manager flat out, "I loved Mel Ott and I'll tell you right now I'm gonna knock your brains out in the paper."

It wasn't any better at Ebbets Field, where Leo thought there might still be some lingering allegiance for the years spent piloting the Dodgers. Instead, he found himself vilified by the Flatbush faithful, booed voraciously upon his return, called a traitor and a bum. Finally, there was the dirt runway.

A high fence on either side of a long dirt runway that led from the locker room to the bench was all that separated the fans from the players on their way to the playing field. When Durocher was a Dodger, he called the walk down the open runway a "triumphant processional." Fans would reach through the fence to shake hands or pat the players on the back. And their remarks only served to glorify their heroes.

As a Giant, Leo quickly discovered the triumphant processional had become something close to running the gauntlet. In *Nice Guys Finish Last,* he described his trips down the runway as a Giant.

"They spat on you. They threw dirt at you, rocks, hot dogs covered with mustard. Anything. They sprayed you with Coca-Cola. They called you every filthy name they could think of."

So early in 1949, nothing was going right for Leo or the Giants. Then a bizarre incident seemed to make everything worse, though it would soon turn into a catalyst for the better. After an early-season game, Durocher was leaving the field when a fan who had been razzing him unmercifully made a grab for his cap. Durocher thought the man was taking a swing at him and went after his perceived assailant. But as Leo related later, "I hadn't taken more than two steps toward him before I was cut off by Freddie Fitzsimmons."

Notwithstanding the intercession of Durocher's pitching coach, the fan sued Leo for assault, claiming the Giant manager had punched and kicked him. Before there was a legal decision, Commissioner Chandler jumped into the fray. He suspended Leo for 15 days, effective immediately, and apparently did it without conducting a hearing or investigation, or even making a phone call to Durocher to get his side of the story.

Suddenly, Chandler became the villain and Leo the martyred hero. The press lined up solidly behind the beleaguered manager, and the fans demanded his return. Chandler's impulsive actions were being questioned in every corner. Finally, the commissioner had no choice and lifted the suspension. The man who had accused Leo later admitted in court that the manager hadn't come near him. This time, Durocher returned to the Polo Grounds a hero and received a thunderous ovation from the fans. They had finally accepted him. It had taken another confrontation with Commissioner Chandler, but Leo was now their main man.

The situation now made it easier for the manager to deal with

Horace Stoneham, to convince him to start making changes. Leo used an old Branch Rickey routine. He told Stoneham that the arrow for the Giants was pointing down, while the Dodger's arrow was pointing up. In other words, the gap between the two rivals was growing. The Dodgers were building a powerhouse team, while the Giants were going nowhere. In effect, Leo was telling his owner, let me put together a team that can compete with them.

Leo remembers how he explained to Stoneham why he had to change the face of the team. "I told him we have a guy like Johnny Mize, good hitter and nice man," Leo relates. "But suppose he hits a single. Now, I've got Walker Cooper coming up and I can't hit and run. I can't do what I want to do. I have to wait until he hits one out. I said that's no good and repeated to him, 'Back up the truck.' "

So the truck backed up. In mid-June, Walker Cooper was traded to Cincinnati for veteran catcher Ray Mueller, although the man Leo would use behind the plate was Wes Westrum, who had been a backup to Cooper. Westrum was already an outstanding defensive catcher and excellent handler of pitchers.

Then in August, Mize went, sold crosstown to the Yankees, where he would become an outstanding pinch hitter and part-time player. In return, the Giants got some much needed cash. The team finished the season in fifth place, at 73–81. But Leo could accept a sub-.500 finish because he felt things were beginning to go his way.

Bobby Thomson had emerged as the star in '49, hitting .309 with 27 homers and 109 runs batted in. Whitey Lockman also had a fine year, hitting .301 with 65 RBIs. Henry Thompson became the Giants' first black player, and, later in the season, was joined by Monte Irvin. Leo was gathering players he knew could win for him. But it was in December, after the season had ended, when the tireless manager made his biggest deal, the one that would transform the Giants into contenders.

Leo didn't feel that shortstop Buddy Kerr was a long-term answer. Kerr had been the Giants' starter since 1944 and was one of the most popular players on the team. But he had hit just .240 in 1948 and .209 in 90 games in '49, both career lows. Leo felt he should go, but Stoneham resisted. Then the manager heard something that almost made him drool with anticipation. He learned that Braves shortstop Alvin Dark, the Rookie of the Year in 1948, was available.

"That's the man I want!" Leo exclaimed, for all to hear.

So the wheels began turning and all the skills and tricks of the deal that Leo had learned from Branch Rickey came into play.

"First I had to convince Horace," says Leo, whose memory of the trade remains vivid today. "He thought Buddy Kerr was the best shortstop in baseball. I said that once we traded him we wouldn't hear much from him again. And we didn't.

"Now I had to deal with Lou Perini of the Braves. I knew just who they would want when I talked trade. They would ask for Sid Gordon. I had someone else beside Dark in mind, too. But I had learned from Mr. Rickey that you don't play your trump card until it's time. The original deal was Marshall and Kerr for Alvin Dark. But then Mr. Perini said, 'Don't you think I should get another player?'

"I said yes and he thanked me for my honesty. He then asked me to make a list and from that list he would make a choice. That's when I told [General Manager] Chub Feeney that he would pick Sid Gordon. Sure enough, Mr. Perini looked at the list and picked Gordon. This was what I wanted. Now it was my turn to deal.

"I said, 'Mr. Perini, don't you think it's a little bit one-sided now?' He said, 'Yes.' So I said, well, I gotta have another player. You've taken my outfielder and two infielders. Gordon was playing third at the time. So I said I wanted another player and he asked me who I wanted.

"What I learned from Mr. Rickey is that first you ask for what you're not gonna get. The Braves had a player named Roy Hartsfield who hadn't played for them yet, but I knew they had paid a lot of money to get him. So I asked for Hartsfield and Perini said, 'Oh, no. He's gonna be our second baseman.' So I said I would take the other guy, Sibbi Sisti, who was a veteran utility infielder. I knew I wouldn't get him, either. Then he offered me Connie Ryan, another infielder.

"I said, 'Hold the phone. Mr. Stoneham already had Ryan here once. You want to get me fired?' Then he said he had nobody left except Stanky. I told him to wait a minute. When Stanky was at Brooklyn and we traded him, he said I stabbed him in the back. I said I didn't know whether Stoneham would go for it. So now I had Perini thinking I was willing to settle for a guy I didn't really want. But, in truth, Stanky was the guy I wanted all along, and I finally got him.

"Of course, I still had to convince Mr. Stoneham. He hedged at first, then agreed. So we sent Marshall, Gordon, Kerr, and a pitcher named Red Webb to Boston for Dark and Stanky. Mr. Stoneham didn't like Stanky and wouldn't speak to him for two weeks. Finally, he came to me and said he wanted to meet him. He did, and that was it. Dark was great and Stanky became the Rock of Gibraltar for me. They were both my kind of player, the scratchers and divers who are always in the right place at the right time."

Now Leo Durocher had reason to smile. Going into the 1950 season he knew his team was coming together. The arrow was definitely pointing up. The Giants were just about ready to challenge the Dodgers . . . or anybody else.

 **BOBBY**

The Early Years

He's our star. Everyone else realized it. When the trading deadline approached and every club wanted to talk business, the
first thing I was asked was: "What do you want for Thomson?"
Can you picture me giving up that guy?
                                        —Leo Durocher, 1949

I held out in 1948. I knew I had a strong rookie year and I wanted a
couple of thousand more than they were offering. So I went to spring
training figuring I would work out with the club while I tried to negoti-
ate a contract. But Mel Ott, who was still managing at the beginning
of the year, wouldn't let Buddy Kerr and myself practice until we
signed. The papers said he was cracking down for the first time in his
managerial career.

Mel came up to me at the hotel one day with a word about Stoneham. "I know the old man, Bobby," he said. "He's stubborn enough to
let you sit out all year."

Then there were stories in the *Mirror* by Ken Smith saying I was
asking for a cut of the gate. Ken was a real Mel Ott fan. So I went to
Mel Ott and said it wasn't true and the *Mirror* retracted it.

But I didn't like the idea of sitting out the season. I was a young kid
who wanted to play ball. Maybe what Mel said about Mr. Stoneham
being stubborn got to me. Anyway, we compromised and I signed for
a reasonable raise and went back to work. I got about $13,000 that
year. And when I hit two home runs in the opening series in Philadelphia I started to read the big prediction stuff again: Thomson's going
to hit 40 home runs this year. Needless to say, it didn't happen.

I began having trouble at the plate early in the season and in those
days I got my back up when everyone and his uncle had advice for me.

We had a coach named Red Kress who said, "Bob, you're not really swinging at the ball." I remember getting pretty teed off with him about that. Soon afterward, I started reading that I was becoming a problem child. What I was was a stubborn, frustrated, immature kid who wasn't hitting.

Like everyone else, I can recall the feeling of shock when we heard Leo was coming over to manage the Giants. I remember that first meeting when he ran his hand across his chest and said, *"Giants!"* We all knew right away this guy meant business and that we had better get out there and hustle. Even though the team wasn't very good then, Leo was the kind of manager who always put pressure on the opposition and always seemed to be one step ahead of everyone else.

It didn't take long for us to realize that Leo wanted to make changes. Walker Cooper wasn't a big Durocher fan and I'm sure the feeling was mutual. I also had the feeling Leo didn't like Buddy Kerr. As far as I'm concerned, Buddy Kerr played as great a shortstop in 1947 as I'd ever seen. But Buddy was a sensitive guy and Leo wasn't his cup of tea.

There were even rumors Leo wanted to get rid of me when I wasn't going well. There were certain things Leo liked in a ball player. He liked guys who could hit with power, throw, and run, and I guess he eventually began seeing some potential in me, especially when I started to snap out of my slump.

But we all knew where Leo was coming from. He wanted us to get out there and play baseball, which to him meant doing things like hitting behind the runner. Al Dark was great at that, but I was lousy at it, especially in those early years. There was one game when we had a man on second and Leo wanted the guy on third. Well, I ended up bouncing the ball right to the shortstop and of course, the runner couldn't advance. Leo really got on my case about that, implying I wasn't trying to do my job.

Leo could yell and holler at you right in front of everyone, but the nice thing was you could yell and holler right back, and the next day it would be forgotten, business as usual. But Leo emphasized fundamentals much more than Mel Ott did. He was more apt to do the little things that won ball games: bunt, squeeze, hit behind the runner— skills that some of us Giants knew we had to master pretty quickly.

Of course, we all knew Leo was something special when it came to being a big league manager. We were aware of his style and pace. His personality was a big part of it. He was loud, but at the same time he was articulate. He was "Hollywood." His fingernails were beautifully done. He was always well groomed. He wore expensive clothes. He was sharp. He always had his friends from the entertainment world coming to the games.

I remember meeting Tony Martin and Cyd Charisse during spring training. Groucho Marx would also visit the team. Life with Leo was never dull.

The 1948 season wasn't very memorable for me. Some people call it the sophomore jinx, but I just didn't feel comfortable at the plate all year, didn't swing well. Maybe it had come too easy the year before. Maybe it was immaturity and not taking the right advice. And there was a little more pressure once Leo got there. In the end, my batting average dipped to .248 and I certainly didn't hit with the same kind of authority as I had the year before.

The off-season that year took an interesting turn. A bunch of major leaguers decided to barnstorm for a couple of weeks. There must have been about a dozen of us and we traveled by car, making a series of stops in the Midwest, playing local teams in front of small crowds. We didn't make a heck of a lot of money, but we had a damn good time. Dick Sisler, who was with the Phillies, organized the trip and took care of the business end. Around the seventh inning of each game, Dick would take himself out of the lineup so he could count the receipts. After the game we would divide it up. We were lucky if we got $25 a game.

Walker Cooper was with us, along with Branca, Ken Trinkle, and Buddy Blattner. Sisler stuttered and Blattner used to kid him about it. It became a kind of running joke throughout the trip. One day we were driving through the countryside when we noticed the gas gauge on Sisler's car was just about on empty.

"Hey, Dick," someone said. "We don't want to get stuck out here in the middle of nowhere. You're supposed to be watching the gas gauge."

Luckily, we came across a little town with a gas station and we all got on Dick's back, telling him to stop and not pass this one up. So he pulled into the station and this little guy stuck his head in the window and said,"H-H-H-H-How many?"

For the first time all day there was complete silence in the car. Then Sisler answered: "F-F-F-F-Fill 'er up."

And the little guy said, "You s-s-s-s-sonofabitch."

We laughed so hard we hurt. It took a while, but we finally explained that Dick wasn't making fun of him, that he stuttered, too. But that's the kind of fun we had.

The trip was only supposed to last two weeks, but I didn't get to finish it. Our tour took us to Buckner, Missouri, which was Cooper's hometown. The night before the game we drank a few beers and the next day at Coop's house, we were relaxing and having a few more beers. All of a sudden I started feeling lousy. At first Coop needled me, telling me I couldn't handle a few beers. But when I told him I was really starting to feel awful, he decided to call a doctor. The diagnosis was appendicitis and they rushed me to the hospital for surgery. That was it for barnstorming. I stayed at Walker's house for a couple of weeks to recuperate. He treated me like a father, and his wife, Doris, was equally great taking care of me.

I knew Coop didn't get along with Leo and he was one of the first to go in 1949. He could knock the hell out of the ball and knock the third baseman down, but he couldn't do those little things Leo wanted. We stayed friends after he was traded to Cincinnati, but I'll never forget the first time I came up to hit when we played the Reds and he was catching. I was digging in, concentrating on the pitcher, and Coop decided to start a conversation.

"Hey, Hoot. Want me to sing a little song?"

"Come on, Coop, knock it off. Let me hit."

"What song do you want me to sing, Hoot? Pick a song. I'll sing it. Come on, pick one."

He kept insisting he was going to sing this song until I was laughing so much I had to step out of the box. That was Coop. A real pistol. But also a Cincinnati Red and trying his damndest to win the game.

The 1949 season turned into a great one for me, but a real year of change for the team. I got out of the gate fast and kept it going for almost the entire season. I started every game in center field and batted third. But the team didn't play well most of the year and Leo began making the changes that we all expected. Coop went, then Mize, and the team finished fifth with a sub-.500 record. I finished up hitting .309 with 27 homers and 109 RBIs, and that got a lot of ink.

Things grew better between me and Leo, too. The fact that I had a good year helped. But he had heard that Thomson had a bad attitude the year before, and that didn't help matters in the beginning.

But late in the season we were playing Cincinnati and the pitcher really decked me. I got up, dusted off, and hit a home run on the next pitch. I learned later that Leo was really impressed by that. There's no doubt he liked tough ball players.

During the off-season the Giants made the big trade, the one that brought Al Dark and Eddie Stanky to the ball club. They were a matched pair, one just as aggressive as the other. And they were needlers. There's no question that after we got those two we became as aggressive as anyone else.

Don't get me wrong. Even under Mel Ott the game could be rough. We were playing the Cards one day during my rookie year when Harry Brecheen hit Johnny Mize smack in the head. We had a left-handed pitcher named Monte Kennedy who could throw hard, but always had trouble finding the plate. When Brecheen came up, Mel told Monte to hit him in the knee. I remember thinking that Monte was sometimes lucky if he got 1 out of 10 over the plate. How was he going to hit Brecheen in the knee? But Monte wound up and, sure enough, hit him in the leg. Brecheen started trotting to first and I began doing a slow burn, thinking this was hardly a tradeoff for hitting Mize in the head. Then halfway to first base Brecheen fell down and they had to help him off the field. Monte had gotten him pretty good after all.

So it was a tough game before Leo. Leo just took it one step further. He was a "two-for-one" guy, especially against the Dodgers. He'd say, "Let's not start at them. But as soon as one of their guys comes up under our chin, I want two for one." He wasn't about to take a backseat to anyone. And, conversely, everyone had it in for Durocher. Charlie Grimm, for example, was a good manager and as nice a man as you wanted to see. Other guys wanted to beat Charlie, but those same guys wanted to *kill* Durocher. It was a difference, and sometimes not too subtle a difference. Dark and Stanky also added a combative element to the team. They thought Larry Jansen wasn't aggressive enough, wanted him to throw inside more and used to needle him about it. That wasn't Larry's nature, but Leo encouraged that kind of thing.

Al Dark was a real athlete, and a good hitter. Defensively he wasn't the kind of shortstop who could go into the hole like Pee Wee Reese. And he wasn't a quick-release guy with the ball. But he was a very confident, aggressive player who took a lot of pride in his work. And that was a very big plus for us.

Stanky was "the Brat" through and through, with us and with our opponents. One day Eddie came into the dugout teed off about something and kicked over a bucket of ice water. Luckily he kicked it toward Wes Westrum, a sturdy, even-tempered man who was sitting quietly minding his own business. The ice water went all over him. What was really comical was the way the water dripped from the peak of Wes's cap as he said, "Come on, Eddie, cut it out." A big guy like Wes with a bad temper could have torn little Eddie apart.

Eddie really knew how to set on the opposition. He was always doing something to screw up the other team. Sometimes he'd jump up and down at second, waving his arms, trying to distract the hitter. I had never seen that done before. We were playing the Phillies in a close game one day late in the 1950 season and he started into this act when their catcher, Andy Seminick, was up. Seminick got sore and it ended up in a huge argument. The umpire threw Stanky out and later in the inning Seminick, who had got on base, slid hard into Bill Rigney at second. They came up swinging and it turned into a real brawl. Of course, the real perpetrator was safe and sound in the locker room. But that was the Brat for you. All three of them—Leo, Dark, and Stanky—could antagonize the opposition, but all they really wanted to do was win the game.

The Giants were a different team in 1950. And Thomson was having another lousy year. I couldn't explain it. Maybe I was pressing again. Mel Ott came in to work with me at the end of August. He shortened my stance and made me conscious of the fact that my weight was on my front foot instead of the back. And it helped.

I was hitting only .231 going into the final month and I managed to get my average up 21 points before the season ended. So I felt a little better about myself at the end. And like everyone else, I looked forward to starting over in 1951.

The Rivalry and Charley Dressen

By the spring of 1950, the pieces for the 1951 pennant race were in place—almost. The Dodgers under Burt Shotton were defending National League champions, having topped the Cardinals by a single game. Though the Brooks were beaten by the Yanks in a quick, five-game World Series, the team from Flatbush was clearly considered the class of the National League, an already fine ball club with the potential to be great. Their basic, eight-man lineup had all-star–caliber players at nearly every position.

The Giants, on the other hand, would be starting 1950 with a revamped lineup, and a different kind of team. Mize, Kerr, Gordon, and Marshall were gone. Stanky, Dark, outfielder Don Mueller, and a combination of Tookie Gilbert and Monte Irvin took their place. Durocher was still juggling players and lineups, still looking for the right combination. And the veterans, players who had been there since 1947, had to adjust to Durocher's new kind of game.

Al Dark, who took over at short for the Jints in '50, remembers the kind of team they were when he was still with the Braves.

"Playing the Giants was no problem," Dark recalls. "In 1947 and '48 it was a home run or nothing. If there was a ground ball hit with a man on base, it was an automatic double play. They were that slow. Bobby was about the only one who could really run.

"As a shortstop, it made a big difference playing a team like the

69

Giants. You didn't have to worry about stealing and you didn't have to worry about the hit and run, so you weren't as itchy in the field. Against a team like the Dodgers you could never go to sleep out there. Every time they got a guy on base you'd have to keep your eye on him until the pitcher had the ball on the way to the plate. *Then* you went to the plate with your eyes. None of that was necessary against the Giants. That was one of the first things Leo changed. He wanted more defense and more speed.

"I roomed with Eddie Stanky at Boston and we talked baseball all the time. He's the one who first told me about Leo from their Brooklyn days, the kind of manager he was and what he expected out of a ball player. Winning was the only thing that mattered. That was fine with me, because as far as I was concerned winning was the fun part of the game. If you didn't win, nobody in the clubhouse was doing a backflip or worrying about next year's salary. Our deal was to win and that was it. That was all Leo cared about, too. That's why I liked playing for him."

But winning didn't come easy for the Giants at the beginning of the 1950 season. The pitching wasn't deep and some players were still trying to get used to the new manager. In addition, Bobby Thomson had gotten off to a slow start and wasn't producing the numbers he had in '49, when Durocher called him "our star."

"These kinds of slumps were always tough on Bobby," said Bill Rigney, who was a teammate in 1950 and would later be his manager. "He always wanted to achieve something for the team and he played as if he loved the game. There was no dog in Bobby. There was also no chance of Leo trading him when he cleaned house because Bobby was already a fine center fielder. Leo needed Bobby's talent because he wanted a team that could do everything."

The 1950 Giants could certainly do more than in the past. Westrum was now the regular catcher. In the outfield, Thomson was flanked by Lockman and Mueller, youngsters who could hit. Stanky and Dark were a fine keystone combination. The only weaknesses in the starting team were at the corners. Henry Thompson was more or less the regular third baseman. He hit with some pop and had a good year at the plate. But he was often erratic in the field and not always reliable on a day-to-day basis.

First base was the second problem spot. Monte Irvin, a 31-year-old veteran of the Negro Leagues, and a player with great hitting potential, played there part of the year but didn't really like the position. Young Tookie Gilbert, 10 years Irvin's junior, saw more action at first, but Gilbert just didn't hit and didn't look as if he would hit. Leo couldn't decide between them and kept making changes.

But on the whole, the starting lineup was potentially a good one, the kind of lineup that would do well if there was a little more power to back it up and some adequate pitching in front of it. By the second half of 1950, that pitching started to come. Right-hander Larry Jansen continued to be the workhorse of the staff as he had been since his great 21–5 rookie year of 1947. He would wind up 19–13 in 1950. But the success of the staff, and ultimately the team, came from two unexpected pitching sources. One started the year with the Giants but hadn't been regarded as anything special. The other came in a July trade.

There's an old Buddhist proverb that says, "When a pupil is ready, a teacher will appear." Fortunately for the Giants, proverb became prophecy with a pair of right-handed pitchers who had seemed little more than journeymen.

Sal Maglie was already 33 years old when the 1950 season began. His major league record up to that time was 5–4, compiled in 13 games with the Giants back in 1945. The next year, Maglie became one of a handful of big leaguers to jump to the outlaw Mexican League and was subsequently banned from the majors for five years by Commissioner Chandler. The jumpers returned from Mexico in 1947 and by 1950 the commissioner had shortened the suspension to three years, allowing Maglie to rejoin the Giants.

Early in the year, Maglie pitched mainly out of the bullpen, most often in mop-up roles. It took a few months for Durocher and his coaches to realize this wasn't the same pitcher who had gone south of the border four years earlier. Unlike others who found the Mexican League experience frustrating and unrewarding, Sal Maglie found himself a guru, a former major league hurler named Dolf Luque who taught the competitive right-hander the art of pitching. Luque was one of the first native Cubans to achieve success in the majors, pitching from 1914 to 1935 and winning 193 games. He knew what hurling was all about.

"Dolf Luque taught Maglie the art of using the curveball," said Jack Lang, who covered the Dodgers for the *Long Island Press* in the early 1950s. Well known today as the secretary of the Baseball Writers

Association of America, Lang remembers the transformation of Sal Maglie and the reason for it. "Dolf showed Sal how to work inside and outside, and not to be afraid to push people back with it. That came natural to Sal. He was a nothing pitcher until he went to Mexico. And when he came back he quickly became dominant. To Sal's credit, he never hesitated to tell people that Luque was the one who turned his career around."

In the second half of the 1950 season, Maglie was moved into the starting rotation and was suddenly all but unbeatable. He would finish the season with an incredible 18–4 record, completing 12 of his 16 starts. Catcher Wes Westrum marveled at the assortment of curves Sal brought back with him from Mexico.

"Sal had three types of curveballs," Westrum recalls. "One broke four inches, the second six inches, and the third was a big, breaking curve that moved eight inches. He wrapped the ball differently for each one and he wasn't afraid to pitch inside. He would throw a high, inside pitch to a batter, shave him close. Then when he got the ball back from me he would play this little game. He'd say, 'This ball is slippery. Give me a new one.' As if it was the ball's fault that it came in tight."

Reclamation project number two was a six-foot-three right-hander named Jim Hearn. From 1947 through 1949, the hard-throwing Hearn had a mediocre 21–16 record with the Cardinals. He was just 0–1 in six games with the Cards through July of 1950 when the Giants bought him for a modest price. The question was what to do with him. Durocher knew. He told two of his coaches to take over.

So Hearn came under the tutelage of Frank Shellenback and Freddie Fitzsimmons. Shellenback had pitched for 20 years in the Pacific Coast League, where he could legally throw his spitter, and for a couple in the bigs. Fitzsimmons, known as Fat Freddie, was a major league hurler for 19 years, winning 217 games. These two veterans had a ton of experience and were invaluable to the Giants. Jim Hearn remembers what they did for him.

"When I came over from St. Louis I was basically a straight overhand pitcher," Hearn recalls. "I threw hard and had an overhand curve, but I wasn't having a lot of success. Then I hooked up with Frank and Freddie. After they watched me for awhile they told me to drop down a little with my delivery. So instead of throwing directly overhand, I threw from the three-quarter position. The ball came off my fingers at a different angle and my fastball started to drop. It became like a sinker with the new angle and I started to win."

Win, he did. After going 0–1 in half a season with the Cards, big Jim was 11–3 with the Giants and wound up with a league-best 2.49 earned run average (1.94 with the Giants). With Maglie, Jansen, and Hearn all pitching well, the Giants unveiled a big three in the second half of 1950 that could keep pace with anyone. Now the team had a semblance of a real staff. That took the pressure off guys like Dave Koslo, Monte Kennedy, and Sheldon Jones.

Proof came in the final two months of the season. To be precise, from July 21 to season's end, the Giants won 49 games and lost just 22. They were the hottest team in the league, maybe the best team. While everyone was watching the developing race between the upstart "Whiz Kids" Phillies team and the Dodgers, the Giants were sneaking up. They finished at 86–68, 5 games behind the Phillies. It was a 13-game improvement over 1949.

In fact, Leo had the Giants playing so well that more than one observer remarked that had the season lasted another week to 10 days, the Giants would have taken it. The discovery of Maglie and the resurgence of Hearn along with the steadiness of Jansen played a big part. But guys like Westrum, Lockman, Mueller, and Hank Thompson joined Stanky and Dark in putting together solid seasons. The biggest offensive disappointment had to be Bobby Thomson, who hit just .252 with 25 homers and 85 RBIs. But Bobby had also finished strong the final month and, like everyone else, was now feeling good about the entire ball club.

Of course, the Giants weren't involved in the main scenario in 1950. That was between the favored Dodgers and the upstart Philadelphia Phillies, a team that had finished 16 games out in 1949. The Whiz Kids, as they were called, became one-year wonders. They would drop below .500 in 1951, but in 1950 they shocked everyone by staying at or near the top most of the way.

The Dodgers didn't have a strong year, either. The team hit well, but the pitching wasn't deep. Still, the ball club managed a late-season charge. With two games left, both with the Phils, the Brooks trailed by just two. They had to win the pair to tie, but were already on a roll, having taken 13 of their last 16 games, while the Whiz Kids had lost 8 of 10. When the Dodgers won the first game at Ebbets Field, 7–3, things looked good. Now it was down to one.

The year before, the Dodgers had to beat the Phils in the final game to preserve their one-game pennant advantage over the Cards. Now Brooklyn's (and Philadelphia's) fate hinged on a single contest. A Dodger victory would force a best-of-three playoff. The game was a classic pitcher's battle between right-handed aces, Don Newcombe of the Dodgers and Robin Roberts of the Phils. It was tied 1–1 going into the bottom half of the ninth inning. Now it was the Dodgers' game for the taking.

Cal Abrams opened with a walk and Pee Wee Reese promptly singled him to second. Duke Snider was up next, with Jackie Robinson, Carl Furillo, and Gil Hodges to follow. Sound baseball strategy called for a sacrifice. But Manager Shotton had the Duke swing away and for a few seconds the bunt was forgotten. Snider had come through with a sharp single to center. The Phils' Richie Ashburn scooped the ball up on the run and fired a strike to catcher Stan Lopata. Abrams, who had raced home on the go signal from third base coach Milt Stock, was a sitting duck. The game-winning, pennant-tying run was cut down at the plate.

Roberts then gave Robinson an intentional walk to load the bases, retired Furillo on a pop to first and Hodges on a fly to right. The Phils had dodged a bullet.

Newcombe was still pitching in the top of the tenth and gave up a leadoff single to opposing pitcher Roberts. No hook from the Dodger bench. Eddie Waitkus then looped a single to center. Ashburn tried to sacrifice but Newcombe fielded the bunt and caught Roberts at third.

Now Dick Sisler was up. With the count 1–2, Sisler connected with a Newcombe fastball and drove it into the left field bleachers for a three-run homer. Roberts retired the Dodgers in the last of the tenth and the pennant belonged to the Phils. The Dodgers, considered the most talented team in the league, went home losers.

But Shotton, the veteran skipper who had taken over from Durocher during his suspension in 1947 and again when Leo was fired in '48, accepted the blame for the loss by saying he should have had Snider bunt. Ralph Branca, who pitched on the '50 team and was never a Shotton fan, agreed, but for a different reason.

"Shotton lost that game," Branca said, "because he never should have had Abrams on the base paths. He had Eddie Miksis sitting on the bench and Eddie was one of the fastest men in the league. He was the guy who scored from first in the 1947 World Series when Lavagetto broke up Bevens's no-hitter in the ninth. But Shotton never made the move."

After the season, third base coach Stock was fired and Shotton went soon after that. Abrams took a lot of flack because some said he hesitated, started back to second for a split second before heading to third. Newcombe, who threw the downtown pitch to Sisler, is rarely mentioned as the goat, probably because most people figured that, one way or the other, the Dodgers should have won it in the last of the ninth. It was a tough defeat and the firings of Stock and Shotton were just two of the repercussions.

There would be two more major changes in the Dodgers in the off-season that would affect the fortunes of the team in both the immediate and long-range future. Walter O'Malley now had complete control of the ball club, having finally succeeded in ousting Branch Rickey in October of 1950. But the Branch Rickey that O'Malley sent packing to the Pittsburgh Pirates was an aging, ill man who undoubtedly realized it wasn't worth waging war to keep a piece of the Dodger franchise. However, the Mahatma played one final trump card before departing. O'Malley had offered to buy Rickey out for the exact amount of money that it cost Rickey to come aboard—$325,000. Rickey threatened to sell his shares to real estate magnate William Zeckendorff, thereby giving O'Malley a partner he did not want. This maneuver forced O'Malley to up the ante considerably, allowing the Mahatma to walk away with a sizable profit.

There is little doubt about the way Walter O'Malley operated. Irving Rudd was the Dodgers' longtime publicist during the period of the 1950s and saw the man they called the "Big O" in action. Still an active PR man today, Rudd has this reflection about those early years when O'Malley put his stamp on every aspect of the ball club.

"O'Malley was heartless in his approach to making money in baseball," Rudd says. "In fact, his approach was just the opposite of Brooklyn fans. To them, the Dodgers were like a religion. The people there had two houses of worship, the church or synagogue of their choice and Ebbets Field.

"But O'Malley was different. Let me give you an example. There was a man named Harold Hickey, who was a director on the Dodgers. He was a strong supporter of O'Malley in the Big O's battle against

Rickey. In 1956, the Dodgers were going on a postseason trip to Japan and Hickey, although he was a sick man at the time, wanted to go and bring his wife along, as well.

"I went into O'Malley's office with Harold Parrott, the team's traveling secretary, to ask Big O if Harold Hickey could go with the team. And there was O'Malley, sitting with that big cigar in his hand, sucking on that cigar, blowing smoke on you for effect. That cigar was a great tool in his hand.

"After we asked him about Hickey, O'Malley paused to puff on the cigar. Finally, he looks at me and says, 'Did you ever stop to think what it would cost to ship a body home from Japan?' That's just one of many stories about O'Malley that show you the kind of guy he was."

It was O'Malley, however, who made the decision to name Charley Dressen as the new manager of the ball club. In doing that, he put the final piece in place, the piece that made the 1951 pennant race possible. It had been a rather circuitous journey, and had A not led to B, which in turn led to C and so on, it certainly wouldn't have happened the same way.

What if Durocher hadn't been suspended in 1947? What if the Dodgers hadn't gotten off to such a slow start in 1948? What if O'Malley and Rickey hadn't become embroiled in a power struggle? What if Stoneham hadn't agreed to let Durocher deal his sluggers and pursue the likes of Dark and Stanky? What if Ashburn hadn't made a good throw and Cal Abrams had been safe at the plate? Just one change, one piece out of place . . .

The final bit of business—the appointment of Charley Dressen as the new manager of the Dodgers—set the stage for the upcoming race. Dressen, once Leo Durocher's self-described right arm when he coached under the Lip, brought with him an attitude that would affect the way the 1951 race was played out. This attitude was described very clearly by Carl Erskine, one of Dressen's top starting pitchers in 1951. Despite the passage of four decades, Erskine's feelings about Charley Dressen's motivations in 1951 are clear.

"While I admired him as a good baseball man and a manager who was always encouraging to me, it was obvious that Charley Dressen was paranoid about beating Leo," says the man Brooklynites affectionately called "Oisk." "Charley felt that a lot of the strategic moves Leo made when he managed the Dodgers were actually his decisions. So when Charley became manager of the Dodgers, he was obsessed by a drive to show Leo and the world that he was the brains and always had been. While the rivalry between the two teams intensified when Leo went to the Giants, the undercurrents of the rivalry were further enhanced with Dressen's appearance on the scene."

Dressen's appearance on the scene didn't happen overnight. A five-foot, five-and-a-half-inch dynamo, Charley began his minor league career playing second base for Moline in 1919. A year later he became an early version of Bo Jackson when he was the starting quarterback for the professional Decatur, Illinois, Staleys, the forerunners of the Chicago Bears. Dressen played three years of professional football, then in 1925 joined the Cincinnati Reds for an eight-year major league baseball career.

Though never a great player, Dressen exhibited toughness, grit, hustle, and a self-assuredness that bordered on the arrogant. Back in the minor leagues during the 1931 season, Charley began looking beyond his playing days, and the future didn't look bright. Then, in the middle of the following year, he heard that the owner of the Nashville team in the Southern League was considering a change of managers. Dressen borrowed money to travel to Nashville, where he sought out team owner Fay Murray and asked to manage a team that was mired in a deep slump.

"What makes you think you can turn this team around?" Murray asked him.

Dressen puffed out his chest and replied, "If I don't win at least half of the remaining games, you don't have to pay me a penny of my salary."

It was an offer Murray couldn't refuse. He hired Dressen on the spot, maybe even hoping to save a manager's salary for the rest of the year. Like a storybook ending, Dressen's fate and his ability to pay his bills came down to one final game. The team was 38–38 under Charley when it scratched and clawed its way to a 12–8 victory in the final game, making the manager a winner and a paid employee at the same time.

"That last game held the key to my baseball career," Dressen would say later.

In 1933, Dressen returned to the big leagues long enough to play 16 games at third base for the New York Giants. The next year Larry MacPhail hired him to manage the Cincinnati Reds. He was fired four years later because he couldn't get the Red into the first division.

Dressen returned to manage at Nashville briefly, but after MacPhail moved to Brooklyn in 1938 and hired Leo Durocher as his manager the following year, Charley got the call to join the team as a coach.

For eight years Dressen and Durocher were a team, a pair of artful Dodgers who played the game in similar fashion. The D & D team stayed together until Leo was suspended in 1947. Dressen also left that year, moving crosstown to coach for the Yankees. Two years later he went to manage Oakland in the Pacific Coast League, winning a pennant there in 1950.

When Walter O'Malley decided that the Dodgers needed new blood after losing to the Phils in the final game of 1950, he picked Dressen, figuring Charley was just the man to light a little extra fire under an already great team.

The ability of the Brooklyn team going into the 1951 season was unquestioned. The players are still well known, reading like a who's who of 1950s stars: Campanella behind the plate, an infield of Hodges, Robinson, Reese, and Cox. In the outfield, there were Snider, Furillo, and then the team's one weak link—left field. At the beginning of 1951, Cal Abrams, Gene Hermanski, and rookie Don Thompson all split time in left.

This was a great offensive team. Campanella, Hodges, Snider, and Furillo all hit with power, and were capable of hitting over .300 as well. Reese and Robinson were the table-setting catalysts who could do the little things both at the bat and on the bases.

Robinson, of course, was an incredibly competitive, aggressive player who drove himself and his teammates. He had been the National League's Most Valuable Player in 1949. Now, no longer operating under Branch Rickey's turn-the-other-cheek gag rule, he was as vocal as he was talented and, more often than not, the focal point of the team.

But because he was so often embroiled in controversy, firing the emotions in friend and foe alike, it was Pee Wee Reese, the captain, who was considered the team leader.

"Pee Wee was the most important Dodger," was the way Ralph Branca puts it, "but Jackie was probably the best overall player we had. He could beat you so many ways."

Duke Snider concurred. "Pee Wee's value to the team went far beyond what he did on the playing field," the Duke said. "He was our captain and unquestioned leader. With Pee Wee around, we all maintained a level of mental sharpness that carried on throughout the entire 154-game season. With Jackie, we became a solid team, and Pee Wee was instrumental in shaping Jackie into a major leaguer."

The Dodgers were also solid on the mound. They had a trio of all-star performers in Don Newcombe, Preacher Roe, and Carl Erskine. The three offset each other. Newk and Ersk were righties, one an overpowering fastballer, the other a guy with a great curve as his out pitch. Roe, the southpaw, relied on guile, offspeed stuff, plus a ball that many opposing batters suspected often contained a bit more moisture than was legal.

Right behind them was Branca, already a 20-game winner, and a pitcher who was as good as anyone when he was healthy. The second-line pitchers were a question mark, but there were certainly enough arms for Dressen to build a staff. Despite their loss to the Phils a year earlier, the Dodgers were heavy favorites in 1951. It seemed that Charley Dressen had walked into the perfect situation.

The longtime baseball man knew what he had. Even before the season began he announced that "the team that beats us can win the pennant, but nobody is going to beat us."

Dressen was also quick to dissociate himself from his predecessor when he told his team, "There was a doghouse in Brooklyn under Shotton, but that isn't my way of managing."

In effect, Dressen was telling his team to relax and play ball, and they would win.

If Charley Dressen was throwing down a gauntlet to the rest of the National League, Leo Durocher was quick to pick it up. He, too, predicted his team was ready to ascend to the top, especially after the fast finish in '50.

"This is my kind of team now," he said to reporters. "We showed what we can do the second half of last year. If we don't win it all this year, you guys can write whatever you want about me and you'll get no complaints. If we don't win this thing, then I don't belong in baseball."

So both managers were firing the first salvo in what would prove to be a race to remember. Not only was it between two outstanding baseball teams. But it was the Giants and the Dodgers. Because there has never been a rivalry like it, before or since, the 1951 pennant race would become unique and special.

The Dodgers and Giants represented the only two franchises in baseball history to compete in the same city in the same league. It was a natural rivalry that, more often than not, became so intense it led to downright animosity.

And it had been going on for years. In 1933, the Giants, under star first baseman Bill Terry, were world champions, while the Dodgers were mired in sixth place. The following spring, sportswriter Roscoe McGowen of *The New York Times* asked Terry which teams might challenge the Giants for National League supremacy in 1934. After Terry mentioned the Cards and one or two others, McGowen loaded up his follow-up.

"How about Brooklyn, Bill?" he asked.

Terry, normally an unsmiling man, grinned and said, "Is Brooklyn still in the league?"

Big laughs. Everywhere but in Brooklyn, that is. Casey Stengel became the Dodger manager that year and Ol' Case made sure his players were aware of Terry's offhand remark . . . and wouldn't forget it. The Dodgers would still finish sixth and under .500, but against the Giants, they played as if their lives—and their pride—depended on it.

Terry's violation of the time-honored let-sleeping-dogs-lie adage came back to haunt him and his team. With two games left in the regular season, the Giants and Cardinals were dead even, tied for first. The Gas House Gang had a pair of games with Cincinnati, while the Giants had to play that sixth-place team from Flatbush.

It was no surprise when the Cardinals came through and won their games against the Reds. The surprise came when the upstart Dodgers went into the Polo Grounds and took the Giants on both Saturday and Sunday. Brooklyn had answered Bill Terry's flip remark. It had proved it was still in the league by knocking the Giants out of the pennant race.

The story of how Terry's remark came back to haunt him got a great deal of ink that year. The lesson should have been learned. And remember, the scene was observed firsthand by two men: Leo Durocher, the shortstop for the pennant-winning Cardinals, and Charley Dressen, the brand-new manager of the Cincinnati Reds. Whether they learned anything from this incident wouldn't be known until 1951.

By that time the rivalry was once again in full bloom. Pee Wee Reese already commented on it when he said there seemed to be some kind of a fracas every time the two teams played. Here's how some of the other participants and observers remember the great rivalry between the two ball clubs.

"The atmosphere was always electric when the two teams played," said the Giants' Whitey Lockman. "It was war whenever we met, even moreso in Ebbets Field than the Polo Grounds. It was undoubtedly a problem for them to come to our ballpark, but everything was so close at Ebbets Field and the fans were more emotional. They were vocal, but not really abusive or profane. Sure, things would creep in once in awhile, but they were just rabid, die-hard Dodger fans who loved it when the two ball clubs played. There was just something special about the games we played against them."

Jack Lang echoed Lockman's war theme. "It didn't even matter if one of the clubs wasn't in the pennant race, it was still war," the secretary of the Baseball Writers Association of America says. "In fact, you simply threw all reason out the window when those two teams played. Maybe the best example I could give you about the Giant-Dodger rivalry came in 1958, when both teams left for the West Coast. That year the Yankees had New York all to themselves and their attendance actually went down. Giant and Dodger fans didn't become Yankee fans. It was the Hatfields and McCoys and people couldn't give it up that quickly."

Al Dark also recalls the strong feelings and the anticipation every-time the two teams were scheduled to meet.

"I was involved with big league baseball for 28 years and I've never seen anything like the rivalry between the two teams. When I was with the Giants I can always remember looking at the schedule and if we were playing the Dodgers in two weeks I started checking on their pitching staff, doing anything I could to get ready for them.

"I can remember when I was with the Cubs in 1958 and I saw Pee Wee and Duke outside the ballpark in Chicago. I was in my car and heading downtown and they hollered to me for a lift. I actually drove a block down the road before saying to myself, 'Oh, hell, I better go back and get them.' I actually wasn't going do it. And when I got them in the car I told them not to tell anyone that I had given them a ride.

"So even when I had gone to the Cubs I still disliked the Dodgers as much as I did before. That was because the Giant-Dodger rivalry was the greatest thing I've ever been involved with in baseball. You re-spected them, but you also wanted to kill 'em."

For Dodgers Don Newcombe and Clem Labine, memories of the

rivalry go so deep that they recall how it affected the teams' minor league ball clubs.

"I had read a lot about the Dodger-Giant rivalry before I even came to the big leagues," says Newk. "I was already looking forward to it when the Dodgers signed me and sent me to the minors. Then when I was with Montreal I realized the same thing existed between Montreal and the Jersey City Giants. We were all aware of it and tried harder against Jersey City than any other team in the league. It was just a natural thing that every time you played the Giants—Jersey City or New York—there was a little something extra that you always tried to do."

"I found the same thing in the American Association when I was with the St. Paul Saints [the Dodger's farm team] and played the Minneapolis Millers [the Giants' club]," said Labine. "The two teams had a great rivalry that I'm sure filtered down from the big leagues, though I don't think it was as intense because we were mostly much younger people. But we all felt something special in the rivalry."

That was the natural part of the rivalry. As the 1951 season got under way it soon became obvious that there was an added attraction—Durocher versus Dressen. The personal rivalry between the opposing managers would give an extra push to an already intense situation and would have a direct bearing on the outcome. Now, as members of both ball clubs got ready, tuning their bodies and their skills in the spring sunshine of Florida, it was almost showtime.

Winkie

I was in Seattle on business when my wife called me and said that Bob and Wink were planning to get married. She said they had set a date of January 10, 1953. I was always sort of an unofficial financial adviser to Bob and when I heard the date they had picked I sent Bob a telegram. It read, "Impossible get married 10th of January. Must get married before December 31, midnight." I figured they might as well be able to file a joint tax return. Bob used to always kid me after that, saying I bought his honeymoon for him.

—Al Corbin

During the early part of my career I still lived at home on Staten Island with my mom. She became a great Giants fan and liked nothing better than to cook for the guys. In the summer, we rented a cottage for a month in Greenwood Lake in upstate New York, about an hour and a half out of the city. When the team was home I commuted to the games from up there.

A few of the guys enjoyed coming up to Greenwood Lake with me, either after a game or on an off day. It was kind of a treat for some of the out-of-town guys who rented a room or lived in a hotel during the season. They could come up there, get a great meal from Mom, do some swimming and boating.

One off day, Larry Jansen, Whitey Lockman, Joe Lafata, and myself drove up to the lake. None of us had been brought up around the water and we weren't exactly experts handling sailboats or canoes, although we thought we were. I was in a sailboat with Lafata and Larry was paddling a canoe. When I tried to bring the sailboat around, Lafata fell overboard. Joe didn't swim well so he was in trouble right away. I was still trying to bring the sailboat around and suddenly I was heading straight for Joe and there was Larry coming at him in the canoe from the other direction. For a second I thought we were going to collide, and all the while Lafata was thrashing around in the water

83

yelling for help. Somehow, we got him out, but we must have looked like a bunch of city slickers trying to survive up in God's country.

In retrospect, I lived a pretty calm and quiet life in those years. We gave everything we had on the field. Away from the ballpark we didn't create a whole lot of excitement like some of the players today. Maybe it was the guys I hung out with. A lot of us had been in the service, the older guys had lost some years of their careers, and we were all worried about making enough money. Of course, there were some party guys, but I wasn't one of them, especially during the season.

Then I met Winkie. Like so many meetings of this kind, it began by chance. After my first full year in organized ball, in 1946, I decided to take a few classes at St. Lawrence University in Canton, New York, up by the Canadian border. Hal Schumacher, the old Giant pitcher, was a great St. Lawrence alum and was instrumental in my going there.

Once I arrived I made a group of friends, guys and gals, and we used to go out on the town together, have a few beers and a good time. One of the gals in the group was from South Plainfield, New Jersey, and every New Year's Day her parents would throw a big party. She invited me and eventually said she'd like me to meet a friend of hers.

Wink grew up in North Plainfield and the first year she was supposed to be at the party, she didn't show up. But the next year, New Year's Day in 1951, she was there. We chatted at the party and before I left I asked Wink if I could call her again. She said yes, but I didn't call for about two or three weeks. Finally, I called, we went out once or twice and then I left for spring training.

At that time, Wink admitted she wasn't really interested in baseball. But when I got back from spring training we started seeing each other throughout the 1951 season. By then, Wink was hooked on the ball club and tried to come to as many games as she could. In those days, it was quite a journey from North Plainfield, New Jersey, to the Polo Grounds.

Believe it or not, Wink wasn't there when I hit the home run. She worked in the social services department of a New Jersey hospital and couldn't get off that day. The interns at the hospital knew she and I were dating so they invited her up the back stairs to the interns' quarters, where they listened to the game on a tiny transistor radio. When things looked so bleak in the ninth inning, Wink promised all the interns champagne if the Giants pulled the game out. She figured she was pretty safe, but didn't complain later when she had to pay them off.

The funny part was that after the home run, my name began appearing in some of the gossip columns, calling me the number-one bachelor in the New York area. These stories had Wink wondering about our relationship, especially after one story appeared during spring training of 1952 that said Leo wished Bobby Thomson would pay more attention to baseball than to a certain singer in the Sammy Kaye orchestra. I believe her name was Barbara Benson and the story had us as a couple, or as they said then, an item. Some story. The truth was that I never even met her.

When I got back from spring training that year, Wink and I resumed dating and we ended up getting married that December, on the twenty-seventh, to be exact. We had a wonderful wedding on Staten Island, because when we changed the date we couldn't reschedule for New Jersey. Our first child, Nancy, was born October 31, 1953. Our other two didn't arrive until I had retired, Bobby Jr., on February 15, 1962, and Megan on March 23, 1963.

Now that I was a married man, there had to be some changes in my life. Fortunately, Wink loved to travel, so she always came with me to spring training and was with me wherever I played. After our daughter was born, we continued to try to stay together as a family. But that didn't mean it was easy. There were times when being a baseball wife—even one who was willing to go almost anywhere—could be a difficult job.

For example, things became more difficult the last few years when I began going from team to team. As Wink said, you change towns, you don't have a home, and you're always looking for a nice place to rent. That kind of constant change takes some adjustment and you never quite get used to it. Even our first move—from New York to Milwaukee—proved a harrowing experience for Wink.

I was traded prior to the 1954 season and that was the year I broke my ankle in Florida during spring training. But even before that happened, Wink began having problems of her own. Shortly after we arrived in Florida she began experiencing terrible back pains, really awful. We had rented a nice little cottage on the water and it should have been a relaxing and enjoyable month for both of us. But Wink was waking up in the middle of the night with excruciating pain. At first, she couldn't believe it was something serious.

"Bob, I'm 25 years old and healthy," she kept telling me. "It can't be anything more than the mattress."

Then I broke my ankle and they took me over to a hospital in St. Petersburg. We knew a minister's wife who was a wonderful baby-sitter for us. When she heard about my accident, she told Wink she would watch the baby if Wink wanted to be near me for a couple of days. So Wink took a room in a house around the corner from the hospital just as I was about to have surgery. She figured she would stay about two days and at least be able to give me moral support.

After she visited me at the hospital the first night following the surgery, she had dinner and went back to her room. In the middle of the night she awoke with the worst back pain yet and knew she couldn't make it until morning. Because she didn't know a soul at the rooming house she decided to walk to the hospital herself—at 2:30 in the morning! When she got there, no one would open the emergency room door. She kept pounding on it until someone let her in. An intern examined her and didn't have the slightest idea what was wrong.

He told her a specialist would have to look at her in the morning and gave her a shot of morphine to ease the pain. More tough luck. After she walked back to the rooming house, Wink had a terrible reaction to the morphine and began feeling as if there were insects crawling all over her. Somehow, she got through the night and then in the morning found out her problem was her gallbladder.

The irony of the whole thing was that all the while Wink was suffering and struggling to get to the hospital in the middle of the night, I was lying upstairs getting the royal treatment, special attention from everyone. Hey, I was a major league ball player. Poor Wink was just a ball player's wife and I never knew what she was going through. She finally went home to have surgery and when she was well enough, rejoined me in Milwaukee.

So despite what some people think, it wasn't always a glamorous life. But Wink has shared it with me without complaint for a long time.

Stumbling Out of the Gate

The 1951 baseball season opened on April 17, with the Giants playing at Boston and the Dodgers hosting Philadelphia. Durocher called his team the best-conditioned squad he ever took out of a spring training camp. His opening day lineup had Stanky at second, Lockman in left, Henry Thompson at third, Irvin at first, Bobby Thomson in center, Mueller in right, Dark at short, Westrum catching, and Larry Jansen on the hill.

For opening day, after all the positive predictions, the script couldn't have been more perfect. Jansen twirled a five-hit shutout and the Giants won, 4–0, getting nine hits. Bobby Thomson had a pair of RBIs and the only negative note was a pair of errors by Irvin at first. But the bottom line was the victory, making everyone from Leo on down very happy.

Not so in Brooklyn. It was a chilly 50 degrees at Ebbets Field as Borough President John Cashmore threw out the first ball. Opening day ceremonies included a marine color guard and baritone Everett McCooey singing the national anthem. In his debut as manager, Dressen presented an opening lineup that contained a couple of surprises.

Rookie Don Thompson led off in left, followed by Furillo, Snider, Robinson, Hodges, Campanella, Reese, then rookie Rocky Bridges at third in place of Cox, and Erskine on the mound. It was a great lineup even with the two rookies, but it went for naught as Phillies ace Robin Roberts went the distance for a 5–2 victory.

But what's opening day? Early-season emotions can roller-coaster from day to day—a win, a loss, a few more wins; hey, a great start, then three losses, back to .500—or they can stay in the background until a definite pattern emerges. So when the Giants were beaten the next day, 8–5, as the Braves' Sam Jethroe slammed a three-run homer off Dave Koslo, no one got too excited. But it wasn't an easy loss. For one thing, Sal Maglie was hammered pretty good and for another, the Giants had fought back to tie it in the ninth only to lose it.

In Brooklyn, just the opposite happened. The Phillies took a one-run lead in the top of the ninth, only to have the Dodgers rally and win it on a two-out triple by Snider and a single by Robinson. The 3–2 final gave Preacher Roe his first victory, and both New York teams were at 1–1. A fresh start. But a start of what? It would take just two more days to find the answer to that question. Not only would it once again underscore the exigency of the Giant-Dodger rivalry, but it would also set the stage for a managerial chess game that would soon turn personal and set the tone for a pennant race that would go down to the final inning of the final game.

Because it was Patriots' Day in Boston, the Giants had an April 19, day-night doubleheader with the Braves. The Dodgers were set to play the Phils again at Ebbets, but the game was inexplicably canceled. Wasn't it coincidence that the Dodgers were scheduled to head into the Polo Grounds the next afternoon for the first of their 22 annual wars with the Giants?

As Roscoe McGowen wrote in the *New York Times,* "By calling off yesterday's series final with the Phils at Ebbets Field, Dressen now had big Don Newcombe ready to toss at the Giants. Pitching plans and lack of attendance must have influenced the cancellation, because it was rather a nice afternoon with some sunshine and a mild temperature."

Could a game be canceled on a whim? In those days, it was totally up to the discretion of the owner. Even today, the home team has the option. The umpires only took control of the game once play began. Bobby Thomson remembered a time when Giant owner Horace Stoneham got his back up at Manager Durocher.

"One Sunday morning we had a game and it was raining a little bit," Thomson recalls. "I don't know if Stoneham had been home even to go to bed, because he had the reputation of spending the night on the town. He walked into the locker room as we were getting ready to play, and he started talking about calling the game. As soon as he said that, Durocher lit up.

" 'Call the game,' he bellowed. 'You can't call the game!'

"But with Stoneham's personality all you had to say was: 'You can't!' As soon as he heard that, Stoneham said, 'I can't, huh? It's called.' And it was. It turned into a beautiful afternoon and I went out and played golf with Wink."

So the Dodgers-Phils game was called and Dressen immediately concentrated on the Giants. He talked about his two rookies, Don Thompson in left and Bridges at third. "I've got to go with those two boys awhile," he said. When asked about the three straight games his club had lost to the Giants at Miami during spring training, he dismissed them with a wave of his hand. "That didn't count. It's tomorrow's game that we're after," he said.

But the Giants had to deal with the Braves twice more before worrying about the Dodgers. They won the day game handily, as Jim Hearn, using that three-quarter delivery the Giants' coaches had taught him, spun a seven-hitter and came away with a 4–2 victory. The losing pitcher was Boston's ace southpaw, Warren Spahn. But the satisfaction was short-lived. The night game was an exhausting, 10-inning donnybrook that saw 25 runs cross the plate, the Braves finally winning, 13–12.

Durocher decided to give the start to Jack Kramer, a 33-year-old right-hander who had won 18 games with the Red Sox in 1948. He was one of those maybe-he'll-help pitchers that Leo wasn't sure about. Kramer was wild, lasted just one-third of an inning, and the Braves came away with a 5–1 lead. It would be Kramer's only start of the year and after appearing in relief in four more games, he was gone.

The Giants fought back with five runs in the eighth, highlighted by Monte Irvin's grand slam, and a 10–9 lead. Boston bounced back with three in the bottom of the inning to reclaim the lead, only to see the Giants tie it in the ninth with another pair. It was still knotted at 12-all in the last of the tenth as Dave Koslo took the hill for the Jints.

His old friend Buddy Kerr opened with a base hit and a sacrifice bunt put him on second. Roy Hartsfield was walked intentionally, and Sam Jethroe drew a pass unintentionally. Then Earl Torgeson slammed a Koslo offering off the center field fence and the issue was settled. On the positive side, the Giants had scored 12 runs. The negatives included the fact that six Giant pitchers threw with minimal effectiveness, and they had to face the Dodgers the next day.

Because Leo was looking to the Dodger series, he had sent Sal Maglie and Larry Jansen home to rest up for the Brooks. Jansen remembers Leo talking to them when he returned after losing two out of three to the Braves.

"When Leo saw us he said, 'Boys, you got out of your uniforms for the last time this year. If I had either one of you in Boston we'd have won that second game.' From that point on we were always ready. Either one of us could have helped because you can always come back and throw an inning or two."

Arthur Daley, writing in *The New York Times,* noted that the upcoming Giant-Dodger tilt held a vestige of hope for Giant fans, who hadn't celebrated a pennant since 1937. Wrote Daley, "The hustling Leo Durocher finally has assembled a team of hustlers, and hope actually is blazing in the lee of Coogan's Bluff." Daley went on to say that most experts considered the Giants and Dodgers the two strongest teams in the National League. He then added a note of caution, inferring that the Giants were missing one element, which he equated with the much-heralded arrival of rookie outfielder Mickey Mantle with the crosstown New York Yankees.

"There will be no precocious youngster such as Mickey Mantle on the premises," wrote Daley. "That is not to say, however, that Leo the Lip couldn't use a Mantle if he could be lucky enough to find one."

It was obvious that no one yet knew about a 19-year-old kid named Willie Mays who was about ready to start tearing up the American Association.

On game day no one cared about the future. Only the moment was important as Don Newcombe squared off against right-hander Sheldon Jones. Jones had won 44 games over the past three seasons. While he was just 13–16 in 1950, he was one of the second-line pitchers that Durocher hoped he could count on for a solid season. By starting Jones in the opener, Durocher could give Jansen and Maglie yet another day of rest.

Nearly 31,000 fans gathered at the Polo Grounds on that sunshine-filled spring day, a day New York City also welcomed General Douglas MacArthur back from Korea. Marine Pfc. Walter Townsend, Jr., of Jackson Heights, wounded three times in the Korean conflict, threw out the first ball as Dressen and Durocher stood beside him. On the field, it would be war of another kind.

Newcombe, who had some stiffness in his elbow during spring training, looked shaky the first several innings. The Giants had him on the ropes several times, getting a run in the first and two more in the fourth. But the New Yorkers couldn't deliver a knockout punch, and after the fourth, big Newk dusted off the cobwebs and began getting stronger.

Jones, on the other hand, yielded a pair of runs in the second, then came apart in the fifth. Newcombe led off with a single. After Don Thompson walked, Irvin misplayed Furillo's sacrifice attempt and threw widely to Jones covering first. The sacks were loaded. Then, after a force-out at home, Robinson singled in a pair of runs and Hodges walked, filling the bases again.

Campanella's long fly got the third run home and when Dark booted Reese's grounder, the fourth run scored and Jones gave way to another righty, George Spencer. The score was now 6–3, and what made it tough to take for the Giants was that three of the four Dodger runs were unearned. Leo Durocher teams weren't supposed to crack like that. Speed, defense, and sound fundamentals were sacred with the Lip.

When the Giants showed some signs of life in the seventh, Charley Dressen stepped out of the dugout and sent a message to his former boss that also set the tone for things to come. It was 7–3 as the Giants batted in the bottom half of the inning. With one out, the New Yorkers loaded the bases against Newcombe and now Durocher sent up left-handed hitting utility infielder Artie Wilson to hit for Spencer.

Wilson was a black player, a 20-year-old kid who had done well in the Pacific Coast League the previous season. To many, he was a player with potential. But Charley Dressen knew Wilson from his own Pacific Coast days with Oakland, and he felt the young infielder was not a threat to pull the ball. What he did next, many felt, was completely out of line.

"As far as I'm concerned, Charley Dressen put on the biggest act I had ever seen," said Bill Rigney, then a utility infielder with the Giants. "He got up on the dugout steps and called time. Then he motioned to Carl Furillo to come in from right field. He had him play where Robinson was at second. Then he moved Robinson to the other side of the bag, put his third baseman Cox right on the line and Reese in the third base hole. Then he motioned to his left fielder to play close to the line. Snider was practically moved to left field. All this took several minutes and Durocher was about to throw a fit."

With the pressure on young Wilson, all he could do was hit a one-hopper back to Newcombe. Dressen's exaggerated shift had apparently worked. Charley said he did it because he knew Wilson didn't pull the ball. But it was the way he did it that caught everyone's attention, his deliberate gyrations in moving his players one at a time. "Grandstanding" was the term some people used. Others felt Dressen had fired the first shot in a season-long attempt to prove he was the smarter manager. Jack Lang was one who espoused this theory.

"Charley always liked to prove how smart he was. He was a cocky guy and this was just one way he did it. He knew Wilson from the PCL and what he did was sound baseball. If it happened today, with all the scouting reports, no one would make a big deal out of it."

Maybe it would have been forgotten if it stopped there. The Dodgers won the game, 7–3, with Newk going the distance. The next day, with General MacArthur in the stands, the Dodgers won again by an identical 7–3 score. This time they beat Larry Jansen and did it with a three-run eighth. Ralph Branca pitched hitless ball over the final three innings to get the win in relief. It wouldn't be the last time Branca relieved against the Giants. The results, however, wouldn't always be the same.

Once again, the undercurrents of the rivalry surfaced. Robinson, the competitor, hit a long homer. Campanella was decked twice by Jansen and ended up in a shouting match with catcher Westrum. Umpire Augie Donatelli had to step between them. Stanky knocked the ball out of Reese's hand when stealing second. Rocky Bridges bowled over Bobby Thomson with a shoulder block on a pickoff attempt. Hank Thompson had words with Dodger starter Chris Van Cuyk after he was sent to the dirt. And Bobby Thomson was hit by a Branca fastball.

Besides all these extras, something else was becoming clear. The Giants were not playing good baseball. It didn't help when the next day the Dodgers swept the series by winning on a Carl Furillo homer in the tenth, 4–3. Maglie went the distance in the loss and Dressen, again showing how important it was to beat the Giants, used Newcombe in relief on just a day's rest. Newk threw three scoreless innings to get the victory.

Once more, the Giants lost in a damaging way. They held a 3–1 lead going into the eighth, but the Brooks got single runs in the eighth, ninth, and tenth against the tiring Maglie to win it. Why didn't Durocher go to the pen? It could be that he didn't have the confidence that his second-line pitchers could do the job.

The Giants had now lost four in a row. When they traveled to Philadelphia for the first night game of the season and were beaten 8–4, they had a bona fide losing streak. In this one Hearn was treated roughly, and Leo began playing with the lineup. He inserted Clint Hartung in right and Jack Lohrke at third. Thomson hit his second homer of the year, but the club was never in the game.

It continued to get worse. The Phils made it six losses in a row when they won the next game, 6–4, with Durocher throwing six pitchers into the fray. Once more the Giants looked unsure and ragged in the field. Owner Stoneham showed up at the game and gazed at the proceedings with an unsmiling visage from the press box. Both manager and owner denied that they were alarmed by the sudden early-season turn of events.

There was a glimmer of hope the next day. The ball club played a sound game, only they didn't hit in the clutch. The Phils beat Larry Jansen, 2–1, despite the fact that the Giants outhit them, eight to five. It was loss number seven in succession, plunging the team into the National League basement at 2–8.

Back home, things continued to go downhill. Braves curveballer Johnny Sain worked his magic to the tune of a six-hit shutout—his 100th major league victory—Maglie taking the 3–0 defeat in a route-going performance. Eight straight losses. This time Stanky was benched and Artie Wilson played second. When the writers asked Durocher about the move, he played it down.

"The club is going badly," was all he said, "and some of the stories in the papers haven't helped us. For the time being I won't say anything. Wilson is playing second, that's all."

Fortunately for the Giants, the Dodgers were also struggling a bit to find their baseball legs. While the Jints were suffering at 2–9, the Brooks were a 5–4 team, though just a game out of first.

For Leo Durocher, there was one bit of news on this day that perhaps cheered him. Baseball Commissioner Happy Chandler, the man who had suspended Leo in 1947, did not have his contract renewed by the baseball owners and was set to resign his office.

Though he may have felt vindicated, Leo was still trying to find a way to get his team back on the track. It didn't happen the next day when the club lost to Spahn and the Braves, 7–3, their ninth setback in succession. Stanky was back at second; Ray Noble took over behind the plate, and a player named Jackie Maguire was in right field. Oddly enough, both Noble and Maguire hit homers, but the club got just three other hits.

None of the formulas was working. The club wasn't hitting and—guess what?—they had another three-game series upcoming with the Dodgers at Ebbets Field, definitely not the Giants, most favorite ball-park. Former Giant Walker Cooper remembered the feeling from his days with the ball club.

"It was a rough place to play. They had that band, the Sym-Phony, and they would razz you all the way back to the bench. And if you beat them, the fans would follow you to the clubhouse, cussing and yelling at you, telling you how they would get you next time. That could only happen in Brooklyn because they had that runway back to the club-house."

For Larry Jansen, Ebbets was just a difficult place for him to win. "Because it was a small ballpark, I always had a tough time pitching there. I threw too many long flies and just didn't get enough outs. Maglie was great at Ebbets, and Leo sometimes juggled the rotation so I wouldn't have to throw when we were in Brooklyn."

For Bobby Thomson, Ebbets Field presented something that got the adrenaline pumping. "There was a difference playing the Dodgers at Ebbets Field," Bobby said. "There was nothing like it, always an extra feeling of excitement and nervousness. The fans at Ebbets treated you differently than the fans in Chicago or St. Louis. It was like walking into the lion's den. It was such a small ballpark. Playing third, you could almost look over and talk to the fans in the first row. It seemed as if they weren't more than 30 feet away."

The Giants were forced to go with a youngster, Roger Bowman, while the Dodgers had Preacher Roe ready. Roe wasn't at his best, but he was good enough to beat the Jints, 8–4, sending the team to its tenth straight defeat. It was also Charley Dressen's fourth straight victory over Durocher and the Giants in a still-young campaign.

When the combination of Erskine and Clyde King beat Larry Jansen and the Giants, 6–3, the next day, the losing streak had reached 11, an incredible, almost unfathomable tumble for a team considered a serious pennant contender. Jansen, as usual, didn't pitch well at Ebbets and his record fell to 1–3. Snider hit a pair of homers and Hodges one as the Brooks put on another power display to sink the Durochermen.

Robinson was hit by a Jansen pitch in the sixth, right before the Hodges homer that broke a 2–2 tie. Jackie talked to Jansen from the time he went to first until he reached the dugout trotting out the homer. He then continued his comments from the bench. And it still wasn't finished. The clubhouses in Ebbets were separated by just a wooden door. After the game, the Dodgers began reveling in their victory at the expense of their vanquished opponents.

Monte Irvin says, "I can remember hearing Carl Furillo and Jackie saying, 'Eat your heart out, Leo, you sonofabitch. You'll never win it this year.'

"Durocher heard it as well and said, 'Fellas, you hear what they said. If that's not an incentive to go out and play like hell, what is?' "

The Giants were now at 2–12, in last place, 7½ games behind front-running Boston. The Dodgers, at 8–4, were just half a game behind. A look at the batting averages of some of the regulars explained part of the problem. Bobby Thomson was hitting .193, Hank Thompson .194, Lockman .200, Mueller .216, Irvin .245, and Westrum .250. No wonder they weren't winning.

The Dodger averages were almost the opposite. Robinson was hitting .396; Reese, Cox, and Gene Hermanski were all at .333; Hodges was at .304, and Snider at .280. The team average of .264 was some 40 points higher than the Giants' .223.

It would be Maglie and Van Cuyk in the Monday finale, the only major league game scheduled that night. Because they didn't play until the following evening, Durocher decided to shake things up a little differently. Bobby Thomson remembers Durocher talking to the team before they left the locker room after that eleventh straight loss.

"Leo said, 'Let's shake things up. You guys who have been staying out at night, stay in. You guys who have been staying in, go out and raise hell. I don't know how many guys did it, but Leo was just trying to keep everyone loose and maybe looks for a new formula. He was never a guy to stand pat. Change, change, change, change. That was Leo's way. His theory was: Let's not sit in this rut; let's try something different, *anything* different."

Leo's shake-up speech helped break the tension, and the team finally came out of the skid. It wasn't easy. Maglie needed help from

Jones but beat the Brooks, 8–5. He was helped by a six-run first inning and a two-run second. At least they got it done early. Though they were outhit, 10–8, and saw the Brooks belt three more homers, the big thing was the "W."

Stanky and Lockman opened the game with singles. Thomson then doubled home a run and the floodgates opened. Van Cuyk was replaced by Earl Mossor, making his major league debut. He was wild and the Giants finished off their six-run inning. Because the top of the first took so long, Maglie cooled off and gave up homers to Hermanski and Robinson in the bottom of the inning.

Later there was a typical Maglie-Robinson confrontation. Robby thought he was being thrown at and dumped a bunt down the first base line. Though it rolled foul, he managed to bump Maglie hard as the pitcher came over to field the ball, and the two exchanged heated words, although nothing more came of it. The losing streak finally ended, but the question became: Where would the Giants go from here? Arthur Daley, writing in the *Times,* was among those who thought the 11-game losing streak had already sealed the Giants' fate.

"It would take a miracle for the Giants to win the championship now," penned Daley. "The losing streak represents a far greater disaster than the faltering start a year ago. At that time Durocher was fumbling for the right combination. He was still experimenting. But at this time he knows he has the best possible varsity on the field. And still, he's deeply and incomprehensibly imbedded in last place."

Daley went on to say, "The Dodger power-hitting can dominate the pennant race as it hasn't been dominated in decades."

For the Giants, was it already too late?

 **BOBBY**

The Giants of 1951

Bobby was the guy who nicknamed me "Nappy." It happened
after he had a real bad game and was pretty upset about it. I
told him even Napoleon had tough days. He looked at me and
laughed. "Okay, Napoleon," he said, "I get the message." He
started calling me Napoleon and after awhile shortened it to
Nappy. Then the other guys began picking up on it. There are
guys today who still call me Nappy and don't know where the
name came from.

—Wes Westrum

I can remember going into the 1951 season and thinking, hey, we're
going to win this thing. In a sense, you feel that way every year,
because if you didn't you might as well not start the season. But in
1951 I felt we really had a better all-around team and my own expectations were high, too.

By now I was a confident center fielder. I felt I could run and catch
the ball with any of them. Heck, I could run *better* than any of them.
Plus I had good hands and instincts. I've already said what Dark and
Stanky meant to the team. By 1951, their contributions were obvious
to everyone. But we had other guys who could play, too.

Whitey Lockman was a quiet guy who just went out and did his job.
He was a good outfielder before he moved to first base. It didn't take
him long, though, to make the transition. In New York at that time, all
you heard about was Gil Hodges. Gil was a great fielding first baseman, but Whitey was great, too, and I always felt he was underrated.
You didn't hear about him much as a first baseman because of Gil. I
know that when I was playing third, Whitey saved me a lot of throwing
errors by scooping the ball out of the dirt. And he could wield the bat,
too. A good man.

Don Mueller was another nice quiet guy who maybe wasn't Leo
Durocher's type of player. But Don showed up and waved that magic
wand of his, putting the ball in play all over the place. He used the

whole field, and if he wasn't the fastest runner, he was far from the slowest.

I always played a shallow center field for two reasons. I hated to give anybody cheap hits in front of me and I also had the confidence and ability to go back and get the ball hit over my head. Because of this, I hated to see anyone playing too deep and I'd always be moving Don in. I'd hold my two hands down by my knees and push forward, trying to signal him to move in. Don had a great sense of humor and used to give me the same treatment, put his hands by his knees and signal me to move in. Don's the one who used to call me Hawk, because, he said, I could really hawk the ball.

We were playing in Cincinnati one time and it happened that there was a ball hit over Don's head. Don steamed after it and I yelled something like "Plenty of room!" Don kept going full tilt and ran right into the fence. He got a bad cut on his chin that left a nice scar and after that whenever he saw me he'd say, "Plenty of room, Hawk, plenty of room." He also says he thinks of me every time he shaves.

I don't think Leo appreciated Don as much as he should have. He didn't seem to get half as upset when someone knocked Don down as when someone threw a ball within a foot of Willie Mays's head. But Don Mueller was a fine man for our club and always in the lineup.

As for Monte Irvin, he was unquestionably our strong guy. I've always thought that Monte was the one who got us there in '51. He was a quiet man whom we all respected because he played hard every day. He wasn't a pop-off guy. He could run and get the ball, had a big arm, and was built like a panther. Monte was so strong that as a batter he could take a ball that would nearly hit him on the fist and muscle it over the infield for a single.

Wes Westrum's biggest asset was his ability to keep guys off second base. But make the mistake of throwing him a curveball and he was liable to whack it into the seats. Wes always had trouble with his hands, getting them all beat up as many catchers do. But Leo continued to play him because he needed him behind the plate. I can recall times when Wes couldn't even put all his fingers around the bat. But Wes was a tough guy who hung in there. He could also catch the knuckleball better than anyone I ever saw. We didn't have Hoyt Wilhelm until 1952, but when Wes caught him he was so loose his whole body seemed to move in rotation with the ball.

Henry Thompson was a little guy with great wrists who could

pump the ball a long way. He could run, too, a good all-around player.

Mays was such a young, innocent kid in '51, but it was obvious he was going to be a great ball player. After he came up, we just sat back and watched him. You could see by some of the plays he made that he was going to be something special. He had great instincts and a great arm. He was streaky with the bat when he first came up, but he sure didn't hurt us with his glove.

As I said before, Dark and Stanky were the leaders, the holler guys, the needlers, a special twosome. Maglie was "The Barber," a leader by performance when he was pitching. But Sal wasn't a role model when it came to getting himself in shape. He never did much running, never killed himself exercising. He'd always tell Leo, "Hell, you can't run the ball over the plate." When he wasn't pitching he sat quietly in the dugout. But on the mound it was his combativeness that led the way.

Larry Jansen was a gentleman, a fine pitcher with great control, a very smart baseball man. Dark and Stanky would needle him, try to get him to pitch inside more. But Larry did what he had to do, even pitching tight.

For opponents, Jim Hearn was a pain-in-the-ass pitcher. He was always a fussbudget on the mound. He had to rub the ball up just right before he made the pitch. But he could pitch. So could Dave Koslo, a tough guy and a good left-handed pitcher.

It wasn't all peaches and cream, though. We'd sometimes get into battles with each other. Most ball clubs that mean business have that kind of thing. You're out there battling and you all want to win. No one wants to make mistakes, but they will happen. And there are going to be times when some guys don't think others are trying as hard as they should.

But it was Leo who set the tone, and that rubbed off on all of us. He was always out in front, always on top of everything. You could always *hear* him. He never walked around with his head down. If he had something on his mind he would tell you and we all appreciated that. You could sit down and have it out with him, then start over fresh the next day. There was something else, as well. Any time you're playing for a pennant, you're not thinking about yourself; you're thinking about the ball club. When you played for Durocher, you had to *learn* to subordinate yourself to the ball club. That's one of the things I learned from him that I'll never forget.

Like everyone else, Leo was easier to get along with when things were going well, and that's something else I've always said about Leo. Give him the right guys and he could run the heck out of a team.

Looking back, I realize something else that I wasn't aware of in 1951. The Dodgers were a much closer team than the Giants, more like a family. Brooklyn was such a small, closely knit community and most of the players lived close to each other. The Giants were all over the place. I lived on Staten Island, other guys went to Westchester, some stayed in Manhattan. Most of the Dodgers hung together, their families did things together. Even the people in Brooklyn considered them part of the family.

I came to realize that after I was voted in the Brooklyn Dodger Opponents Hall of Fame a few years ago. Just going to a couple of functions there gave me a feeling of what it must have been like playing in Brooklyn and the close feeling the fans had for the team.

That doesn't mean the Giants weren't like a family on the field. We were out there pulling and fighting for each other, and on the field I don't think you could say the Dodgers were closer than the Giants. But our problem early in 1951 wasn't togetherness. It was winning. The 11-game losing streak was tough. A lot of guys, myself included, weren't hitting. It was certainly too early in the year to think we were out of it. But we knew we'd have to start turning things around pretty quick. Hell, we were sitting in the basement.

A Pressing Need for a Kid Named Mays

In 1951, a young reporter named Charley Feeney was covering the Giants for the *Long Island Press*. He witnessed the team's 11-game losing streak as well as other up and down periods in the Durocher years. During that time, Feeney observed something he thought of as odd about the Giant manager.

"Durocher was often easier for the writers to deal with when the team was losing," he said. The stories about Leo being a bastard when the club was losing just weren't true. He might blow up once in a while when the club was losing, but when he had a winning team he would sometimes be arrogant, with a "screw you" attitude after the game, just get dressed and leave. In those days, though, most managers didn't sit around the clubhouse for an hour after the game answering questions. You'd be better off catching them later, when they were having a drink somewhere. You just didn't talk in the clubhouse. Everything was get up and go, and that's the way Leo was."

During the 11-game losing streak, Leo Durocher didn't have time to worry about the press. His problem was getting "my kind of team" to win. No one, in their wildest imagination, would have guessed that after 14 games the Giants would be mired in last place with a record of 2–12. The victory over the Dodgers broke the streak, but that was bound to happen sometime. The question was how the team would react in the upcoming month. If they were going to claw their way back into the race, they had to do it soon.

Even when they won on May 1, topping the Cubs, 5–3, on an Al Dark grand slammer, many key players still weren't hitting. Thomson was at .188, Mueller had dropped to .182, Lockman was at .203 and Irvin at .232. These were four key hitters. If they didn't snap out of it soon the ball club would continue to be in trouble.

The club got a lift on May 2, when George Spencer went the route to defeat the Cubs, 8–1. It was the Jints third win in a row. At the same time the Dodgers lost to Pittsburgh, dropping back to 8–7. They weren't tearing up the league, either. The Brooks also made some off-field news when Jackie Robinson and the ball club clashed with National League president Ford Frick.

Frick had admonished Jackie for his part in the bumping incident with Sal Maglie, when Robby pushed the foul bunt toward first and ran into the Giant pitcher. Robby had claimed too many pitchers—especially on the Giants—were dusting off Dodger hitters. Walter O'Malley was quick to defend his star player.

"I have no reason to be dissatisfied with Jackie Robinson, his conduct on the field or his spirit—and I have seen all the games at Ebbets Field and the Polo Grounds," O'Malley said. "He has the full support of this organization."

Robinson continued to defend his actions with a verbal assault on the National League president. "The pitcher throws at your head and if he scares you, he's got you with the curveball," Robby said. "I'm willing to take it as long as I can give it back. If they don't want me to give it, then I think there should be legislation that I don't have to take it."

But it was Frick who had the last word, and it came as a warning to Robinson and the Dodgers.

"I'm getting tired of Robinson's popping off," said the former sportswriter and soon-to-be commissioner. "I have warned the Brooklyn club that if they don't control Robinson, I will."

This was just the beginning. The Brooklyn club and especially Jackie Robinson would be involved in a number of abrasive and antagonistic incidents as the season wore on. To some, it might have seemed like good, old-fashioned competitive baseball. But it would also create an atmosphere around the National League that may very well have helped influence the outcome of the race.

Durocher was ejected the next day in a May 3 loss to the Pirates. Leo got into it when he backed coach Freddie Fitzsimmons (who also got the thumb), but as abrasive as Leo could be, his outbursts with the umpires were often the same as his outbursts with his players. Once it was over, it was forgotten.

As Sal Maglie threw a one-hitter at the Pirates the next afternoon, the Dodgers lost to Cincinnati. In that game, the Dodgers got into a rhubarb with plate umpire Frank Dascoli. Before it ended, Dascoli banished pitchers Don Newcombe and Dan Bankhead from the Dodger bench. It wouldn't be the last time the Brooklyn team clashed with Dascoli. Before the season ended, Dascoli would make a critical call that some Dodgers say cost them the pennant.

During the next week the Giants continued to show signs of snapping out of their early-season malaise, while the Dodgers still hadn't made a real move to take control of the race. On May 5, the Dodgers blasted five homers in a 12–8 win over the Reds. The next day the Jints split a pair with the Reds as Whitey Lockman fell victim to the old hidden ball trick, perpetrated by Reds' second sacker Connie Ryan.

On May 10, the Giants completed a three-game sweep of the Cardinals, while the Dodgers triumphed over the Cubs. Since breaking their 11-game losing streak, the Jints had won 9 of 11 to pull to 11–14 and within four games of league-leading Boston. The Dodgers were second, a game out at 13–10. Now, only three games separated the two ball clubs.

Despite his propensity for being the center of controversy, Jackie Robinson was leading the National League in hitting with a .396 average. Al Dark was fourth at .370. Dark and Monte Irvin had 18 RBIs each, two behind leader Andy Pafko of the Cubs. And Gil Hodges led the league in homers with nine. As a team, the Dodgers were batting .270, while the Giants had worked their way up to .254. Both Lockman and Irvin had improved their averages. Thomson had reached .238. Only Don Mueller continued to struggle at .160. There wasn't much separating the two clubs at this point.

In the May 13 edition of *The New York Times,* Arthur Daley quoted Cubs' manager Frankie Frisch on a bit of strategy the old Fordham Flash said he followed.

"Let sleeping dogs lie," Frisch said. "I don't want to wake the other team up and get them mad so that they play over their heads against us. Let 'em slumber. They're softer pickings that way."

Daley used the quote to make an analogy with Leo Durocher. "Leo Durocher operates on a different principle," he wrote. "He kicks every sleeping dog in the teeth, even the bigger and more ferocious dogs. The Dandy Little Manager loves excitement. If it isn't there, he creates it." Daley went on to cite some instances when Leo managed the Dodgers, how he had often inflamed the opposition with beanball tactics or verbal baiting.

But Leo had not yet done anything like this in '51. As the season continued, however, there would be a strange twist. It would be Charley Dressen and not Leo Durocher who would kick the sleeping dogs, then kick them again and again. And it wouldn't be long in coming.

The same day Daley wrote his column, the Dodgers topped the Braves, 12–6, and slid ahead of Boston to take the lead by percentage points. At the same time, the Giants' aces, Maglie and Jansen, whipped the Phils, 11–2 and 4–2, giving the New Yorkers a 13–15 record and leaving them just three games out of the top spot. Jansen evened his record at 3–3 and Maglie moved to 4–2. The team seemed to be coming on.

Even though the Giants were winning, Durocher wasn't happy with his team. The ball club wasn't the smooth-running machine he thought it should be. Maybe that's why there was a reported increase in behind-the-scenes "activities." Despite the team's .500+ record since the disastrous losing streak, owner Stoneham came to New York and called a conference with Durocher. There was speculation that the Giants were trying to work out a trade for Yankee third sacker Billy Johnson, enabling Leo to platoon him at third with the lefty hitting Henry Thompson. Instead, Johnson was sold to the Cardinals.

On May 19, the Giants won at Cincinnati, 3–2, as Monte Kennedy went the distance. The victory brought the Giants within a single game of .500 at 16–17 and within just two games of Brooklyn. The Dodgers were 16–13 and in a virtual tie with the 17–14 Braves. The entire eight-team league was bunched within three games of one another.

And there were still no hints of the rumored shake-up on the Giants, although Durocher was reported to be "at wits end" over the season-long slump of Bobby Thomson. Bobby's average had dropped to a lowly .223 and the manager moved his center fielder to the eighth spot in the order. Mueller, hitting even less at .203, was in and out of the lineup.

To the casual observer, the Giants were doing okay. They had bounced back from that 11-game slide to move within a couple of games of the lead. The Dodgers won a doubleheader the next day, but even though the Giants lost to the Cards 8–7, the headlines were occupied with matters other than bottom line results. Instead, Durocher was busily denying reports that he took a swing at umpire Lon Warneke after the game.

Stanky had been bounced out of the game by Dusty Boggess and Leo went berserk when Warneke let Red Schoendienst stay in the game after a big argument with the St. Louis second sacker in the eighth.

"As I went off the field through the runway, Warneke was behind me," Durocher said. "I turned around and told him what I thought of him, but I did not raise a hand and there was no fight of any sort. I went my way and he went his."

Another umpire, Babe Pinelli, backed up Leo, saying "there was no threatening gesture of any sort."

Meanwhile, in Cincinnati, another story broke saying three anonymous letters threatening Jackie Robinson's life had been received, one of which was sent to police headquarters. The letters said that someone intended to "shoot the Negro Robinson." One went so far as to say he would be shot "from a window." The threats were taken seriously enough to send the FBI as well as local authorities into action.

"When I arrived here it was the first I knew of it," said Jackie, who had been under this kind of pressure ever since he broke the color line back in 1947. "They told me they thought it was the work of a crank, but that they couldn't take any chances."

The police checked out several buildings that had clear views of the Crosley Field playing field. Additional police were placed on duty at the stadium during the doubleheader. Fortunately, nothing happened. But plenty would happen during the next several days. It would not be business as usual, especially on the Giant front.

First, Leo was fined $100 by Ford Frick for using "vile and abusive" language to Lon Warneke. But even Warneke admitted that maybe Leo had a kick coming. "It was a pretty rough decision not to eject Schoendienst and I wish I had another look at it. However, Schoendienst did not use abusive language. Durocher's was pretty rough."

At the St. Louis ballpark the next day, Leo surprised everyone. When the Giants took the field against the Cards, Monte Irvin, who had been playing first base all year, trotted out to left and left fielder

Lockman came out and stationed himself at first. It was the first major change in the club's basic alignment. As everyone would soon learn, it was just the beginning.

"I never liked playing first base," Monte Irvin recalls. "I had originally been a third baseman with the Newark Eagles in the Negro League and I could play the hell out of it. In fact, back then I could play anywhere. But I developed an inner ear problem and kind of lost my coordination for the infield. The ball just got on me too fast. In the outfield there was time to recover from a mistake and I realized it was my best position. It just took awhile for the Giants to realize it."

Whitey Lockman, the other half of the switch, was moving to a completely new position and a surprise.

"Leo just walked up to me in St. Louis one day and asked if I had a first baseman's glove," Lockman remembers. "I said no. He said get one, so I borrowed Monte Irvin's, who was absolutely delighted to get rid of it.

"Playing at first was more of an adjustment than I thought it would be. I used to fool around taking balls in the infield before some games, but not at first. So the defensive positioning on cut offs and relays, things like that, were completely foreign to me. It was quite an adjustment defensively and sometimes that makes you take a step back offensively. But we started to win and that can be a great equalizer.

"The best piece of advice I got came from Earl Torgeson, who was the first baseman for the Braves. He told me to forget all the fancy footwork, just get over there and put my right foot on the bag and take the throw. Forget all the stuff about straddling the bag, shifting feet, all that. It really made sense. Monte was a hell of an outfielder, better than me and with a stronger arm. He was more of an outfield type, a real offensive player with power. Plus Monte wasn't hitting when he played first, didn't like it there. I'm surprised the move wasn't made sooner."

It wasn't magic time quite yet. Despite the presence of Irvin and Lockman in new positions, the Giants lost to the Cards, 5–2. But what no one knew then was that Phase Two of Durocher's realignment was just around the corner. The team traveled to Chicago, where rain canceled the Tuesday game. But the manager reiterated to the press corps that the Irvin-Lockman shift was not a temporary one.

When the ball club returned to action on Wednesday, Irvin slammed a two-run homer, enabling Maglie to win his sixth straight.

The Giants got just 4 hits to 10 for the Cubs, but they won, the mark of a good team. The ball club was 17–19 for the year, but 15–7 since the losing streak ended. Eddie Stanky had been on base in all 35 games he had played.

In Pittsburgh, Brooklyn defeated the Pirates, 11–4, as Billy Cox connected for a home run with the bases full. Two other things of note occurred. Dressen got into it again with umpire Frank Dascoli, the second time in a little over two weeks. And before the game, the Dodger players, jumping the gun a bit, met to decide on a split of television money from the World Series. Ralph Branca, the club rep, said the players couldn't decide whether to throw the money into the pension fund or the Series jackpot.

Thursday, May 24, was an off day. But the Giant camp was far from quiet. This was the day the ball club made an announcement of far-reaching implications. It had called up a barely 20-year-old out-fielder named Willie Mays from Minneapolis, a move that took most people by surprise. Willie Who? was the question many fans asked.

Once the facts were known, curiosity about Mays spread through-out the league. Here was a kid who was signed out of high school in Alabama less than a year before in June 1950. His father, Willie, Sr., had been an outfielder with the Birmingham Black Barons in the Negro Leagues. In fact, the elder Mays had the nickname of Kitty Cat because of the quick and quiet way he would sneak up on fly balls.

Young Willie had played a bit for the Black Barons in 1948, '49, and '50, but times had changed and now he had the opportunity to play in the bigs. Ironically, Dodger catcher Roy Campanella had played against Mays during a barnstorming trip through the South following the 1949 season. In that game, Willie made one of his patented, rocket-like throws to cut Larry Doby down at the plate. Campy was so impressed he implored Dodger scouts to head south to sign the kid.

"The Dodgers took my advice," Campy reported in his biography, *It's Good To Be Alive;* "that is, to the extent of sending a scout to look Willie over. The scout, Wid Matthews, came back with his story of Mays. You know what he included in the report? 'The kid can't hit a curveball.' "

Fortunately, the Giants didn't make the same mistake.

After he signed in 1950, Willie finished the year at Trenton in the International League, where he batted .353 in 81 games. He had been toiling at Minneapolis in 1951 where he had played in just 35 games and was hitting an incredible .477. They said he could do it all—run, throw, hit, hit with power, steal bases. Just who was this guy, anyway, superman?

"Leo had only seen Willie once, in an exhibition game in Sanford, Florida," said Ernie Harwell, the veteran baseball broadcaster who shared the Giants announcing booth with Russ Hodges in 1951. "But once was enough. He fell in love with the kid and wanted to bring him up immediately."

Durocher said he had been told in the spring by two scouts that the team had a potentially great player in their system. But when the manager asked to bring the kid to preseason camp, the front office said no. He wasn't ready. That's when a special game was arranged between Minneapolis and Ottawa, both Giants farm teams, at Sanford. Mays didn't disappoint. He made a couple of outstanding catches, gunned out a pair of runners, and belted a long home run.

So while the story never made the paper, Leo was privately lobbying for Stoneham to bring Willie up all year, especially after the team floundered so badly at the beginning. The answer continued to be no. One reason was the Korean War and the draft. Owner Stoneham said that Willie might be called at any time. Leo's answer was, Fine, but why not let him play for us until that happens?

But some felt there were reasons other than just the fear of losing Willie to Uncle Sam. According to Harwell, Stoneham had a good working arrangement with the Minneapolis team and was hesitant about taking away their star player. Then there was still another factor, one that can sometimes be easily forgotten with the passage of time.

The Giants already had four black players on their roster—Irvin, Henry Thompson, Artie Wilson, and catcher Ray Noble, who was a native Cuban. Mays would make five. Early in the year, only Irvin and Henry Thompson were regulars. Wilson was a seldom-used utility infielder and Noble, along with Sal Yvars, backed up West Westrum in the catcher's position. But suppose Mays came up and circumstances suddenly led to four or even five blacks in the lineup at the same time? Was it possible Stoneham and his front office staff were concerned about fan reaction, both at the Polo Grounds and around the rest of the league, if that kind of situation developed?

This may be a difficult concept to grasp, especially with the multiracial makeup of sports that is taken for granted today. But in 1951, the situation was different. It had been only four years since Branch Rickey's "noble experiment" had brought Jackie Robinson to the Dodgers.

In writing about the 1951 pennant race, the names of Robinson, Campanella, Newcombe, Irvin, Thompson, and Mays are mentioned regularly. These were key people, integral parts of both ball clubs. The Dodgers also had pitcher Dan Bankhand for part of the year. But contrary to what some people might assume today, there was no stampede around the rest of the league to sign black players. In fact, besides the black players on the Dodgers and Giants, the 1951 season saw just one other black man on the six other National League rosters. He was Sam Jethroe, the center fielder of the Boston Braves and National League Rookie of the Year in 1950.

So a question of how fans would react to a team with four or five blacks on the field at one time was conceivably a legitimate concern. Integration at the major league baseball level had not come easy. Robinson's ordeal in 1947 is well documented. The players who followed might not have suffered quite the same kinds of insults and indignities, but the face of prejudice was still evident. Very much so.

"When Jackie was brought in by Branch Rickey in 1947, every team was against Rickey and dead set against the color line coming down with the exception of Bill Veeck at Cleveland in the American League," said baseball historian and writer Donald Honig. "Horace Stoneham was a little more progressive and forward looking than some other owners and he brought Thompson and Irvin to the Giants in 1949. He also saw the success the Dodgers were having at the gate and on the field with their black players.

"Then the Braves brought in Sam Jethroe in 1950. Other teams took longer. For example, the Cubs didn't bring in any blacks until 1953, the Pirates, Reds and Cards until '54, and the Phillies waited until 1957."

Honig also noted that Jackie, because of the nature of his personality, paved the way for the others in more ways than one.

"Robinson, in a perverse way, made it easier for Campanella and Mays, and the other blacks, because they were not like him. They were easygoing guys. Jackie raised a lot of hackles. He put off a lot of people with his strong personality. He was very abrasive, a very provocative guy, and because of that there was a lot of hatred for him."

Even some of the sportswriting of the time reflected a latent prejudicial tone, a tone which in those days was considered normal and acceptable in dealing with blacks. But it didn't help the situation. Listen to this lead from a May 1949 game story written by Dick Young in the New York *Daily News.*

"Making their two-man act in Chicago the most enjoyable entertainment since Buck and Bubbles, Jackie Robinson and Roy Campanella had the large proportion of Negro fans among the crowd of 15,579 screaming and waving hands overhead like an old-fashioned revival meeting," wrote Young.

Looked at today, this is stereotyped, offensive racial writing, much in the way the old "Amos 'n' Andy Show" or the slurring, shuffling movie roles of Stepin Fetchit and Willie Best are considered racially stereotypical and offensive. But back in the 1940s and 1950s, these were perceptions accepted by much of the population. Yet Young is depicting Robinson and Campanella as vaudeville entertainers in a minstrel show and the fans as chanting and screaming Negros at a revival meeting. He is singling them out from the white players, much in the way the word Negro was so often used as an adjective in describing the black players of the day.

Donald Honig says this kind of thing was the result of the newness of blacks in the game. "You've got to remember that this was a new experience, a new chapter in social history," said Honig. "Dick Young actually handled it better than most. Young was a supporter of Robinson in his early years, as well as being extremely liberal in his social attitude back then. So I feel there was no offense intended and maybe even none taken back then.

"As I said, dealing with black ball players was a brand new experience. Some people covered themselves with glory, but many didn't."

That still didn't make it any easier on the players. Sam Jethroe, for instance, was the top rookie in 1950, batting .273 with 18 homers, 58 RBIs, and a league-best 35 stolen bases. His numbers were almost identical the next year, 18 homers, 65 ribbies, a .280 average, and a league-leading 35 steals. But when he slumped to .232, 13, 58, with 28 steals in 1952, something happened. Bill Bruton was the new Braves center fielder in '53 and Jethroe would get only one more major league at bat, with Pittsburgh in 1954.

It was said that Jethroe was a liability in center and that he struck out too much, but it seemed that some team could have used his talents. He did put up some outstanding numbers in the minors after that, yet despite repeated promises, was never recalled.

"I was sick over the winter of 1952," Jethroe recalls, still with a trace of bitterness. "I had a fistula operation, but the doctor said I was as good as new. Management decided to send me to Toledo anyway where I had a great year, hit .307 and helped them win the pennant. But I was never recalled."

He was finally traded to Pittsburgh, where Branch Rickey, Jr., told him he'd be called up, but the call never came despite continued outstanding seasons in the minors.

"Boston was prejudiced for a long time," Jethroe says. "Even in 1951 when the Dodgers and Giants were in the playoffs there was a tremendous amount of prejudice in the National League. I once got a call from Branch Rickey and he said he was considering using me. The one question he asked was did I live clean? I said I lived as clean as anybody else.

"I didn't room with anyone my first year in 1950. In Chicago, the team stayed at the Edgewater Beach Hotel and I had to stay at a black hotel. The next time we went through, Duffy Lewis, the traveling secretary, had me room with him at the Edgewater Beach, but I couldn't eat with the rest of the team. They sent the meals to my room.

"The fans in Boston took a liking to me because I could steal bases and they used to yell, 'Go! Go! Go!' whenever I got on base. The rest of the league did a lot of hollering at me, too. I could have talked back, but didn't. And I didn't like it when Charlie Grimm, my manager at Boston in 1952, and others called me Sambo. If one of my teammates called me Sambo, and they did, I would say, 'Watch it. I'll get a bat and there'll be no one left in this clubhouse but me.' "

Jethroe is convinced it was prejudice that caused his early exit and kept him from returning to the majors.

"Even though I was no Willie Mays in the outfield, I could have pinch hit and pinch run for some team. There were a lot of utility players kept around for those reasons, but players with lesser ability and lesser stats stayed up because they were white.

"In those days if you were black you had to be almost a superstar to stay with the team. I know I talked back to my manager when he called me Sambo and in those days you didn't do that. As a result I wasn't up long enough to get a pension and I'm still angry about that today."

The early blacks were all talented players. When Stoneham finally acquiesced and allowed Durocher to send out the call for Mays, the player dropped was Artie Wilson, the black utility infielder. Was Wilson simply the best candidate to go, or was there a kind of unspoken quota system to limit the number of blacks on the team? Monte Irvin, who saw the entire situation develop firsthand, thinks that there was.

"They'll deny it, but I'm sure there was a quota system," says Irvin, who spent a good number of years working in the commissioner's office after his retirement and is one of the most respected men in the game. "In 1950, we needed a third baseman. The Giants had Ray Dandridge playing in Minneapolis, one of the greatest players in Negro League history. We told them that Dandridge was the man for the job, but they said he was too old. [Dandridge was nearly 36 when signed in 1949, hit .363 that year and then won the Most Valuable Player award with Minneapolis in 1951.] What the hell do you care how old he is as long as he can play?

"We also needed a relief pitcher and Satchel Paige was available after he left Cleveland in 1949. All management had to do was pick him up anytime in 1950. But my feeling is that they didn't want more than two or three blacks playing then. Dandridge never made the majors and he's always been bitter about it."

Don Newcombe, who joined the Dodgers in 1949, also remembers those years vividly. Newcombe, too, is aware that the Dodgers and Giants were isolated islands in a sea that was predominantly white in those early years.

"How could anyone expect that by 1951, after just four years, something that had existed for more than 100 years was going to just go away?" said Newk. "Jackie Robinson, Roy Campanella, Don Newcombe, Monte Irvin, and Larry Doby were not going to erase it. All we wanted to do back then was play baseball. We didn't realize how it was going turn out as far as civil rights were concerned. But we played a very important part in the civil rights movement just by playing baseball.

"I think the record shows that the black players on the Dodgers and Giants brought those clubs together and helped make them the best. People sometimes forget the conditions under which we had to play, the things we had to endure in places like St. Louis, where we had to live in substandard hotels because the Chase Hotel wouldn't allow us to stay with our teammates.

"I think that kind of thing gave us more determination. We were angry and the only way we could vent that anger was on the ball field. Because of that, we'd come to the ballpark with a decided edge. The white players were relaxed because they were living in their own world. We were trying to penetrate their world and to do that we had to be better and continue to be better, because if we weren't better we would not be there very long.

"Do you know how it was for a great athlete like Jackie Robinson, Roy Campanella, or Don Newcombe to be told we can't stay in a hotel or they don't want us swimming in their swimming pool? Do you know what it does to people, to a man? It's like someone taking a bag of crap and hitting you in the mouth with it. 'And that's what you deserve, Mr. Robinson, because we are superior to you and don't want you around.'

"So we excelled because we were black. We had the need to excel, to show people we were as good or better."

There's little doubt about the quality of the early black players. Robinson, Newcombe, Jethroe, and Mays were all Rookies of the Year. Robinson, Newcombe, Mays (twice), and Campanella (three times) were Most Valuable Players. And Don Newcombe was baseball's first Cy Young Award winner back in 1956. With the exception of Jethroe, these were the players involved in the 1951 pennant race.

Even the great Stan Musial, whose Cardinals battled the Dodgers for the top spot during most of the 1940s, saw the coming of the black players as changing the balance of power in the National League. Said Musial, "The Dodgers continued to win because they signed the three best black players in baseball."

Stan the Man was alluding to the late '40s signings of Robby, Campy, and Newk. Players like Irwin and Mays helped bring the Giants up to that level. When Leo Durocher finally convinced Horace Stoneham to call up Willie, he knew he was getting an exceptional player, but one still in the embryonic stage of development.

Ernie Harwell remembers when Willie joined the team in Philadelphia. As the youngster came out to take batting practice, Harwell saw something very unusual take place.

"We were at old Shibe Park," says Harwell, "and when Willie came out for the first time everyone on the field stopped what he was doing and watched Willie hit. A lot of the guys didn't even know who he was. But he was just a natural and I guess something about him just caused everyone to watch. I had never seen that happen before and haven't seen it since."

Willie Mays was a five-foot-eleven, 170-pound package of enthusiasm. He had just turned 20 earlier in the month and was almost overwhelmed by his sudden elevation to the big leagues. Wide-eyed and bursting with energy, Willie called his manager "Mis-a-Leo" right from the first, a practice that gave Durocher's critics the opportunity to call him a racist and claim that he maintained an Uncle Tom relationship with his young star. Monte Irvin, the ball player closest to the situation, says this wasn't so.

"When Henry Thompson and I joined the Giants in 1949," Irvin recalls, "Leo had a little meeting and introduced us to everybody. He said then that he didn't care whether you were black, green, or yellow. If you could play baseball, you could play on the Giants. That was the only thing he said about the racial situation, but that basically said it all. We had a good number of white southerners on the team, but we got along with those guys just fine.

"When Willie came up, Leo wanted me to help him in all kinds of ways. I was about 12 years older than he was, took care of myself, didn't drink or carouse, so Leo felt we were made for each other. It was like the old vet teaching a rookie. We developed great habits and enjoyed being with each other. But there was absolutely nothing racial on the ball club."

Now that he had Mays, manager Durocher had to solve his one remaining problem. Bobby Thomson had been the Giants' center fielder since his rookie year of 1947. He was considered one of the better outfielders in the league. Mays, too, played center. While it's never easy to pull a veteran out of his position, one thing that made it easier for Leo was Thomson's .229 batting average. He still wasn't hitting. Neither was Don Mueller, so in effect, there was an outfield position open. The decision was made quickly to install the rookie in center, shift Irvin from left to right, and make Thomson the left fielder.

"I think the main reason for the shift of Bobby to left and installation of Willie in center was Willie's throwing arm," said Monte Irvin. "Bobby was a good outfielder who could do it all. He could run like hell and was probably faster than Willie in a straight race. But Willie probably got a better jump on the ball. Bobby never threw many people out and Willie was capable of doing that, too. He was just a born center fielder."

Al Dark, who was also right on the scene, said the change had to be a blow to Bobby.

"Outwardly, Bobby didn't seem to resent the change. He was a good team man. But inside I'm sure he resented it because no one could cover more ground in center field than Bobby Thomson. Defensively, the only difference at that time in their careers was Willie's throwing arm. Bobby's was good; Willie's was outstanding and very accurate. He also got rid of the ball very fast."

With Mays in the lineup, the Giants rallied for five in the eighth and defeated the Phillies, 8–5, as Whitey Lockman slammed a bases-loaded double in the decisive frame. The rookie took the collar in five trips, although he did hit two hard shots to the outfield. A day later the ball club reached .500 for the first time since the fourth game of the season. Jansen blanked the Phils on seven hits, 2–0, beating Robin Roberts and evening his record at 4–4.

Mays was hitless again, but Bobby Thomson slammed his seventh homer of the year to break a scoreless tie in the seventh. Durocher had to be happy. He finally had Mays, his team was at .500, and Bobby Thomson was showing signs of life with the bat. The Dodgers had lost to the Braves the same day, bringing the Giants to within 3½ games of the top. Durocher and the Jints were starting to feel pretty good about everything.

When Sal Maglie threw a two-hit shutout to complete the sweep of the Phils the next day, the ball club was over .500 and seemed to be making a genuine move. Mays went 0-for-4, making him hitless in 12 trips, but Bobby Thomson had another pair of hits. Amidst the revelry following the victory, however, there was a minicrisis. The rookie Mays wasn't used to failure at the plate. After a dozen tries with nothing to show for it, he sat in front of his locker and began to weep.

When manager Durocher asked him what was wrong, Mays, in his high-pitched voice, said he didn't feel he could play in the majors and asked Leo to send him back to Minneapolis. Durocher, who had seen every type of player since coming into the big leagues a quarter of a century earlier, immediately knew what he had to do.

He put his arm around the rookie and said, "Willie, I brought you up here for one reason. To play center field. You're the best center fielder I've ever seen and you're gonna be out there tomorrow, next week, and next month. Just play center for me and don't worry about the hits."

As Leo had said before, there were players who needed a kick in the ass, others had to be angered, and a few needed to be babied. He knew immediately that Willie Mays had to be babied and encouraged, and that's the way he would play it the rest of the year. The question was: Would it work?

The ball club returned to the Polo Grounds the next night as 23,101 fans turned out to see the Giants and their much-publicized rookie. On the mound for the Braves was the crafty Warren Spahn. Spahnie got a quick edge when Boston jumped on Sheldon Jones for three first-inning runs. He then took the hill and quickly retired Stanky and Lockman. Now May was up. Spahn, who seems to remember every pitch he threw during his long, highly successful career, takes over the story from here.

"When we came into the Polo Grounds the story was that Mays couldn't handle the breaking ball away," recalls Spahn. "The thing they forgot to tell me was that the breaking ball away was from a right-hander. I tried to break my curve straight down over the outside corner and I found out later that Willie kind of gave against right-handers, pulled out a bit, but he didn't against lefthanders. He just waited in.

"So he got that little outside curve and hit it up into the seats. I can remember kidding Willie when he was inducted into the Hall of Fame, telling him he wouldn't have gotten there if it wasn't for me giving him confidence. And, of course, after that I had to pitch Willie differently. Like all great hitters, I had to pitch him all over. Great hitters can't be pitched one certain way."

So Mays slammed his first big league hit high up onto the left field roof. Then Spahn, an obvious student of the art of pitching, settled down and defeated the Giants, 4–1. To many, the loss didn't matter. Mays had connected off one of the best pitchers in baseball. That was the big story. But there were no proclamations from Durocher, no statements that his team was on its way.

Maybe Leo had a premonition that the Giants still weren't out of the woods. Though they were close enough to get back in the race at the end of May, the toughest days of the season still lay ahead.

 **BOBBY**

Leaving New York

Johnny Antonelli was a good looking pitcher and Charlie Grimm asked me if I would trade him for Bobby Thomson. I said of course. Potentially, Bobby was a .300 hitter and had great defensive skills. He could go from first to third better than anyone I ever saw. I felt that man for man, we got the better of the deal. My respect for Bobby Thomson was stupendous. He was a versatile ball player, who could do all the things you needed on a ball club.

—Warren Spahn

There's still so much to tell about the 1951 season and I don't want to jump the gun on that story. So this might be a good time to move forward and talk a bit about what happened after 1951, especially about what was probably the biggest change in my entire career—my trade by the Giants to the Braves before the 1954 season.

After 1951, the Giants became a different team. We had more real hitters with Monte, Willie, Al, Whitey, Don, Henry Thompson, Wes. They could all pop the ball. Even though Monte broke his ankle in the spring of '52 and Willie went into the service, the team was still pretty potent. I was older and more mature, as well.

In my early years, in 1948 and '49, I would often take flack in the press when I wasn't going well and I'd be a liar if I said some of it didn't bother me. But it bothered me more when I knew I wasn't helping the team as much as I could.

In some ways, I didn't have the easy ride back then. After my rookie year expectations were high and when I didn't live up to them, it made news. There were no coattails for me to ride on and I had no right to expect any. I had to ride on my own. When I went 0 for 4, everyone knew it. But I think after 1951 I had the confidence and maturity to get past that. And, of course, we had more players to pick up the slack. Being able to handle pressure is part of being a ball player. You've got to reach a point where you don't think about it.

There's always a nervous excitement before every game, but it should disappear once you take that first hard run, make a defensive play, or take a hard swing.

But some of that pressure returned in 1952. One day during spring training, Leo said "Gee, Bobby, I just have the feeling you're going to hit one every time you're up." He was referring to the big one, of course, and that home run did put me in a spot where people always seemed to expect something to happen. It was a feeling that would last for a while.

Early in the 1952 season we were playing the Cards at the Polo Grounds. The game came down to the ninth inning and we were losing by three runs with two out, bases loaded. Guess who came up and guess what he did? Thomson hit a grand slam homer to win the game. I can remember leaving the clubhouse early. I was walking across center field and some die-hard fans who were still in the stands gave me a great ovation. I'm sure a lot of them were remembering my homer the year before. It was as if I was continuing the heroics.

But while a grand slammer like I hit against the Cards was a real thrill, the '51 homer was a once-in-a-lifetime thing. So you can't make that comparison. As a ballplayer, you get a thrill every time you do something special. I made a catch in Philadelphia one Sunday when I was still playing center with the tying and winning runs on base. It was an over-the-head catch of a ball while I was running away from the plate, similar to the one Willie made in the '54 Series. That was a real thrill for me, especially because it ended the game with the winning runs on base.

A catch like that really just happens. You follow your playing instincts. I was an outfielder who could take his eyes off the ball and run to the spot where the ball would come down, then look up. That's what Durocher would call a three-base catch. It's an instinct, a comfortable feeling, a confident feeling. I've gone out in old-timers' games, not having played ball or caught any high flies in front of 60,000 people and I didn't know whether I was going to get hit in the head or not. No confidence. Of course, this was when I was 60 years old. But it's a great feeling to have that confidence, to know you can do whatever you want out there. And that's the way I used to feel.

Whenever you do something heroic—a big hit, a great catch—you think about the game first. The game situation is the thing. Naturally, what you did sinks in afterward and you enjoy the moment. It's certainly personal satisfaction, but the biggest satisfaction is when you do something like that and win. That's because you know you're doing your job and feel good about yourself, helping your team to win.

On the other hand, if you screw up and the team still wins, all is forgotten. But if you screw up and you lose, well, no one likes to be the donkey. It's part of the game, though, and you just have to rationalize about it. That's the good thing about baseball. If you have a bad day, you've got the chance to come back the next day and do the whole thing all over again. What you did yesterday is old news.

So 1951 was already old news. In '52 we played without Mays and Irvin for most of the year and still finished second, just 4½ games behind the Dodgers. Leo did a great job with that ball club. Jansen fell off that year, but we had Hoyt Wilhelm and he went 15–3 and pitched in a slew of games. I was the only guy with more than 20 homers and 100 RBIs, even though I only hit .270. Leo had me swinging back and forth between third base and the outfield that year. Stanky had gone to manage St. Louis and Davey Williams was playing second. But we were still a scrappy team and really made a run at it.

In '53, things began to fall apart. Monte made a pretty good comeback, but Willie was in the service all year. Yet most of the guys hit well. It was the pitching that went downhill. Maglie was beginning to show his age, Jansen had a bad back, Hearn just plain didn't do well. They all had losing records and high earned run averages. When I look at my record it was one of my best seasons, a .288 average, 26 homers and 106 runs batted in. Yet I don't remember it that way.

I had a strange feeling I was over the hill. I can't explain it because I wasn't 30 years old until that October. But I wasn't the only one. I remember watching TV during the off-season. Some sportswriter was being interviewed and he was talking about me as if I was washed up. Why is it that when a guy hits 30 he's supposed to be on the downside? I can't explain it.

I had been back in center field the entire '53 season with Willie gone and enjoyed it. I also knew that when Willie returned, it would be his position again. I realized I would always be subordinated to him, although it never occurred to me I'd be traded. But with Mays coming back I was undoubtedly one of the only guys who was still strong enough to bring something worthwhile in return—and also a guy they apparently could do without.

The trade came on February 1, 1954, just before the start of spring training. I knew the team needed pitching, and when they had the chance to get a promising young left-hander named Johnny Antonelli from the Braves, they took it. That's when I got the phone call I never expected.

At first, the news was devastating. It hurt. Bad. Players have always said that the first trade is the hardest to deal with and brother are they right. Especially in my case. You've got to remember that I grew up in New York and was a Giant fan long before I signed with them. So in that sense, playing for the Giants was a dream come true, a dream that was suddenly being shattered. The few days after I got the news were among the roughest of my life.

I can recall some of the stories in the press, asking how the Giants could do it, how they could trade a guy who had played so well for them and had produced the most dramatic single moment in the team's history. Even though I knew that most players were traded at some time or another, I was asking myself that same question, too. How could they do it?

There are so many things to think about. How would my family take the news? Where would I live? How was I going to fit in with a new team? What was it going to be like leaving old friends? That was one of the toughest parts. I had been with guys like Whitey and Larry since 1947. I enjoyed having them as teammates and enjoyed hanging out with them. There were others, too. Even Leo. As tough as he was, I knew I'd miss him. I wondered how I'd feel coming back to the Polo Grounds in another uniform and playing against those guys. All these things went through my head and believe me, it wasn't pleasant.

But you also knew that, as a ball player, you had to accept a trade. There was no free agency then and if you wanted to play, you played where they told you to play or you didn't play at all. That meant it was off to Milwaukee for Thomson. But it was extremely difficult and the hurt didn't go away overnight.

I wasn't with the ball club when the trade was made, so I wrote Leo a letter and told him it had been a pleasure to play for him. Writing him like that made it sink in all over again, seem more final. I was leaving the Giants, leaving New York, leaving the Polo Grounds where, just a little over two years before, I had hit a home run that was still being talked about. And, of course, the newspapers recounted it all over again when the trade was made.

If there was any consolation at all it was that I was going to a good team. The Braves were an up-and-coming ball club, had just moved from Boston to Milwaukee the year before, and already had a nucleus of solid players. Plus, to give up a very promising pitcher, they proved they wanted me. That was the final reality, the thing that allowed me to accept the whole thing. The Giants didn't want me anymore; the Braves did.

Eventually, the pain goes away. You're a professional ball player and have a job to do. You've got to do that job whether it's in New York, Milwaukee, or Oshkosh. So you eventually accept what happens, try to fit in and do your job to the best of your ability. And like I said, it helps if you're dealt to a good team.

The Braves had Bill Bruton in center then, so I was going to be the left fielder. I reported to spring training with mixed emotions, but was greeted warmly and began feeling pretty good about things. Then came the game that probably changed the course of my whole career. We were playing the Yankees in St. Petersburg. Mel Allen interviewed me before the game and was telling me how good I looked. I thanked Mel and told him I had been pretty lucky because I had always stayed free of serious injuries. Me and my big mouth!

Whitey Ford was on the mound for the Yanks and my first time up I rapped a base hit. Whitey was a great pitcher and because he was in the American League I didn't face him much. Getting a base hit was a good feeling. Now I was leading off first and the next hitter bounced one back to Ford. Instead of just sliding into second and becoming a routine out, I stayed on my feet trying to foul up the shortstop, Woodie Held, into making a bad throw to first.

It was a case of "overhustling," trying to show my new ball club that I was serious about playing for them, and that they had made the right move by getting this guy Thomson on their team. But the next thing I knew Woodie Held had his arm cocked and was ready to hit me squarely between the eyes with the ball. Instinctively, I fell out of his way and half slid toward the base. Somehow I jammed my right foot into the ground. It bent to the side to where it was almost perpendicular to my leg, then snapped back.

I knew something had gone wrong and let out a holler. While I was on the ground Monte Irvin's injury in 1952 flashed through my mind. After he slid into third his heel was where his toes should have been—his foot had completely reversed itself. That's what was running through my mind and I was afraid to look at my ankle. When I did get the courage to look, it seemed to be lying flat on the ground, no twists or grotesque turns. Hey, I thought, it looks perfectly fine.

There wasn't even a lot of pain. By this time everyone was out there looking down at me and then three or four guys came with the stretcher. The guy closest to my foot picked up my leg just above my ankle and when they raised me up, my foot just stayed on the ground! Uh-oh, I said to myself. I got a problem.

It didn't start hurting until they got me to the hospital. Fortunately, I had a wonderful doctor, Dr. Lonergan, a man I'll never forget. Lou Perini, the Braves' general manager, had him consult with his orthopedic guys in Boston. Together they decided how best to treat the injury. Then, just before I was supposed to go into surgery, they brought in a guy who'd had a bad accident with his lawn mower. He was bleeding profusely and they had to take him first. I can remember waiting to go into surgery when Lou Perini came in. I looked up at Lou and said, "Boy, that was a great trade you made." I really felt awful about it.

After the surgery all I wanted was to get the leg back in shape. The doctor told me there wasn't any reason I wouldn't recover fully with the right kind of therapy, but for a while, nothing seemed to go right. Once the cast came off they taped my leg, and they put some brown gunk on my leg to make sure the tape stuck. So what happened? I get a reaction to the brown stuff and broke out in a rash. Now I was scratching it all the time and spread the damned rash to my face.

But my ankle finally started to heal and I worked hard to rehabilitate it. I returned in August to play in 43 games, 26 of them starts. But I still wasn't 100 percent and didn't hit all that well.

It so happened that in my first game back we were playing the Giants in Milwaukee and I was available for pinch hitting. Sure enough, the game was on the line with the winning run on third when I got the call. I was wearing a big, high shoe to protect my ankle and Hoyt Wilhelm was on the mound. Hoyt, of course, was one of the greatest knuckleballers ever and he threw the flutterball almost exclusively. I went after the first two and didn't come close. But the next one didn't knuckle and I slammed it into left for a base hit to win the ball game.

After the game I had a sandwich with my old teammates Whitey and Larry. In talking about the game, Larry mentioned how Leo gave Wilhelm hell for letting me hit the ball with an 0–2 count. Then Larry went on to say, "Well, if we had to get beat, I'm glad you were the one who did it."

Oddly enough, what really shook me up was my first trip to Ebbets Field with the Braves. I came out of the dugout and there were about half my new teammates kibitzing with the Dodgers out by the batting cage. I couldn't believe my eyes. When I was with the Giants we never talked to the Dodgers. We talked to other teams, but never the Dodgers. Old habits die hard and I just stayed in the background.

In a lot of ways, playing for the Braves was a new experience. For openers, the mood of the team was completely different from that of the Giants. The Braves were a much looser club, with a lot of kidding around and practical jokesters. I was the new guy, coming from New York, and there are always guys who liked to kid people from New York. I didn't see myself as a hotshot, but maybe some of the guys thought I did. It added up to a kind of strange situation for me.

One example. Out first year in Milwaukee, Wink and I rented a house right on Lake Michigan. Most everyone else on the team lived on the west side of town. The only reason we got the place was that a friend of ours from home arranged it. I guess the lake was considered to be on the upper class side of town. So right away some guys saw me as different, and maybe as a New York hotshot. There were even some remarks about it, not a whole lot, but enough to make us feel a bit uncomfortable.

Overall, though, Milwaukee was a great place and at one point we even talked about settling there permanently. The people were great. If you remember, 1954 was just the second year the Braves were in town and it was unbelievable the way all of us were treated.

The ball players and everyone connected with the team were looked upon as heroes. Even the clubhouse kids who shined the shoes were signing autographs. People on the street recognized all the players. Golden Guernsey was the big dairy farm in Milwaukee and they gave the players milk, eggs, and butter on the house. Sibby Sisti, who was a utility player coming to the end of his career in 1954, had six or seven kids and getting those dairy products was like a godsend to him. It was really unbelievable the things they did. Bill Bruton was one of the first out there and they practically gave him a new house.

One thing I still recall is my role in Hank Aaron getting his start. When I broke my ankle that spring, Hank was called up to replace me and had a fine rookie year until he broke his ankle late in the season.

Whenever I see Hank I remind him that he might never have made it if I hadn't been hurt. I'm joking, of course, because he was one of the great talents in the game.

He was also a quiet guy who just went out and performed. The team had a number of players like that while I was there. Bill Bruton was the same way. So was Eddie Mathews, a great home run hitter who showed up and did the job, day after day, both at the plate and at third base. The biggest character among the everyday players had to be Johnny Logan, the shortstop. John was a guy who marched to his own drummer and always seemed to take the opposite direction from everyone else.

Before each game we would have a meeting to go over the hitters. If Spahnie was pitching, he'd talk about how he was going to pitch each hitter and where we should play each guy. Logan would invariably pipe up and say, "Well, you guys do what you want. I'm gonna play him my way." It wasn't unusual for John to have a mind of his own, especially when it came to playing the hitters.

I don't think Spahnie minded too much because he knew how John was. Besides, Spahnie was just a great guy. He liked to have fun and when you put him together with Lew Burdette you had a couple of real clowns. One year they exchanged gloves when the Topps people were taking pictures for baseball cards. I don't know how many they took before they realized that Spahnie had a glove on his left hand, posing as a righthander, while Burdette passed himself off as the southpaw.

When they weren't pitching, everything was fun and games. As a matter of fact, I had one incident with Spahnie my first year in Milwaukee where I kind of lost my cool. We were in Pittsburgh and Spahnie had pitched the day before, so he was sitting in the dugout, very jauntily, with a big wad of chewing tobacco in his mouth. He didn't always chew tobacco, but you never knew what Spahnie was going to do.

You've got to remember that it was a very different time back then. A lot of guys chewed tobacco. It was part of the game, maybe a leftover from the rough-and-tumble days of the 30s, the Gas House Gang and teams like that. So while it might sound pretty disgusting today, it wasn't unusual for guys to be spitting tobacco juice all over the place.

Anyway, there were a set of about five steps into the dugout at old

Forbes Field and when I came in from the outfield I sat down on the steps to watch the game. All of a sudden, I felt something on my leg. I looked down and there was a big, dirty drip of tobacco juice on my leg and down my sock. Right away I looked at Spahnie and there he was with a big goofy grin on his face.

So I said, "Come on, Spahnie, you jerk. Don't do that. That's terrible." Then I turned around to watch the game and, presto, he did it again, another splatter on my socks.

"Spahnie, what the hell's the matter with you?" I said, getting even more annoyed. "That's not right. Knock it off. What the hell is the matter with you?"

Now Spahnie is sitting there with that sheepish grin on his face. To him, it was a big joke. He enjoyed life and this was fun. So here he goes again, splatter all over my leg. That's when I blew my stack. There was a batting helmet sitting right there on the steps. I grabbed it and just swung it backward, hard as I could, because he was right behind me. Wouldn't you know, it hit him square in the middle of the forehead. Fortunately, it was with the round part of the helmet and not a glancing blow with an edge that could have cut him. But it had to stun the heck out of him.

By that time everyone was wondering what was going on. There's old Spahnie sitting there, a little dazed, but he survived and came out of it pretty well. I remember Del Crandall saying, "Warren, what the heck did he do to you?" But Spahnie accepted the fact that he had it coming and that was the end of it. I've always respected the way he handled the whole thing because it shows the kind of man he was.

Spahnie might have had a happy-go-lucky attitude, but on the mound he was all business. When he wasn't pitching he was loose and easy. In fact, the whole team could be that way, and that's what distinguished them from the Giants. As a group, the Giants were more serious. There wasn't the same kind of clowning around. Guys were more apt to be paying attention to the game.

A lot of that came from Durocher. Leo was all business. So were Dark and Stanky. They didn't want anyone fooling around. Charlie Grimm was the Braves' manager when I got there. Old Jolly Cholly. He was nothing like Leo. Charlie was a great guy who used to tell us not to make too much of the game.

"All it takes is a bat, a ball, and a glove," he would often say. I remember when I first heard that I almost fell off the bench because

I had just come from Durocher. And now I was going to a bat, a ball, and a glove.

But everyone has his own way and there really isn't any one formula for success. Unless it's talent. The Giants were serious and they won. The Braves were a loose team, a fun team, and they would be winners, too. When I got there they were a club on the brink of doing some really good things. Unfortunately, I wouldn't be there when they finally got to smell the roses. My problem was simple. During my entire stay in Milwaukee, as good as it was, the numbers just didn't come. They didn't seem to be there anymore.

The Dodgers Make Their Move

On the morning of June 1, the Dodgers were in first place with a 24–15 record. While the Giants sat in fifth with a 21–21 slate, they were just 4½ games behind, certainly within striking distance. The three teams in between—the Cards, Cubs, and Braves—weren't considered serious contenders over the long haul. They just didn't have enough firepower to match up with Brooklyn. But up to this point in the season, the Giants didn't appear to have it, either.

Dodger power jumped out at you, much in the way the baseballs were jumping out of Ebbets Field. The team now had a collective .297 batting average. Robinson was leading the majors with a .407 average; Reese, Campanella, Snider, and Hodges were all hitting over .300. Snider and Hodges were one-two in RBIs, while Hodges led the majors with 15 home runs. Offensively, the team was a juggernaut, ready to steamroll anything in its way.

The Giants were no longer a team of patty cakes, but their run-scoring muscle couldn't approach that of the Brooks. Dark was still the only .300 hitter at .331, but Stanky, Lockman, Westrum, Irving, and Henry Thompson were all hitting better. Bobby Thomson was up to .244 and showing signs of life as well, but Mays still had only a single hit, the homer off Spahn. Willie was 1 for 21 and while Durocher had pledged never-ending loyalty to the youngster, there were still questions whether or not Mays could handle big league pitching.

Maglie won his eighth straight to start the month of June. The Barber was ferocious on the mound, delivering the goods nearly every time out. Though Mays was hitless again, it took a great catch by the Pirates' Pete Reiser to keep it that way. A Dodger loss to Cincinnati cut the lead to 3½ as the top six teams in the league were still within five games of each other.

During the next week the Giants got a real boost. Willie Mays began hitting. By June 7, he raised his average to .200, with 10 hits in 50 trips. But the club, at 25–25, was having a tough time shaking the .500 mark. There was also bad news when third baseman Henry Thompson dislocated his left thumb; he would be lost for a week.

On the Dodger front, Dressen learned he had been fined $100 for "failure to leave the bench when ejected from yesterday's game and for masquerading in the dugout." Using a combination of imagination and sheer nerve, the Dodger manager donned the garments of a groundkeeper and unobtrusively stood in the dugout, hoping to escape detection. Discovered and banished again, Dressen then appeared in a field box adjacent to the Dodger dugout, causing Cardinal manager Marty Marion to protest the game. So it was Dressen who was running afoul of the league officials as much or more than Durocher. But the Dodgers were beginning to move. They won six straight before losing to the Pirates on June 9, and with a 30–17 record were six full games in front of the Giants, whose victory over the Cubs brought them to 26–25. In that game, Durocher moved onto the third base coaching lines—anything to shake up the team, get it going.

By June 15, the Giants had moved into second place, still six games behind Brooklyn. The Dodgers were gaining momentum at 34–18, while the Giants were now four games over .500 at 30–26. In an 11–6 victory over Cincinnati, Jansen got his record up to 7–5. More importantly, Hank Thompson was back in the lineup with three hits and Willie Mays, with three more hits, had now hit safely in 10 straight, jacking his average up to .280, second to Dark's .332. Mays was beginning to give everyone a preview of things to come.

A Dodger victory over the Cards came on Gil Hodges's twentieth home run of the year. The big first sacker was showing awesome power and there was talk about him challenging Hack Wilson's National League record of 56 home runs and even Babe Ruth's still sacred 60.

Besides checking the box scores, there was something else fans always looked for on June 15. At midnight, the trading deadline would pass, and everyone wondered if either of the two ball clubs would make a deal. Durocher indicated the Giants would stand pat. "I don't see anything in sight," was the way Leo put it. "Whenever we talk with other clubs they ask for a top player while offering a second-stringer in return." Nevertheless, the betting line was that the Giants were more likely to make a trade than the Dodgers—but it was the Brooks that provided the big surprise by announcing a major deal. In one shot, the Dodgers apparently solidified the only weak spot in their lineup—left field—and in the eyes of most observers they also won themselves a pennant.

The man they acquired was Andy Pafko, the hard-hitting left fielder of the Chicago Cubs. Pafko was coming off a great 1950 season in which he had slammed 36 homers, driven home 92 runs, and hit .304. He was a lifetime .295 hitter and was batting .278 at the time of the trade. The Dodgers also got pitcher Johnny Schmitz, catcher Rube Walker, and infielder Wayne Terwilliger. Going to the Cubs were left fielder Gene Hermanski, catcher Bruce Edwards, pitcher Joe Hatten, and utilityman Eddie Miksis.

But Pafko was the main man. He would give the Dodgers still another power hitter as well as a versatile veteran player who, much like Bobby Thomson, had also spent time in center and at third base.

Reaction to the trade was swift. Manager Dressen couldn't hide his elation. "I think the deal is going to improve us a lot," he said. "Schmitz is a good pitcher, steadier and more experienced than Hatten. In Andy Pafko, I have an outfielder who will end for me the daily problem of switching from a left- to a right-hand hitter."

Strangely enough, Andy Pafko was not elated when he heard he was going from a second-division team to one of the best in baseball.

"The crux of it was," Pafko says, looking back, "that my wife and I loved Chicago. At the time of the trade I don't think it mattered that it was the Dodgers. It could have been any other team and I still wouldn't have been happy. I don't think any player likes being traded once he is established in a city. And people in Chicago still talk about it, saying it was a bad trade.

"But it didn't take me long to realize I had come to a great team. People sometimes forget that I was also a member of the '57 Braves, a fine team that won the World Series. But I don't think they were as talented as the '51 Dodgers. Man for man, that Dodger team was the best I ever played on."

Another veteran Dodger, Duke Snider, remembers the Pafko deal as giving the ball club the final piece of a superb, eight-man starting lineup.

"We had truly a great team in 1951," the Duke of Flatbush remembers. "Pafko joined me and Carl Furillo in the outfield. Both Andy and Carl had also played center field at one time during their careers. So now we had three center field–quality outfielders. Both Billy Cox and Jackie Robinson had been shortstops. Add Pee Wee, and we had three terrific, shortstop-quality glovemen in the infield. Hodges at first was as good as they come, and Campy was an MVP catcher. The offense was tremendous; the pitching staff was excellent. I'm not saying this was the greatest team of all time, but we certainly rank right up there."

Pee Wee Reese agrees with the Duke. "When we got Pafko," recalls Pee Wee, "I can remember some of the opposing players saying, my God, you guys are way out in front and you pick up a guy like Andy Pafko. Now you'll probably win it by 30 games."

Did the Pafko trade assure the Dodgers of a pennant? Many felt that way at the time, and there were some indications that Leo Durocher, at least privately, was among them. Sources said that Leo was extremely disappointed when he heard about the trade, though he didn't concede the pennant outwardly to his archrivals. But the Lip had known Pafko was available and said later that the Giants had offered three times as much as Brooklyn for the Chicago outfielder.

Was Leo blowing smoke? The evidence says no, and a small, almost filler-type blurb that appeared in the October 10, 1951, edition of the *Sporting News* adds another interesting twist on the '51 season that can be placed into the What If column.

The item was headed, "Leo's Peeve at Cubs Ended." The short paragraph went on to say that Durocher had stopped talking to Cubs' manager Frankie Frisch after Frisch turned down Leo's offer for Andy Pafko and traded him to the Dodgers instead. This was followed by a single sentence that contained a kicker that had not appeared at the time the story first broke. It simply said with no further explanation, "Among the players Durocher offered the Cubs was Bobby Thomson."

Leo has admitted getting many feelers about Bobby through the years. As he was reconstructing the club in 1949 and 1950 he had said repeatedly that he would not even consider trading Bobby. But after a sub-par 1950 season and his tortoiselike start in '51, it would not be unlikely that a major June trade package could have included Thomson. Even Bobby recalls having a kind of eerie premonition at that point of the season, especially after losing the center field job to Mays, then being benched briefly before eventually taking over at third.

"I had a funny feeling that Leo was getting tired of a Thomson who would perform, then wouldn't perform," Bobby said. "It wasn't anything Leo said or did, but simply a feeling I had. He never pointed a finger. But you have to remember one thing. Leo didn't sit on failure and he was never averse to change. When I got back in the lineup after sitting a few days I remember saying to myself, 'Here's your chance. If you blow it now, you may be sitting for a long time.' "

The facts add up. Bobby was a stronger player than Gene Hermanski, the outfielder the Cubs received in the package. Hermanski was, at best, a part-timer while Thomson, like Pafko, was a frontliner and a player who still had star potential. Had Thomson been part of a Giant offer, it certainly would have been stronger than the Dodgers' package.

One other thing. Go back to 1937 when Frankie Frisch was the aging second baseman for the Cardinals and also the team's manager. The Redbirds' shortstop that year was none other than Leo Durocher—who, on more than one occasion, told Branch Rickey to "get that old man off the field." Could it be that Frisch, some 14 years later, was playing a little payback game with Leo? It's an intriguing question, especially since the October 10 *Sporting News* blurb said that Durocher refused to speak to Frisch after the trade was made.

Of course, the bottom line is even more intriguing. Had Bobby Thomson been traded for Andy Pafko in June of 1951, the entire course of the pennant race would have been altered.

The Dodgers were in Chicago when the trade was made, so the eight players involved simply switched locker rooms. The game that day was filled with irony. Pafko did his job, belting his thirteenth homer of the year in his first game as a Dodger. Hodges also continued his hot hitting with home run number 21. But the day belonged to the discarded Bruce Edwards. The second-string catcher slammed a three-run circuit off Erskine in the seventh inning to provide the margin of victory in a 6–4 Chicago triumph. The loss ended a Dodger four-game winning streak.

In Pittsburgh, the team that didn't make a trade won its game. Sal Maglie became the first National League pitcher to win 10 games as the Giants beat the Pirates, 6–1. Durocher continued to juggle his lineup. Thomson was back in the third spot, with Westrum batting cleanup. Irvin, Mays, and Lockman followed them. Despite frequent lineup changes, the cast of characters seemed to be stabilizing. The Giants now trailed the Dodgers by five games and by seven in the loss column.

On June 19, Dressen and the Dodgers won a minor victory when National League President Ford Frick denied the Cardinals' protest of the June 6 game in which Dressen didn't leave the dugout when ejected, then appeared in a nearby field box.

"Games should be won and lost on the field," Frick said, in rendering his judgment. He went on to point out that the score of the game remained the same from the time Dressen was ejected until it ended. Charley may have won this round, but was it worth the price? The Dodger manager obviously thought he was being clever in his attempt to circumvent the rules. But, in reality, his masquerade would be construed as showing up the umpires, something no smart manager wants to do. Sooner or later, this kind of behavior was bound to backfire, because it's the men in blue who always have the last laugh.

Nevertheless, the Dodgers continued to gain momentum on all fronts. Preacher Roe was putting together an amazing season. The veteran lefty was still unbeaten at 10–0. Just a little more consistency from the rest of the staff and the feeling was the Dodgers would make the race a runaway. Meanwhile, Mays was looking more and more like a diamond in the rough. He blasted three-run homers in two straight games and had his average up to .287. That meant he was batting well over .300 since his horrible start.

Bobby Thomson, however, continued to struggle. Even Don Mueller had righted himself and gone on a tear that had his below-.200 average up to a respectable .278. But Bobby's hitting had dropped 22 points in as many days to .222. Durocher was using him to pinch hit or as a late-inning defensive replacement. No wonder Bobby began to feel he was down to his last chance.

On June 24, the Giants completed a 14-game road trip with a 10–7 victory over the Cubs, while the Dodgers were stopped twice by the last-place Pirates, 10–7 and 5–4. Erskine fell to 6–7 by losing the first game, while Clyde King took the loss in the nightcap after relieving starter Erv Palica. The double-dip loss cut the Brooks' lead to six games, but no one on the team seemed especially worried.

The Giants closed their trip with a strong relief job by George Spencer, who had become a dependable stopper for Durocher. Mueller had hit a blazing .415 on the trip, followed by Mays at .389, Lockman .352, Dark .345, and Irvin .326. But Westrum's hands were getting beat up again and that always affected his hitting. And Bobby Thomson continued to slump.

Both ball clubs had exhibition games the next day. The Dodgers played the Yanks in the Mayor's Trophy Game, while the Giants traveled to Fenway Park to play a benefit game with the Red Sox. Arthur Daley, writing in *The New York Times,* evaluated the season thus far and concluded that the boys from Flatbush were running a "juggernaut" and that the Giants were the "nearest and least feeble pursuers."

Daley also concluded that the Giants were no longer the disorganized team that had lost five of six to the Dodgers during the early-season 11-game losing streak. Then he added: "Leo Durocher has brought his stumbling heroes back on their feet and the boys are starting to hit at long last—except for Bobby Thomson, who seems to have lost the secret."

Manager Durocher had one other worry. Henry Thompson, who was playing third, was also in a horrendous slump. His average was down to .247, he was 0 for his last 13 at bats, and hit just .189 on the road trip.

On June 26, after the exhibition pause, the two ball clubs went head-to-head at the Polo Grounds. Maglie continued his mastery over the Dodgers, handing Roe his first loss by throwing a three-hit shutout as the Giants won, 4–0. In this game, Durocher replaced the slumping Thompson at third with Bill Rigney. In the second contest, Newcombe won his tenth of the year as the Dodgers turned on the power and took a 10–4 victory. Hearn was routed in this one and his record was now a disappointing 6–5.

Mays continued to excite. The Dodgers had scored four times in the fourth and were going for more when the rookie center fielder made a tumbling, acrobatic catch of Furillo's blooper into short right-center. Willie did a complete somersault and came to his feet with the ball in his glove and his cap in his bare hand. It wouldn't be long before the young center fielder would make a habit of running out from under his cap as he chased fly balls or scampered around the bases. It soon became a trademark of one of the most exciting players to watch in the major leagues.

The third game was a hard-fought affair in which Monte Irvin blasted two home runs off Ralph Branca. It was the second one that did the real damage, a three-run shot in the eighth that brought the Giants from a 4–2 deficit to a 5–4 triumph. This time Durocher got fine relief pitching from Sheldon Jones, who bailed out starter Dave Koslo to get the win. The loss dropped Branca's record to 5–2.

The victory brought the Giants to within five games of the front-running Brooks. When the Dodgers dropped a 3–2 decision to the Phils a day later, the lead narrowed to 4½ games and the Giants were right back in the topsy-turvy pennant race. With midseason approaching, no distinct pattern had yet emerged. The Dodgers were now 41–25; the Giants, 38–31.

However, June ended with a pair of blowouts. The Giants dropped a 19–7 decision to the Braves, Boston scoring its final 15 runs in the seventh and eighth innings. The loser was Sal Maglie, the league's best pitcher. The same day, the Dodgers crushed the Phils, 14–8, turning on the power to score 13 of their runs in the third, fourth, and fifth innings.

July began with Bobby Thomson hitting a three-run homer in the second inning to spearhead a 4–1 victory over the Braves. The homer was Bobby's tenth of the year, but his first in a month. He had been in and out of the lineup and pinch-hitting since mid-June and Durocher had indicated that unless he started hitting he might take a more permanent seat on the bench. But it would still be three weeks before Durocher would make a decision that would contain one of the keys to the season.

Bobby suddenly went on a tear. He homered in four straight games, six of the next eight, and began resurrecting his place on the ball club. But just as suddenly the Giants were digging themselves into a hole. In a big, July 4 doubleheader, the Dodgers whipped the Giants 6–5 and 4–2, coming back to win the opener in 11 innings and taking the nightcap on a route-going performance by Ralph Branca. Dressen was up to his old tricks, getting tossed in the first game and then appearing in Walter O'Malley's private box, causing Durocher to threaten a protest. The double victory, however, upped the Dodgers' lead to 6½.

Before the doubleheader, Jackie Robinson paid unexpected homage to Sal Maglie, one of his archrivals and antagonists, calling the Barber "the best pitcher in the league." Pee Wee Reese, on the other hand, questioned Durocher's strategy of always having his starters in the bullpen, shooting the works every game.

"Durocher was so anxious to beat Philadelphia that he had all his starters for the Brooklyn series—Maglie, Hearn, and Jansen—in the bullpen. I can't understand it."

Leo spent the pregame time scratching his arms, which had broken out in a nasty rash. "It's an allergy," the manager told reporters. "I get it when I become upset, kind of external ulcers. Know what caused this eruption? It was the 19 runs the Braves scored off us Saturday."

When Newcombe topped the Giants the next day, 8–4, it completed the sweep and upped the Dodgers' lead to 7½ games. John Drebinger, reporting on the game in the *Times,* wrote, "With this triumph, Chuck Dressen's Brooks have just about made a shambles of the National League pennant race as it moves into the halfway mark next Sunday."

Dodger domination was reflected in the All-Star Game selections. Hodges, Robinson, and Campanella were voted onto the starting lineup. Snider and Reese were substitutes, and Newcombe and Roe were on the pitching staff. The seven selections from the Brooks represented the largest group from one team in either league. The Giants were represented by Al Dark, starting at shortstop, with Maglie and Jansen picked as pitchers.

At the time of the July 10 All-Star break, things were looking good for the Dodgers. They had a 50–26 record and an 8½ game bulge over the 43–36 Giants. Brooklyn's team batting average of .282 was well above the Giants' .258. And Bobby Thomson, despite his homer barrage, was back down to .231. Leo Durocher's ball club still had a big hill to climb.

The Nationals won the All-Star Game, an 8–3 triumph over the Americans as Hodges, Bob Elliott, Ralph Kiner, and Stan Musial all homered. The winning pitcher: Sal Maglie.

Now it was on to the second half of the season, and it didn't begin well for the Giants. The Cardinals' Gerry Staley blanked the Durochermen on four hits, topping Larry Jansen, 2–0. The loss not only dropped the Giants 9½ games behind the winning Dodgers, but also bumped them back to third, percentage points behind the Cardinals.

There was a noticeable change in the Giant lineup. Young second baseman Davey Williams, just recalled from Minneapolis, started in place of Stanky. Rumors were already flying that the Brat was ticketed to become the Cardinals' manager in 1952. The elevation of Williams was looked upon by some as a sign that Durocher was conceding the season to the Dodgers and beginning to think about next year. But anyone making that kind of speculation didn't know Leo Durocher.

The 22-year-old Williams was reputed to be a slick fielder, and handled eight chances flawlessly in the game with the Cards. When the Dallas-born second baseman belted a grand slam the next day, it looked as if he might be in the lineup for some time.

Bobby Thomson hadn't gotten into a game since July 8, prior to the All-Star break. When the Scot returned to the lineup on the fourteenth, no one knew how long he would be there. But when the Giants lost to the Cubs on July 17, a small item appeared after the game story in several papers. It said that manager Durocher was toying with the idea of trying Bobby at third in place of the still slumping Henry Thompson. The Giants were now eight behind, a sizable gap, but it could have been even worse had the Dodgers not picked this time to drop a pair of doubleheaders on successive days.

First the Cubs turned the trick, winning both ends of the twin bill, 5–4 and 11–7. In the nightcap, the Dodgers failed to score on two occasions when double plays snuffed out a pair of bases-loaded rallies. The next day Cincinnati rolled into Ebbets Field and topped the Brooks 5–2 and 6–5. Roe was beaten for just the second time in the opener, while the disappointing Johnny Schmitz lost the nightcap.

Still, to those observing National League action from afar it didn't look like much of a pennant race. Despite the four straight losses, Brooklyn appeared to have things well in hand. In the coming weeks, the Dodgers would reaffirm what appeared to be the obvious. The Dodger lead would continue to lengthen, and the inevitability of the finish became more apparent. But to those closer to the scene, there were some interesting events taking place. Some were overt, others subtle, but all would begin to indicate the difference in the way the two ball clubs, and especially their managers, were operating.

On Wednesday, July 18, the Dodgers got into a slugfest with the Pirates. Before the game ended, 25 runs crossed the plate. Unfortunately for the Brooks, the final two came in the Pittsburgh ninth and the Bucs won, 13–12, sparked by three Ralph Kiner home runs. The losing pitcher was right-hander Erv Palica, who failed to hold a one-run margin in the final frame.

Palica was a 23-year-old who had first pitched for the Dodgers as a 19-year-old in 1947. After a 13–8 season in 1950, a year in which he showed his versatility by making 19 starts in his 43 appearances and throwing 200 innings, expectations for him were high. But Palica hadn't pitched well in 1951, and perhaps spurred by the Dodgers' sixth loss in seven games, manager Dressen ran out of patience.

"I never saw a fellow with so many alibis," Dressen announced in the press room after the game. "If it isn't his groin, it's his arm, or something else." The manager then outlined plans to pitch Palica in an upcoming exhibition game the following Monday and then in another exhibition on August 6. In between, he would work on his pitching in the bullpen.

The next day Dressen again jumped on Palica in a clubhouse meeting. "I've never talked about a player to newspapermen before," he said, "but this time I did. When you're ready to throw the ball hard you can pitch for me again. Until then, no. It's all up to you."

The Dodger manager was also bellyaching about minor injuries that had slowed Newcombe and Branca. "Eight games in front," he said, "yet if Newk and Branca had been all right we'd be ahead by eleven, at least."

Dressen's words had the hollow sound of an alibi, which was strange in itself because his team had a sizable lead. More significantly, the Dodger manager had turned his back on one of his springtime proclamations: that there would be no doghouse in Flatbush as there had been when Burt Shotton was the manager. Erv Palica was not only in Dressen's doghouse but had been subjected to public humiliation.

Ralph Branca remembers the incident and says it was indicative of the way Dressen handled his pitchers. "Whenever one of the pitchers would complain of a sore arm or another ailment," Branca recalls, "Charley's stock answer was, 'It's all in your head.' He used to say that all the time. I can remember him starting Palica after Erv said he had a sore arm. But Dressen, who knew more than his pitcher did, said it was all in his head. By the end of the year it got to be a joke. Someone had a sore arm? Hey, go soak your head in the whirlpool."

The Palica incident was the first sign of a crack in the Dodger machine. It wouldn't be the last, although cracks have a way of remaining hidden while a team is winning.

Meanwhile, the Giants were also making off-field news. On July 18, the ball club announced that Henry Thompson had been optioned to Ottawa in the International League to make room for a right-handed pitcher named Al Corwin. Thompson had been slumping badly as well as battling an injury, and the pitching staff needed a fresh arm. Oddly enough, Corwin wasn't the guy Leo wanted. The manager had dispatched pitching coach Frank Shellenback to Ottawa under the assumption that Shellenback would return with another right-hander, Alex Konikowski.

Charley Feeney, who was covering the Giants at the time for the *Long Island Press,* remembers why the scenario changed. "Shellenback went to Ottawa to try to find mound help," Feeney recalls. "Everyone figured that Konikowski was the guy who would get the call. He had been up before and was having a fine year at Ottawa. Al Corwin, on the other hand, was having a mediocre season to that point, with a couple of more losses than wins. Yet when Shellenback called in his report, he told Leo the guy who could help them was Corwin. The Giant brass were skeptical, but Frank held his ground. He said Corwin threw sidearm and because of his delivery it would take a few trips around the league for the hitters to get used to him.

"I remember thinking that it took a lot of guts for Shellenback to take that kind of a stand. Everyone knew Konikowski was the big gun. It also took guts for Durocher to go along with his coach's recommendation. But they did and Corwin went on to win five games for the ball club during the second half of the year."

Unlike Charley Dressen, who would rely more and more on himself as the season wore on, Durocher had enough respect for the people around him to consider their opinions before making a move. That's what he did when all roads were leading to Konikowski.

A day later, on July 20, two more pieces of Giant news hit the papers. Though the team still trailed the Dodgers by eight games, owner Stoneham extended his manager's contract through 1952. This vote of confidence served to take some of the pressure off Leo in the final months. No matter how it ended, he knew he would be back.

More importantly, with Henry Thompson in Ottawa, Leo wasted no time in naming Bobby Thomson his new third baseman, beginning with the game against the Reds that same day. Leo remembers:

"I didn't know if Bobby could play third. When Thompson got hurt and stopped hitting, I began looking for a third baseman. I was tripping over Bobby every day until someone reminded me that Bobby had played second when he first came up. Bobby was always a good team man, and when I made the suggestion he said he'd give it a try. Know what? He was sensational."

Bobby played errorless ball in his first game at third, but perhaps more importantly, contributed three hits and a pair of RBIs. Some players, switching to a new position for the first time, concentrate so hard on defense that they almost forget how to hit. The Giants won, 11–5, as Maglie notched his thirteenth victory. Though the Dodger margin was still eight games, Stanky had returned to second and the Giant realignment appeared to be successful.

The next day, Bobby Thomson showed he wouldn't become a liability at the hot corner. Cincinnati was again the opponent and in the eighth inning Bobby booted a Bobby Adams grounder for an error. But on the very next play, he went quickly to his left, fielded Joe Adcock's tricky bouncer, and turned it into a bang-bang, 6-4-3 double play. The Giants won again, 3–2, as Jansen upped his record to 12–8.

At the same time, the Dodgers topped the Cards, 3–2, with Don Newcombe winning his thirteenth. Big Newk seemed on course to win 20 and it was difficult to see what Dressen had complained about. The lead was still eight games and the Dodgers were off on a tear that would result in a 10-game winning streak. During that same period, the Giants also played outstanding baseball. They were 10–3 from July 20, to July 31, but still lost another game and a half to the Brooks. As August dawned, the Giants were as far back as they had been all year, 9½ games.

Third Base and a New Stance

Bobby's mother played a big role in the 1951 season. She knew that Bob was feeling pressure and tried to make his life as smooth as possible. She would always have dinner in the oven for him. Sometimes she would go out to dinner with him. She understood how tough it was getting through that season.

—Elaine "Winkie" Thomson

I felt lousy when I wasn't hitting. Slumps will do that to you and the first half of 1951 was nothing but one long slump. No one has to tell you that you're not hitting. You're aware of it every day. But that doesn't stop your teammates from making suggestions, and you read about it in the papers, if you read the papers. Sometimes, when you're not playing well, you don't want to read them.

There was never any doubt in my mind I was going to start hitting. The question was: when? Since I had put some good numbers up before, there was no reason I wouldn't put them up again. I can recall one of the local writers—Arch Murray, I believe—quoting Leo in a story that said the Giants were a different team when I was hitting.

I know Leo tried to light a fire under me. He did that with a lot of guys. In '51, I didn't feel as much pressure as I had in '49 or '50, because we were a different team now. Dark and Stanky were established and Monte was the big guy. But that still didn't help me. When you're hitting .230 and you're supposed to hit .280, there are no excuses and, sometimes, no answers. I think the Giants were getting tired of my inconsistency. There's got to be a certain amount of frustration when you're dealing with someone who has the potential to play well and just isn't doing it. I know how I felt and I can imagine how Leo and the front office must have felt.

When they brought Willie up I knew immediately that he would be

140

the center fielder. He had to play there. Maybe the other guys realized it would be tough on me, because Al Dark called a meeting and said, "We all know Bobby's a better center fielder than this guy, but this is Leo's decision." None of us really knew Mays then but they all knew what I could do out there. I didn't take a backseat to anyone when it came to covering the wide expanse of the Polo Grounds. Willie, of course, turned out to be a great center fielder. But to get pushed out of your job by a young kid has got to be a bit of a jolt. I like to think I was a team man, so I accepted it despite what was going through my mind. The important thing was staying in the lineup. But where?

I played left field for a while, hit some homers, then slumped again. Pretty soon I was sitting out some games, platooning in others, and beginning to feel like the fourth outfielder behind Monte, Willie, and Don Mueller. I didn't dream Leo would ask me to play third. We all knew that Henry Thompson wasn't hitting well. He had that thumb injury earlier and maybe it was still affecting his swing. So one day Leo asked me if I'd be willing to give third base a try. He made it sound easy. "Hell, you've played the infield before," he said. "You can handle it." Then he took me out for a workout, hit me a bunch of grounders. I was down there fielding them, scooping them up pretty good, and Leo said, "What did I tell you? You can't play any better than that."

So I started at third on July 20. Right away there were people saying it wouldn't work, that I wouldn't be able to field the position well enough and wasn't hitting anyway. But I knew this might be my last chance and was determined to make it work. And it did. I was at third for the rest of the regular season and into the playoffs. Willie, of course, started hitting and remained in center. Willie was a great, great ball player.

Part of Willie's greatness came because he never played safe. If he won a Gold Glove, he did it by going after every flyball that came his way. Some guys prefer to sit back and get the ball on the first hop. Willie never did that, just as I never did. If you can go back on the ball the way we both could, you can play shallow and catch a lot of base hits. Willie not only had a powerful arm, but the ability to catch the ball and throw in one motion. That's a tough combination to beat.

Surprisingly, playing the infield again was an enjoyable experience. You're always in the ball game, can't relax for a second. You're so damned close to the batter, that ball can be on you in an instant.

You're on your toes every pitch, ready to make a quick move to the right or left, charge in for a bunt or slow roller, or just get the glove out in front of you so you don't get killed.

At third you're in the middle of everything. Leo told the infielders, "Get on Maglie! Get on Jansen! Tell 'em to bend their backs," and we'd do it. Sometimes they would get mad and tell us to shut the hell up and let them pitch. Then we'd holler "Let 'er rip! Let 'er rip!" which became our battle cry the second half of the season, thanks to George Spencer, who first used the phrase. Soon, we were all using it and we used it right up to the final game.

The toughest part of playing third for me was the throw to second base. I just couldn't get comfortable making that throw. A guy like Graig Nettles could field the ball and flip it to second and make it look so easy, but it never was easy for me.

I made a few wild ones to first, too. Whitey saved my tail a lot with his glove, but I do remember making a low throw in St. Louis for an error. It was the first inning and I was so mad at myself that when the next ball was hit to me I grabbed it and heaved it with everything I had. I never threw a ball like that before. It started down and then just rose up toward the sky. It's amazing that Whitey was able to catch it. But I had a real live arm then and that's what it could do.

Leo was taking a gamble in another sense when he moved me to third. I still wasn't hitting worth a damn and now I was playing a new position. While some guys concentrate so hard on learning the new position defensively that their hitting falls off, mine didn't have anyplace to go but up. Fortunately, I started to feel better at the plate about the same time I made the switch to third.

Part of the reason could have been because I finally changed my batting stance. Both Whitey, who was my roommate, and Leo had been after me to try a different stance for several months and stubborn Thomson kept resisting. I had a straight-up stance with the bat held high. Leo felt—and Whitey agreed—that I wasn't being aggressive enough at the plate and that a change in my stance would help.

Leo kept saying, "Why not try crouching over a little more as you get ready for the pitch. You've got to be loose up there, ready to spring." He was right. When I began crouching I felt I could spring out at the ball. Maybe some of it is psychological. But you try it and it works and suddenly you've got it in your head that you can hit again and you keep hitting. Had I changed my stance and still failed to hit, who knows what would have happened. I know Leo wouldn't have stayed with a weak-hitting third baseman for very long. He never did.

There was something else in '51 that may have affected my play the first half of the year. I usually came to spring training at about 190 pounds and gradually lost weight when the season started, leveling off at 175. But in '51 I was having a lot of trouble keeping the weight on. My stomach was bothering me and I simply wasn't eating enough. I made an appointment with a doctor who gave me a shot of insulin to stimulate my appetite. I went to the ballpark that afternoon to take some extra batting practice. I was in the cage taking my swings when all of a sudden the stuff hit me—I mean *hit* me.

I never had a feeling like that before—a ravenous hunger that came over me so bad I was shaking. I thought I was going to pass out. I dropped my bat and ran all the way out the center field clubhouse and asked the clubhouse man, Eddie Logan, to get me something, a sandwich, *anything*. Eddie hustled off and came back with a roll and I devoured it like a piranha. After that I was all right.

Fortunately, my weight stabilized. Add that to a new position and new batting stance and I was ready for the stretch run. We all were.

The Lead and the Winning Streak

Charley Dressen must have felt a shiver go up his spine when he read John Drebinger's July 29 column in *The New York Times*. Drebinger said what other people were bound to be thinking. It went like this: While Leo Durocher had to juggle, scramble, change, scratch, improvise, and maneuver just to keep his team in the race, all Charley Dressen had to do was write the names of Reese, Robinson, Hodges, Snider, Campanella, Furillo, Cox and Pafko on the lineup card every day and let them play.

"And so the Dodgers roll on," Drebinger wrote. "Eight games in front. Nine, ten. Soon it will be fifteen and by October it likely will be twenty."

No sweat. But Drebinger also said that because the team was so strong and powerful, Dressen was being denied that which he liked the most—to manage, to use his baseball guile and coax every ounce of ability out of his players and his team.

"All this is denied poor Chuck," was the way Drebinger put it, "who is convinced he could give Casey and Leo cards and spades at this sort of thing and shake rings around them if given only half a chance. But every day it's the same." Drebinger concluded that by running away with the race, the Dodgers were running away with their manager as well. What is more, he isn't enjoying the ride one bit."

Except for his outburst with Erv Palica and his battles with the umpires, Dressen had been subdued, free of any kind of controversy. While his team moved on its merry way to a pennant there was no reason to feel it should be any other way. Such is the life of the front-runner.

But maybe not in Charley Dressen's case. Columnist Drebinger, in a bit of insightful reporting, drew attention to a part of Charley Dressen that had not yet been available for public awareness. Previously described as both arrogant and egotistical, Drebinger pointed out, Dressen liked to be the center of attention. Moreover, he felt that people still viewed him as a Durocher disciple, going back to his days as a Dodger coach. His goal was to show the world that he was the better manager, but because his team was so talented, Dressen couldn't pull enough managerial strings to make him the puppeteer and his players the puppets. Drebinger recognized the paradox; the rest of the baseball world would see it very soon.

Toward the end of July the Giants were playing so well it was hard to believe they were still out of shouting distance. Maglie won his fifteenth game, Irvin stole home for the fourth time in the season, Thomson was hitting and playing well at third. Yet the ball club couldn't gain ground. It's a tribute to the Giants and their manager that they didn't just quit.

The Dodgers made what at first glance seemed like a minor change in late July when they recalled right-hander Clem Labine from St. Paul. Labine had a resilient arm and could both start or relieve. But the 24-year-old rookie had an ankle injury, and reported to the Dodgers on crutches. He became a forgotten man for the first few weeks. Labine, however, remembers the reason the Dodgers called him up, a reason that would become apparent during the final two months of the season.

"I was brought up because the staff was beginning to show signs of overwork," he said. "Even though the club had a big lead, they had some pitchers like Preacher, who were in their thirties. I guess they just wanted a younger pitcher around because the team I joined had a big lead and was very confident."

On August 1, the Dodgers' 10-game winning streak came to an end with a 12–9 loss to Pittsburgh. The Pirates, residents of the National League basement for nearly the entire season, seemed to play like pennant contenders against the Dodgers. They would win the season series from the Brooks and their tenacious play in the final weeks would influence the outcome of the race.

It's an old baseball maxim that a traded player will often return to haunt his former teammates. In the case of the Bucs, it wasn't a traded player. Rather, it was the general manager. Though he still hadn't built his new team into a winner, Branch Rickey had put together a ball club that knew how to beat the Dodgers. For the Mahatma, forced out of the Dodger hierarchy so unceremoniously by Walter O'Malley not even a year earlier, each victory had to be a sweet one.

That same day, the Giants split a pair with the Cubs. In the nightcap, young Al Corwin threw a seven-hit shutout for his first victory. But the Brooklyn margin was still a comfortable nine games.

The Dodgers continued to be an offensive powerhouse. Robinson was second in the league with a .360 average, Campanella fifth at .328. Hodges's 31 homers were still the best in the majors. On the other side of town, Monte Irvin had taken over the National League lead with 73 RBIs, one ahead of Ralph Kiner and two in front of the Duke.

Bobby Thomson continued to hit with the help of his new batting stance. On August 4, Bobby was up to .251 with 20 homers and 65 RBIs, just eight behind league leader Irvin. In his first 17 games since moving to third, the rejuvenated Scot had hit .345 with five homers and 18 RBIs. It looked as if Bobby was coming on strong, something Durocher and the Giants had hoped for all year.

Despite the improved play of the Giants, they failed to gain ground—because the Dodgers continued to win. Then, on Wednesday, August 8, the two ball clubs met at Ebbets Field in a day-night doubleheader, with the final game of the three-game series set for the following afternoon. To most fans and writers, the series represented a last vestige of hope for the Giants. They had to sweep. Anything less just might be the final nail in the coffin. The Dodgers apparently thought so, too, because minutes after that third and final game there was an incident that would become a major turning point in the campaign.

The Dodgers had already beaten the Giants in 9 of their previous 12 meetings. If the Jints considered the afternoon game a must, they got a boost early. Preacher Roe, in the midst of a great season, had to leave after two innings when his arm stiffened up. The Giants had Hearn pitching and the score was tied at 1–1. But Carl Erskine came

That's me in the middle, flanked by two teammates, during my one season with the Jersey City Giants in 1946.

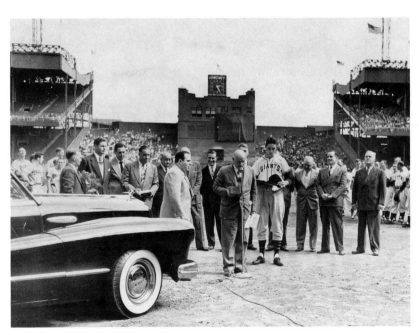

The Staten Island community gave me a day at the Polo Grounds during my rookie year with the Giants in 1947. One of the gifts I received was a shiny new Buick convertible. The photo shows the old Polo Grounds and that unique clubhouse in dead center field.

Early in my major league career I lived at home with my mom on Staten Island.

This is my dad during World War I when he was a member of the Scottish Guards.

By 1953 I was a family man. Winkie and our young daughter Nancy join me in Bradenton, Florida, during spring training with the Milwaukee Braves.

I think the Giants were the only team in the National League using Adirondack bats when we set the home run record with 221 in 1947. That's Hal Schumacher, who pitched for the Giants from 1931–1946, standing with me.

Keeping in shape during the offseason back then involved helping your father-in-law clear property for a house in New Jersey.

You couldn't ask for better teammates. That's Al Dark on the left, Monte Irvin, a guy named Thomson and Whitey Lockman.

Willie Mays was one of the main reasons we turned things around in 1951. Willie's arrival was also the reason I moved to third base, but that worked out well, too.

Jackie Robinson was a player who simply hated to lose. His great catch and clutch home run against the Philadelphia Phillies prevented us from winning on the final day of the regular season in '51.

The Brooklyn Dodgers of 1951 at Ebbets Field, Brooklyn. *Back Row:* Billy Cox, Rube Walker, Carl Erskine, Andy Pafko, Preacher Roe, Clem Labine, Clyde King, Jackie Robinson, Dick Williams, Cal Abrams. *Center Row:* Harold Parrott, "Doc" Wendler, Wayne Terwilliger, Phil Haugstad, Don Newcombe, Erv Palica, Gil Hodges, Johnny Schmitz, Bud Podbielan, Don Thompson, John Griffin. *Front Row:* Rocky Bridges, Duke Snider, Ralph Branca, Jake Pitler, Charley Dressen, Clyde Sukeforth, Cookie Lavagetto, Pee Wee Reese, Roy Campanella, Carl Furillo. *Bat boy:* Stan Strull. *(National Baseball Library, Cooperstown, N.Y.)*

The New York Giants of 1951 at the Polo Grounds, New York.

Back Row: Sheldon Jones, George Spencer, Monte Irvin, Jack Kramer, Jim Hearn, Spider Jorgensen, Clint Hartung, Allen Gettel, Bob Thomson, Monte Kennedy, Larry Jansen, Sal Maglie, Bill Rigney, Whitey Lockman.

Center Row: Wes Westrum, Roger Bowman, Artie Wilson, Dave Koslo, Leo Durocher (Manager), Rafael Noble, Henry Thompson, Don Mueller, Jack Lohrke, Fred Fitzsimmons (Coach).

Front Row: Frank Shellenback, (Coach), Herman Franks (Coach), William Leonard (Batboy) Jack Maguire, Sal Yvars, Alvin Dark, Eddie Stanky. *(National Baseball Library, Cooperstown, N.Y.)*

Here are the two guys who pulled all the strings in 1951. I didn't know much about Charley Dressen then, but it's no secret how the Giants felt about Leo—we just loved the guy!
(National Baseball Library, Cooperstown, N.Y.)

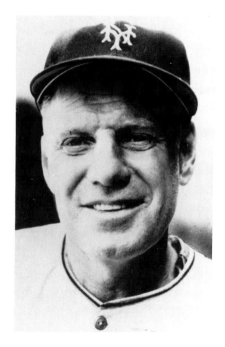

New York and Brooklyn fans might have lived and died with their teams, but they were friendly enemies while waiting for tickets for the second playoff game at the Polo Grounds.

The first inning of *the* game, October 3, 1951. I'd forced Duke Snider at third and fired to first in an attempt to double up Andy Pafko. But Pafko beat the throw.

Ralph Branca.

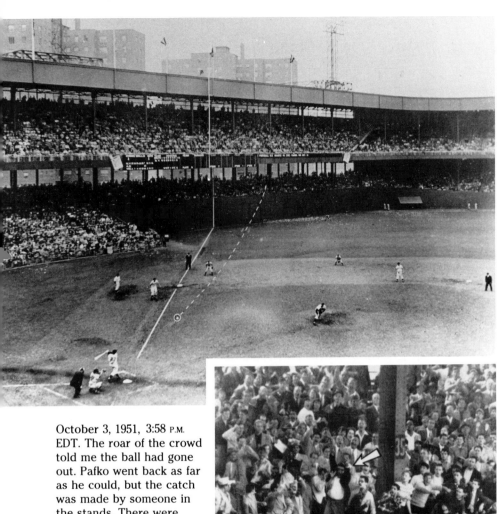

October 3, 1951, 3:58 P.M.
EDT. The roar of the crowd
told me the ball had gone
out. Pafko went back as far
as he could, but the catch
was made by someone in
the stands. There were
dozens of pretenders, but
the ball I hit was never
returned.

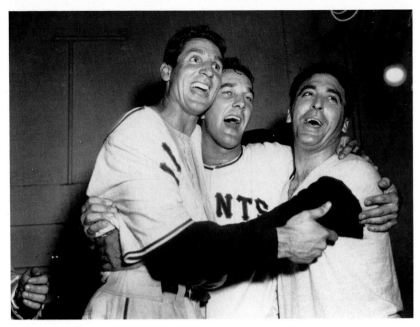

Talk about a jubilant clubhouse! That's me on the left with our two best pitchers, Larry Jansen in the middle and Sal Maglie on the right.

What would a celebration be without Leo? I never saw him so happy. He's hugging me and the Giants' owner, Horace Stoneham, at the same time.

There was no joy in the Brooklyn clubhouse that day. This picture shows Ralph moments after he'd left the field. Sitting beside him is Dodger coach Cookie Lavagetto. *(Barney Stein)*

Coming out on the clubhouse steps and waving to the
thousands of fans who just wouldn't leave the field was an
emotional moment I'll never forget.

We had a family celebration of our own that night at the Tavern on the
Green on Staten Island. Seated at the table from left to right are my sister
Jean, my sister Betty, me, my mom, and my sister Marion. My brother Jim
is standing in the back row, second from the left.

It seemed as if everyone wanted a picture of me at Yankee Stadium on October 4. We had to start the World Series without an off day in between, but I never felt as relaxed as I did during that first game against the Yankees.

The fan mail and telegrams came in droves during the winter of 1951–1952. I tried to answer all of them although I sometimes thought I'd never catch up.

When the Mets began playing at the Polo Grounds in 1962, they held a reenactment of my home run. Some of the Dodgers who returned to relive a moment I'm sure they'd rather forget were *(left to right)* Gil Hodges, Duke Snider, Jackie Robinson, Charley Dressen, Carl Erskin and Roy Campanella, who was confined to a wheelchair after his tragic automobile accident. *(Herb Scharfman)*

Ralph and I have spent a good deal of time together in recent years. We often meet at golf tournaments and sports dinners, but this one was a little different. Here we are at the White House, joined by Mrs. Babe Ruth and one of America's great baseball fans, President Richard Nixon.

in, outpitched Hearn, and shut the door. The Dodgers went on to win it, 7–2, as Erskine raised his record to 12–8.

Now the nightcap was even more critical. The Giants had Maglie going, the one guy who was usually so effective at Ebbets. Only this time the Barber didn't have it. At the end of three the Dodgers had a 4–0 lead. Still, the Giants fought back. Trailing 6–2 against Don Newcombe, they got a run in the eighth, then three more in the ninth to tie the game. Bobby Thomson started the ninth inning rally with a homer off Newk, and Monte Irvin's two-run single off Clyde King brought the Giants even. But it only prolonged the agony.

With Dave Koslo pitching in the tenth, the Dodgers loaded the bases on three singles after two were out. Then Billy Cox slammed a long drive off the left center field wall. Under normal circumstances, it probably would have cleared the sacks. But the Brooks needed only one and the game ended as soon as Andy Pafko crossed home plate with the winning run.

Now the lead was 11½ and the final game had even more of a last-gasp feeling for the Giants. Durocher started Larry Jansen, a pitcher who admitted to limited success at Ebbets. The Dodgers countered with Ralph Branca. Neither would be around at the finish. In fact, the game saw a parade of nine pitchers from both ball clubs and the biggest problem all of them had was finding home plate. The nine gave up 24 bases on balls, a National League record. Dodger pitchers issued 15 of the free passes, but in the end it didn't matter. A Roy Campanella home run off Sheldon Jones in the seventh inning settled the issue. It broke a 5–5 tie and enabled the Dodgers to win the game, 6–5, sweep the series, and increase their first-place margin to a whopping 12½ games. It appeared to everyone that the Giants were dead.

Even the Dodgers thought so and they decided to let their hated rivals know it. Only that single wooden door separated the two locker rooms at Ebbets and the quiet gloom settling over the Giants was contrasted by the unrestrained glee coming from the Dodger side. That was to be expected. So were a few taunts. That had happened earlier in the year. But this time, with the pennant race seemingly over, some of the Dodgers decided to really rub it in.

Suddenly bats were banging against the door and then the taunts came.

The Giants are dead! The Giants are dead! How do you like it now, Leo!

As the Giants listened in amazement and then growing anger there was suddenly a chorus of Dodger voices singing.

Roll out the barrel, we got the Giants on the run!

Over and over again. More laughter, more taunts.

Roll out the barrel, we got the Giants on the run!

It went on for several painful minutes. Leo and his ball players knew the Dodgers liked to revel in victory. They had been doing it all year. It was obvious that Charley Dressen wasn't going to stop them. A manager can control that kind of thing. Dressen not only didn't control it, he encouraged it. Carl Erskine remembers the locker room scene immediately following the ball game.

"Charley came by our lockers," recalls Ersk. "Palica, Branca, and myself all had our lockers close together. Charley came by and was all fired up. He wanted us to go back and sing through that door. I had no desire to do that and I don't think Palica did, but Ralph went."

Teasing, taunting, and jockeying also came easily for Jackie Robinson. Robby had taken a lot in the early years and seemed to enjoy the payback. Like Don Newcombe had said, his anger made him a better player. Other Giants said that Newcombe was there, and Branca and Furillo, as well.

Young Clem Labine, with the team barely two weeks when it happened, also remembers the incident well. "I don't care what other people say, that had to be the worst thing that ever happened to us," Labine recalls. "A lot of us were saying, shut up, leave them alone. Nobody was saying go ahead and do it, but they did it. Dressen was right there with them, so was Jackie, in that little high-pitched voice of his. And Branca, too, with that deep baritone. They were all singing and yelling that the Giants were dead."

On the Giants' side, there was anger. "We all knew they had buried us by sweeping the series," Bill Rigney said. "Because they had kicked our butts we had to sit there and take it. But we didn't forget it. We knew who was singing. We heard Branca and Jackie, and Jackie was pounding on that door with a bat."

Among those listening was the combative New York captain, Al Dark. He is reported to have said, "Human beings can only take so much and we had a bellyfull. You just can't treat human beings like they treated us and get away with it."

And when a reporter asked Leo Durocher if the Dodger sweep would dictate more lineup changes, Leo the Lip sounded off in that loud voice of his, making sure everyone on his ball club could hear him.

"This is my team," he said. "There will be no changes in the lineup. If they go down, I go down with them. If they go up, so do I. This is my team and I'm going to stick with it."

That was all Leo said. He didn't yell back at the Dodgers, didn't tell his players to answer.

"That's one thing that Leo always taught us," said Bobby Thomson. "Let the sleeping dogs lie. Just let 'em lie."

Don Newcombe, one of the enemy, also remembers Durocher as a guy who not only didn't kick sleeping dogs, but didn't encourage his team to gloat. "I know the taunting made the Giants mad, especially when they lost," said Newk, "but they never did it to us when they won. They never yelled the way we did. Leo got angry, too, but he just vowed he would get even."

The New York press corps, much more abundant in 1951 than it is today, was quick to jump on the story. After hearing the Dodgers' taunts in person, the Giant players then had to read all about it once again. And it didn't sit well.

"Pressure by the media helped stir up the Giant-Dodger rivalry even more," Don Mueller remarked later. "Dick Young, who covered the Dodgers for the *Daily News,* stirred up more crap than you can imagine. Between Dick Young, Dressen, and Durocher, something was always happening to make the rivalry even more intense."

Dodger rookie Dick Williams also recalls the effects of Dressen's tactics when they hit the press. "The media used Dressen's quotes kicking the Giants when they were down and I always felt that it served as a launching point for the Giants. All you have to do is look at what happened right after that. The Giants played .800 ball over the last 44 games of the season."

Giant announcer Ernie Harwell also felt the publicity resulting from the Dodgers' locker room outburst had a lingering effect. "Dressen's comment that 'The Giants is dead' appeared in newspapers and was talked about on the radio," recalls Harwell. "It seared itself into the Giant players' brains. But they didn't run off half-cocked. Leo Durocher was a master psychologist and kept his players relaxed, but effective."

Leo did protest the incident to the league office and shortly afterward the wooden door between the clubhouses was permanently bricked. But the damage had been done. The Giants might have been 12½ out, but suddenly they had another reason to win. They might not be able to take it all, but they vowed to play as hard as they possibly could for the remainder of the season.

And there was one other thing that seemingly went unmentioned at the time. Didn't anyone remember 1934, when Bill Terry asked his infamous question: "Is Brooklyn still in the league?" Didn't anyone remember the consequences of that confidence-induced gaffe?

Then came the games of August 11. Looking back now, that day has become more a symbol of the 1951 pennant race than any other mundane statistic of the season.

The Giants returned to the Polo Grounds and hosted the Philadelphia Phillies, the pain of the Dodger sweep still fresh in their minds. They were promptly shut out by Robin Roberts, 4–0. At the same time, the Dodger express took the first game of a doubleheader from the Braves, 8–1, as Ralph Branca ran his record to 10–3.

At that moment, the Giants trailed the Brooks by 13½ games, the biggest margin between the two clubs all year. With roughly a month and a half of the season remaining, it certainly looked as if the Giants *were* dead. It meant little when the Dodgers were beaten in their second game with the Braves, 8–4, reducing the margin to an even 13 games. It is the 13½ that sticks in the mind and remains the barometer to a lead that looked completely insurmountable.

But from this point on, everything changed. Though *The New York Times* game story said the Giants had been "knocked completely out of sight as a pennant contender by the Dodgers earlier in the week," the Giant players managed to regroup. They began with a doubleheader sweep of the Phillies. In the opener, Maglie won his sixteenth, then in the nightcap young Al Corwin further justified the decision to bring him up by winning his third game without a loss. In Brooklyn, Newcombe kept pace by beating the Braves, 7–2, running his record to 16–5, the same as Maglie's.

Both clubs won again the next day. The Giants were now 62–51, but the Dodgers, at 72–36, were playing .667 baseball. And despite a modest, three-game Giant win streak, the margin was still a formidable 12½ games. The only item of note on this day was still another Dodger clash with umpire Frank Dascoli. This time first base coach Jake Pitler was ejected after arguing a close call on an Erskine bunt.

Now the two ball clubs were due to meet again, this time at the Polo

Grounds. With the Dodgers having beaten the Giants 12 of 15 times, they were in a position to deal their rivals the coup de grace. Surprisingly, Dressen went with his "doghouse" pitcher, Erv Palica, who was making his first start since the public whipping, while Durocher countered with George Spencer. Some 42,867 fans flocked to the old Polo Grounds on August 14. It was the third largest crowd of the year. Even though many fans felt their ball club was too far gone to seriously challenge, any Giant-Dodger series had the potential for the kind of excitement not normally seen in a routine, dog-days-of-August game.

The Dodgers played without Reese, who was hobbled by a pulled leg muscle, while Robinson, recovering from minor surgery for the removal of a cyst, played just four innings. Maybe that mattered; maybe it didn't. The Giants hammered Palica early, homers by Mueller and Lockman accounting for three first-inning runs. That was all Spencer needed and the Giants coasted home a 4–2 winner. A minor victory? Maybe. No one had any way of knowing then just how important every single Giant victory and Dodger loss would become.

Hearn and Branca were the pitchers in the second game. Both right-handers had good stuff. The Giants got a run in the first on hits by Dark and Irvin. Brooklyn didn't get to Hearn until the seventh, when they tied the game on singles by Reese and Campanella, followed by a wild pitch. It was still tied in the top of the eighth when hits by Billy Cox and Branca put runners on first and third with one out. Now the dangerous Carl Furillo was up. The right fielder reached for a Hearn curveball and lofted a fly to medium right-center. Mays was off and running for the ball while Cox retreated to third to tag up. Giant catcher Wes Westrum picks up the story from here.

"Willie raced into right-center for the ball," Westrum recalls. "If he got it I knew there would be a play at the plate so I came out and got ready. At first it looked as if the ball was going to drop. It was what we call a dying quail and didn't carry. But Willie kept charging and made a running catch with his gloved hand completely outstretched. Cox tagged, probably figuring Willie didn't have time to set and throw.

"But Willie fooled everybody. He made a complete pivot, turning his body away from the plate, and then came out of it throwing in a single motion. It was almost a blind throw but it came in to me on a line. I blocked the plate and nailed Cox. I remember Dressen telling me later that I should get credit for the out by blocking the plate. But

Willie had made an amazing play to get rid of the ball like that. He was probably the best ball player I ever played with."

Mays's play drew raves all over. It psyched the crowd and it psyched the Giants. In the bottom of the eighth, Mays didn't rest on his fielding laurels. He promptly rocked Branca for a base hit. Westrum was next. The big catcher, who hadn't hit a homer in a month, picked out a Branca curve and sent it over the scoreboard in left for a two-run homer. Hearn held the Dodgers in the ninth and the Giants had a 3–1 victory. Suddenly, the Giants were on the brink of an unlikely sweep.

It was Maglie and Newcombe in the finale and the two right-handers disappointed no one. The Giants struck again in the first, when Stanky singled and rode home on a long triple by Irvin. Then the pitchers took over and there was no further scoring until the Giant seventh. Thomson started it with a walk, went to second on a sacrifice by Westrum, advanced to third on Maglie's ground out, and scored when big Newk uncorked a wild pitch with Stanky batting.

Trailing 2–0, the Dodgers tried to get back into it in the eighth. Billy Cox did damage with an opposite-field homer to right which barely cleared the wall at the 300-foot mark. But otherwise, Maglie's sharp-breaking curves and 34-year-old guile controlled the day. The Giants won the game to complete the sweep and along the way take their sixth straight victory. In the space of three days the New Yorkers had whittled the lead down to 9½ games and were putting together a substantial winning streak.

Suddenly, the team that had been written off just a week earlier seemed to have a foot back in the door. Those who predicted a Dodger runaway had to think twice. One game story said that the lead, while still substantial, was no longer so great that the Giants didn't have hope. It also alluded to the Dodger-Cardinal race in 1942 when the Cards got hot and erased a 10½ games lead over the last month and a half.

The Giant winning streak continued. An 8–5 victory over the Phils made it seven, their longest streak of the year. George Spencer continued to pitch well and got the win in relief of Corwin. That same day the Dodgers split with the Braves, chipping another half game off the lead. Johnny Schmitz, the young pitcher who had come over to the Dodgers in the Pafko deal, couldn't get anyone out while yielding three runs in the first inning of the nightcap. He was bailed out by

Clem Labine, but by then it was too late. Schmitz's record fell to 2–6. He hadn't helped in the way Dressen had hoped.

Jansen shut out Robin Roberts and the Phils the next day, 2–0. The Giants had now won eight in a row, making it a serious winning streak. Though the Dodgers won as well, there was an increasing feeling of optimism in the Giant camp.

"We had decided to just play it one game at a time," Leo Durocher says, looking back to that exciting time. "After each game I just gave them a short talk in the clubhouse. I'd say, 'You're playing great ball fellas. Just go home, get a good night's sleep, and come out tomorrow. Play the way you've been playing and don't worry about anything.' I never told them we were going to win it. It was the team, not me. I did nothing different. I just sat there and let them play. And after the streak reached 10 or 11, I found myself saying, 'Hey, this club can win it.' "

It reached that point very quickly. A 5–4 victory over the Phils was number nine. Corwin won in relief and Bobby clubbed his twenty-third homer. That day the Dodgers were crushed by the Braves, 13–4. But the stories of those August 19 games took a backseat to a game in St. Louis in which Bill Veeck, who owned the American League Browns, sent up a three-foot-seven midget named Eddie Gaedel as a pinch hitter. Gaedel drew a walk from Bob Cain and then left the game. Shortly after, his contract was invalidated by American League president Will Harridge.

Win number 10 was a 7–4 triumph over the Reds, as Spencer won in relief and Stanky, Lockman, and Westrum all clubbed homers. In fact, just to show the intensity level at which the Giants played in 1951, Eddie Stanky would finish the year with 14 home runs. Never a long ball hitter, the Brat wound up with a total of 29 four baggers in his entire career. Nearly 50 percent of them came in 1951.

The eleventh came on August 22, a 4–3 victory over the Reds as Sheldon Jones got credit for a relief win. Suddenly the Giants were winning the close ones and everyone was contributing. When the Dodgers lost to the Cards the next day, 4–2, the once insurmountable lead was down to 7½ games. It was the first Dodger loss to St. Louis in 15 games.

A change in fortunes? Perhaps. The Dodgers were playing sloppy baseball. They made a pair of errors, Newcombe balked in a run, and the ball club twice hit into inning-ending double plays with the bases full. A good case could be made for this being a game they shouldn't have lost. No wonder the Giants were beginning to feel a spark, a new life, sensing that in addition to their own winning streak the Dodgers might be showing some cracks.

"After the All-Star break we were so far behind I don't recall any feelings about a chance to catch them," Whitey Lockman revealed later. "The feeling on the team was to simply go out and play the best you could every day and take it from there. Once we started into the winning streak we found ourselves becoming more conscious of our chances and the excitement began building. Everyone on the club was playing well during the winning streak, especially Bobby, who was driving in a lot of big runs. And it was during the streak that I think everyone finally realized just how good Willie was."

Don Mueller was one member of the team who didn't think there was any real chance in mid-August. "I had already made plans with my brother to go on a hunting trip as soon as the regular season ended," Mueller admits. "None of us really thought we had a chance because we were 13½ games behind and catching a team like the Dodgers just didn't seem possible."

Bobby Thomson echoed the feelings of many Giants when he said that the ball club rallied behind its manager.

"When Leo had said he would make no more lineup changes that day at Ebbets Field after the Dodgers serenaded us and announced we were dead, we really felt close to him. He was saying we were his team, win or lose, and we wanted to win for him."

The streak reached 12 when the ball club rallied for a pair of ninth-inning runs to top the Cards, 6–5. Lockman drove in the tying run with a base hit and Bobby scored the game winner, blazing home from third on a fielder's choice. It was the fourth straight game in which the Jints had come from behind to win.

At Brooklyn, Ralph Branca tossed a three-hit shutout over the Cubs, enabling the Dodgers to go home a 1–0 winner. But, somehow, the Brooks didn't look like the same invincible powerhouse of a month earlier. Then, when the Giants were rained out the next day, the Dodgers couldn't capitalize. They lost a 5–1 decision to the Chicagoans and the lead was down to seven games.

On Sunday, August 26, the New Yorkers rolled by the Cubbies twice, 5–4 and 5–1, extending the winning streak to 14 games. George Spencer, in relief of Maglie, and Jim Hearn got the victories. Hearn threw a six-hitter in the second game and raised his record to 12–7. He was finally pitching the way he did after coming to the Giants the season before, when he had the best earned run average in the league.

As for Brooklyn, the Dodgers once again gave the impression of a struggling ball club. They dropped the opener of their double bill with the Pirates, 12–11, as the Pirates exploded for an eight-run seventh. Though they salvaged the nightcap with a close 4–3 victory, the lead was down to six. It had been an unbelievable turn of events and it wasn't over yet.

A day later, the Giants had a second straight twin bill with the Cubs. Despite a tiring pitching staff, Jansen and rookie Corwin got the job done in a pair of route-going performances. The scores were 5–4 and 6–3 and the New York Giants of "the Giants are dead" fame had won 16 consecutive ball games. In the opener, Jansen threw 12 innings and appeared to be on the losing end of a 4–3 decision when his teammates rallied for a pair of runs in the bottom of the twelfth.

Dark drew a walk to open the inning against knuckleballer Dutch Leonard. After Mays fanned, Irvin singled Dark to third and took second on the throw. Thomson was then intentionally walked to fill the bases. Lockman followed with a bloop single to center, sending Dark home with the tying run. Now Bill Rigney was up, pinch-hitting for Westrum. Knowing Durocher, the Cubs looked for the squeeze play. But Leo crossed them up, ordering Rigney to swing away, and the result was a long fly to left, allowing Irvin to tag and score the winning run. Such is the way winning teams operate.

At Ebbets Field, the Dodgers could manage just a split with the Braves. The only bright spot was a brilliant two-hit shutout by Ralph Branca in the first game. The big righty now had a 12–5 record and seemed well on his way to an outstanding season.

At day's end, Brooklyn had a 79–45 mark and the New Yorkers were 75–51. The margin between the two ball clubs had been reduced to five games. While the Giants were ripping off their 16 wins, the Dodgers played .500 ball, going 9–9 over the same period and losing eight full games off a lead that most people expected to lengthen, not shrink. The numbers, of course, were important. They now pointed to an undeniable fact: What had been close to a runaway some two weeks earlier was now a bona fide pennant race.

"By the time the 16-game winning streak had been completed and the margin reduced to five games, the complexion of the entire season had changed," said Charley Feeney. "A lot of people use the word "miracle" when talking about 1951. But as far as I'm concerned, talk of a miracle ended when the Giants won those 16 straight to cut the lead to five. After that it was simply a damned good pennant race."

On August 28, the streak finally ended. Pittsburgh's Howie Pollet tossed a six-hit shutout and beat the Giants, 2–0, with Sheldon Jones taking the tough-luck loss. Wes Westrum, for one, will always remember the day the streak ended. That's because he had to sit out with an injured thumb.

"I always think about the end of that streak," Westrum says, today. "I had caught all 16 games of the streak, but didn't catch the seventeenth. Sal Yvars caught instead. I came up with a thumb injury and Leo told me to rest. But I didn't like it. I sat in the bullpen wishing I was on the field."

Westrum's feeling echoed that of the entire ball club. The Giants were on such a roll that everyone had become caught up in the excitement, which was beginning to border on euphoria. No one wanted to miss a single game.

At the same time, the Dodgers topped Cincinnati, 3–1, with Duke Snider's two-run homer in the eighth providing the margin of victory. Dressen gave young Clem Labine his first start and the resilient righthander responded with a route-going performance.

With the lead at six games, the Dodgers buried Cincinnati, 13–1, while the Giants behind Jim Hearn topped Pittsburgh, 3–1. In Brooklyn's easy victory, Gil Hodges hit two homers, giving him a club record 36 for the season, and Don Newcombe coasted to his seventeenth victory. The month then ended on an up note for the Brooks. They completed a sweep of the Reds behind Preacher Roe, 3–1, who raised his record to an outstanding 18–2. The Giants, on the other hand, blew a seven-run lead and wound up losing to Pittsburgh and a Ralph Kiner homer, 10–9.

Now there was a month left. The Dodgers seemingly had recovered from the shock of the Giants' 16-game blitz, sweeping the Reds and returning two games to a lead that was once so great. It now stood at seven games, still a considerable margin going into September. But the Giants had shown everyone just how quickly a lead could melt away. Now, with just one more month to play, the two ball clubs were getting ready to meet each other again in an important two-game set at the Polo Grounds.

 **BOBBY**

Some Odds and Ends

One thing about Bobby was that he was so self-critical. He was so conscious about what he did at the plate. He was always telling himself to stay back, not get out in front, don't do this, do that, was his setup just right, the way he held the bat, his stance. He was not always confident enough in himself even though he was so good. In fact, I think his main problem was realizing just how good he was.

—Whitey Lockman

I wore the same pair of undershorts during the entire 16-game winning streak. Don't worry, I washed them, but it was one of those things that happen, a ball player's superstition. So I had these shorts, believe it or not, with a design of ants on them. I was wearing them the day we started winning. So I figured, what the hell, I'll wear the damn things the next day, and we kept winning.

There was a nail right in front of my locker where I'd hang them when I changed into my uniform. It got to the point where the guys would come in and look for the shorts. When they saw them hanging on that nail they felt better.

"Hey, there they are. There's the pants. Let's go get 'em."

It may have been a superstition, but the players really looked for those shorts and it went on for the entire 16-game streak. I was still living on Staten Island with my mother and when she would see me with them she'd say, "You're not wearing those things again?" And I'd say, "Yeah, I've got to keep wearing them." Then once we lost they just became an ordinary pair of shorts again and finally just disappeared. But for those 16 games the shorts with the ants were a part of a great winning streak.

I didn't have a lot of superstitions, things I *had* to do everyday. But there's no doubt some ball players thought about little things that might help—something they might have done before a win: a ritual, like the way they combed their hair, or an article of clothing like my shorts. Almost anything can become a superstition if a player associates it with winning.

One time Leo got to the ballpark so late that the game had already started. The clubhouse at the Polo Grounds was out in center field and the players had to walk across the field to get to the dugouts. With the game already under way, Leo didn't want to walk across the field and draw attention to the fact that he was late, so he decided to make the difficult trek under the stands from the clubhouse, over to the right field line, then down to the lower stands by the dugout. It wasn't easy, ducking under all those girders. You really had to be agile and it took awhile for him to get there. But we won that day and believe it or not, Leo took that same route, going under the stands to reach the dugout, until we lost.

There was *one* thing I used to do. First it was a habit and then became a superstition. It started in '51, shortly after I came in to play third. When I'd come onto the field at the beginning of an inning, I would always touch third base with my foot before taking my fielding position. Soon the touch became a kick. I kicked the base every inning, and I'd always kick it from the foul line toward the infield. Maybe I felt that if I moved the base even a half inch, it might cause the ump to call a close one foul. A silly little thing, but I did it every inning, every game without fail.

A lot of people think that when we won those 16 straight it marked the beginning of the end for the Dodgers. I never saw it that way. Despite the presence of my lucky shorts the Dodgers didn't fold. As far as I was concerned, they were still the Dodgers and still in first place. Sure, there was a chance of catching them and everyone felt the pressure in September, including some of the umpires. I was tossed out of a game in the middle of the month, just the second time in my career I got the thumb.

The first time I deserved it. I was trying to get back to first on a pickoff play in a game against the Cards. Stan Musial was playing first. He had his back to the bag and wasn't looking at me. When Stan took the throw from the pitcher I knew they had me beat. I started diving back to the bag as I saw Stan coming across with a sweep tag. So I held my arms back until the glove swept past the bag, then dove in with both hands. He missed me, missed me clean.

Because the ball was there first, the umpire called me out. I jumped up like a shot. Not only did I argue, but I put my hands on the umpire's chest and left a couple of dusty handprints behind. That's when I got the thumb. Because of the handprints, I couldn't deny what I had done. But the image must have been comical, the umpire standing there with two big handprints on his chest.

The second time was during a doubleheader in Pittsburgh. It was a hot Sunday afternoon, I was up at bat, and Augie Donatelli was the plate umpire. I felt Augie was calling too many high pitches and without turning around I said more than once, "Come on, Augie, get the ball down. The ball's too high, Aug, get it down." That's all I said. Never even turned around once and, boom, I'm out.

No one on the Giant bench knew what was going on. Leo couldn't believe it. "What do you mean he's out of the game?" he roared. "What did he do?" Augie never gave me a warning and that's what made it so strange. Usually an umpire will say, "If I hear another word out of you, you're gone!" But Augie never said it. Just, boom, you're gone.

Whenever something happened with an umpire, Leo was quick to get out there and stick up for his ball players. And if he disagreed with something the umpires were doing, he let them know about it. Thanks to Leo, we didn't have a quiet bench. He wanted us to root for the guys on the field and he would holler at the guys on the bench if they weren't doing it.

I knew that once we reached September in the 1951 season, Leo had to be at his best. So did the rest of us because we all knew we still had a long way to go.

Behind the Scenes

Despite the great run the Giants made at the Dodgers in the final weeks of August, most of the so-called experts—the writers, broadcasters, and opposing players—continued to feel the Dodger lead of seven games was more than substantial. The smart money refused to believe that this great team could lose to the upstart Giants. But to the everyday fan the prospect of a real pennant race that would reach out and tug at the emotions was fast becoming a reality. Those who weren't at the ball game turned on their radios and televisions, as well as gobbling up the many newspapers that rolled off the New York City presses back then. It would be that way all month, as the intensity of the race increased up until the final game.

The pennant race, the standings, the daily results were there for all to see. What wasn't visible to the average fan was the overall mood of each team and the interactions among the varied individuals that made up the ball clubs. Many behind-the-scenes events went unreported or unnoticed by the news media in 1951. They would not be revealed until years later when the passage of time and the emergence of a more candid style of sports reporting cut through the old-fashioned sanctity of the locker room.

Winning teams are traditionally happy teams. The personal animosities, jealousies, finger pointing, and bickering usually remain beneath the surface until a ball club begins to lose. By September, both the Giants and Dodgers seemed to have everything under control. In spite of being the only teams in the league with a number of black players, a situation with the potential to fuel the fires of prejudice, there were no overt racial incidents within either ball club. Bobby Thomson said he realized in later years that the Dodger players were more like a family, both on and off the field. Yet the Giants under Durocher, bonded by a common goal, closed ranks too, especially during the final month and a half of the campaign. Some of the Giants might have carped about what they perceived as special treatment for the emerging Willie Mays. But once they started winning, the team developed its own momentum, a kind of tunnel vision which focused on catching the Dodgers and obscuring nearly everything else.

By mid-August, the Dodgers were quickly approaching a state of euphoria. Bolstered by a 13½-game lead, they were beginning to count their World Series money. But as their huge lead started to unravel like a ball of yarn, sober reality began to replace their self-induced feeling of invincibility. It wasn't long before a growing number of the Dodger players began questioning the tactics of Charley Dressen. Earlier in the year, with that big lead, Dressen often found himself with nothing more to do than fill out the lineup card and make some pitching changes. But once the lead began to shrink, the Dodger manager's tactics, and his personality, would begin to create conflict and resentment.

As for Durocher, he said from the start that the young, immature Mays needed to be babied, encouraged, complimented, and protected. Willie was an exuberant youngster from a small Alabama town who could easily have been overwhelmed by the magnitude and temptations of New York City. Leo assigned Monte Irvin to take the youngster under his wing, on the field and off, and keep him there.

When Mays called his manager "Mis-a-Leo" some were ready to brand Durocher a racist and accuse him of fostering an Uncle Tom relationship with his young star. But Irvin, who had readily become Mays's friend, mentor, and guardian, was one of many who said Leo didn't care about the color of a player's skin, as long as he hustled and played the game.

Team captain Al Dark agreed. It wasn't color that bothered Leo, rather it was players who didn't give their best. "Loafing was the only thing that Leo wouldn't accept," said Dark. "It drove him up a wall. He would only have a meeting if the team was going real bad, or if someone was loafing. Hustle and you could play for Leo. It didn't matter what he thought of you personally or what you were. He wasn't averse to benching anybody if he thought it would help the ball club or the ball player. I even saw him bench Mays once, but not in '51."

Whitey Lockman says that while the coming of Mays certainly helped the team, it also created some lingering resentment among a few of the veterans. "Naturally you stay a little laid back when a new kid comes in and takes over a key position," Lockman explained. "We knew a little about Willie but didn't know whether he would be able to do the job having just turned 20. But after watching him for a while, we could certainly see he was going to be something special.

"Later in the season, there were a couple of players who began feeling a little resentful that Leo paid so much attention to Willie. It was basically a matter of Leo spending less time with these guys than with Willie. Leo wasn't growling at anyone, but he wasn't compliment-ing them when they did something good for the team. Willie got compliments all the time. But it certainly wasn't a major problem for us, especially when we began to win."

There's no doubt Durocher was extra protective of the budding young superstar. Some felt he was more upset when a pitcher threw at Mays than at one of his vets. But the wily manager probably knew his vets could handle it. As it turned out, Willie was like most of the great ones. Throw at him and he would answer with base hits.

Racial tensions, per se, didn't appear to exist within either team in 1951. The blacks on both the Giants and Dodgers played within the team context with no obvious problems and were considered integral parts of their ball clubs. But human nature being what it is, there were times when inadvertent racial remarks were passed between the two teams because of long-standing animosities.

Jackie Robinson could usually be found in the center of much of the controversy. On one occasion, when Jackie was hollering and rapping his bat against that old wooden door in Ebbets, Eddie Stanky became so riled that he began cursing Jackie, then for good measure added some racial epithets. When the Brat turned around he realized that his teammate, Monte Irvin, had heard every word. Irvin, wise enough to understand what can happen in the heat of anger, reportedly smiled and said, "That's just fine with me, Eddie."

Irvin himself indicated that Jackie wasn't one of his favorite people.

"Jackie and I were never close," Monte said. "We got along all right, but whenever I saw him I just said, "How you doing?" and kept going. I didn't know him from the Negro Leagues, but I had seen him play with Montreal and knew he had the potential to be a real star. I also admired the fact that he had taken so much abuse without cracking those first couple of years. Nevertheless, I stayed away from him."

Irvin recalls another time when Durocher said something that more sensitive souls might have construed as a racial slur. "We were playing the Dodgers and Jackie was sitting in their dugout with white guys sitting on each side of him. Leo turned to me and said, 'You know, Monte, this is the first time I realized Jackie was so black.' I just looked at him and said, 'Hell, Leo, no one will ever mistake him for white.' Leo didn't mean anything by it and I took it in the spirit in which it was given.

"But I will say this. Both Jackie and Carl Furillo really hated Leo and there was always a lot going on between them. I remember the time Jackie ran down Davey Williams at first when he was actually after Maglie. He tried that old trick of dumping a bunt down the line, but Williams ended up covering first and Jackie ran right over him, put him out of action because Davey had a real bad back.

"Leo wanted to get even. Jackie was playing third base that day and when we got back to the dugout he said, 'I want the first guy who gets the chance to give it to that sonofagun. If you hit a double, just keep running and go into him at third. We can't let him run us out of the ballpark that way.' Then Leo turned to Hank Thompson and myself and asked what we thought.

"I said, 'Leo, we have Giants across our chest. We play for the Giants, not the Dodgers.' Leo said, 'That's good enough for me.' As it turned out, Al Dark was the guy who got the chance and he gave Jackie a real good jolt when he slid into third." Harking back to his football days as a collegian, Dark looked more like a halfback than a shortstop as he plowed into Robinson.

There was another time when Pee Wee Reese had to restrain Durocher from moving out of the third base coaching box to go after Jackie at second. Pee Wee said at the time that the language passing between Leo and Jackie actually caused him to blush. With those two, the words always flew and so did the baseballs.

Leo's favorite war cry was "Stick it in his ear!" He would often yell that to his pitchers, especially when Robinson or Furillo was up. He did it to a lot of other guys around the league, but when the Giants were playing the Dodgers you could always hear his loud voice cutting through the crowd noise.

Two years later, in 1953, Furillo was having a great season. He was hitting well over .300 and in the running for the batting title when the feud between the two reached a breaking point. Duke Snider says it went back to Leo's days with the Dodgers, when he platooned Furillo because he felt Carl couldn't hit right-handers. As was usually the case, Leo was on him that day, bellowing out the usual, "Stick it in his ear!"

Ruben Gomez, a rookie right-hander was pitching. Furillo came up to bat and, *bang*, he got hit with a pitch. Jim Hearn picks up the story from there.

"Today, a hitter who thinks he is being thrown at intentionally will drop his bat and head for to the mound. But Carl turned around toward Leo, who was sitting on his little raised spot at the end of our dugout. He sat there so he couldn't be seen from the opposing dugout when he was giving signs. Carl yelled at him, 'Leo, you caused this.' And Leo, who always had to have the last word, yelled back, 'What do you want? I didn't hit you.'

"Then Carl trots down to first base, but all the while he's looking into our dugout. By this time we had all focused back on home plate because the next hitter was up. All of a sudden we heard the sound of running feet, pounding toward our dugout. Two or three of us stood up on the top steps of the dugout, but Carl dove right at Leo and got him in a headlock. Monte Irvin and I tried to be peacemakers. Leo couldn't move and Carl was choking him so hard Leo was turning purple. We were trying to get them apart when I saw Pee Wee, Duke, and Erskine running over. I jumped up because I thought they were going to jump us. But they said, 'Let 'em go at it. Let 'em fight.' That's the absolute gospel. They wanted to see Carl hurt Durocher. That's the kind of hatred that existed between our two teams.

"While we were trying to break it up, someone stepped on Carl's hand and he was out for the year with a broken bone. Some say I stepped on his hand. I didn't. I know who did, but I'm not going to say. I played golf with Carl years later and told him there had been only two of us trying to get him off Leo, but it wasn't me who stepped on his hand."

Don Mueller told the same story with a slightly different twist.

"Dressen and Durocher stirred up a lot of hoopla. They made every series between our teams seem so crucial. Leo didn't give an inch when Carl came charging in, a 30-year-old man coming after a 45-year-old manager. Jim Hearn intentionally or unintentionally stepped on Carl's hand, but that probably helped Carl win the batting title, even though he didn't play again that year."

And Duke Snider confirmed that he and his Dodger teammates did exort the Giants to "Let 'em go. Let 'em fight." He also said that "Hearn stepped on Furillo's hand. He didn't mean to, but he did."

The fight between Durocher and Furillo was one of the most blatant explosions between the two ball clubs. Like so many other incidents, it started with a beanball. Durocher had the two-for-one rule. If the other team threw at a Giant, two players on the other team would go down. Charley Dressen, it seems, gave the same instructions to his pitchers.

"Dressen had a theory," says Carl Erskine. "Give them two for one. The first time someone threw at one of us, he would tell us we owed them two. So we had to play the two-for-one game and those kind of things can get crazy. Sometimes it would take three or four hours to finish a game because of that nonsense."

Clem Labine, a rookie in '51, came to the majors fully prepared to pitch tight. "It was never against my grain to brush somebody back," Labine said. "It's a matter of ownership. The hitter wants ownership of the plate and you want ownership of it, too. So you've got to make him respect you by throwing inside. If you didn't do it you'd be in the minor leagues all your life. Asserting yourself on the mound doesn't mean you're going to hit someone in the head. It merely means that when I'm out there, you're not gonna take advantage of me."

"There was an unwritten rule," Erskine adds. "Pitchers never threw at pitchers even though that would seem the logical thing to do. But the manager usually asked us to throw at the catchers. I can remember a number of times when I was told to throw at Wes."

Maglie, of course, had no compunctions about coming in close. Although Leo sometimes complained that Jansen wasn't mean enough, other Giant players said Larry would indeed pitch inside when the situation called for it. Before Labine arrived, Newcombe and Branca were the two Dodger hurlers who wouldn't hesitate to knock a guy down.

"When Bruce Edwards was catching for us he used to kid me,"

Branca remembers. "He'd say when I was going to knock somebody down my eyes would get big as saucers. But it's true that Newk and I wouldn't hesitate to protect our hitters. Today, the umpires don't give you the inside pitch because they don't want to make a judgment whether you're throwing at a hitter or just pitching inside. If I was pitching today I would have to tell the umpires I'm pitching inside. It's the only way."

As for Newcombe, he went inside whenever the situation dictated it. According to publicist Irving Rudd, he would also go at someone as payback for a racial slur.

"Newk never got outwardly upset the way Jackie did," Rudd explained. "But if he didn't like something an opposing player said or did, he would throw at him. He could and he would."

Big Newk admits even today that throwing at hitters wasn't difficult. "I was taught how to do it in the Negro Leagues," he says. "You had to knock guys down there, too. I was a fastball pitcher with pretty good control so I could hit a guy anytime I wanted. I used to tell Willie, for example, that he was a first ball hitter and Dressen would fine us $50 if we let him hit the first pitch. So what are you going to do with that first pitch?

"Willie was what we called a Bible hitter. A Bible hitter says thou shall not pass. He lets nothing go past him. So the first pitch goes right at him. I used to tell him I was gonna knock him down with the first pitch and he better be ready. Once Willie became a seasoned veteran he would holler right back, 'I don't give a damn. I'll get up and hit the second pitch.' And he would.

"One time during his rookie year, Campy and I decided to have some fun with him. His first time up I knocked him down. Willie got up and told Campy to knock it off. Then I knocked him down again. This time Willie's really upset and in his high-pitched voice he starts asking Campy all over again why we're knocking him down. By then Campy's trying not to laugh and he stepped up and whispered something to Willie. Well, Willie just burst out laughing. Leo, who was coaching third, called time, and asked Willie what was so funny, but Willie wouldn't tell him what Campy said. It was simple. Willie was laughing because Campy had said I was throwing at him because I didn't like niggers."

But when he was serious, Newcombe knew exactly what he was doing. "The best target was the ribs," he said. "If I threw at a guy's ribs

I could hit him ten straight times if I wanted to. It isn't that some pitchers don't want to come inside, they just don't know how to do it, so they let the ones who know how take care of it. We had to protect our hitters because our hitters were always in the dirt."

Then there were the managers. There's little doubt that Durocher and Dressen played a constant, never-ending game of one-upmanship during 1951. The Artie Wilson incident early in the season, in which Dressen took nearly five minutes to restructure his defensive align-ment, was just one example. The brushback pitches, with both skip-pers operating with the same two-for-one philosophy, prolonged the games, causing countless stoppages for arguments and bickering. And the bench jockeying never ceased. By late in the season, many of the players were getting tired of the game, and they didn't mean the game of baseball.

"There's no doubt that Leo and Charley slowed the game down," Bobby Thomson said. "If it wasn't something major, like the Wilson incident, it was a lot of little things. I can remember one day at Ebbets Field. Leo was coaching third and he fielded a foul ball. The stands were so close to the field there that he simply turned and flipped the ball into the crowd. The next time we're at the Polo Grounds, Dressen's coaching third and gets hold of a baseball. What does he do? He makes a big deal of walking over and tossing it into the stands because Leo had done it. The difference is that at Ebbets the coach is almost by the rail. At the Polo Grounds, there was a lot more distance, and it was obvious what Dressen was doing.

"I'll never forget a game we were playing against the Dodgers and I was up at bat," continued Bobby. "Campy was shaking his head. 'I wish someone would send those two guys home so we can finish this game,' he said. You know, it's 10:30 and we're still in the third inning."

Clem Labine, only with the Dodgers since late July, was quick to see what was happening between the two managers. "They were con-stantly trying to show each other up and the first people to see it were the ball players," Labine remembers. "We were much more likely to see it than the fans. If it was the kind of game where Leo used 10 pitchers, Charley would have to use 11. I was told they used to be good friends, yet I remember they wouldn't even look at each other. Charley even had Pee Wee take the lineup cards to home plate so he wouldn't have to look at Leo.

Whitey Lockman also found the constant interplay between the two skippers annoying. "I remember a few guys saying they wished the two guys would settle down and let us play," said Lockman. "I had that same feeling on more than one occasion. It seemed as if they were always overmanaging against one another, with hit-and-runs and squeeze plays all the time. But maybe some of the blame should go to the players because we didn't exactly love each other, either.

"I remember talking to Billy Loes. Billy pitched for the Dodgers and Dressen after 1951, and he told me that Charley had once ordered him to knock me down. Billy told Dressen I wasn't crowding the plate and was hitting good pitches, so why should he knock me down. He refused to throw at me. Dressen really got upset with Loes, but it shows that the players could have controlled some of it if they wanted to."

Herman Franks, Durocher's longtime coach and friend, admitted that Leo did learn from Dressen when they were together on the Dodgers. "Charley was always a good baseball man," Franks said, "and he taught Leo a lot when Leo was breaking in as a manager. But Leo was more motivated than Dressen. He was a very intense man and I always felt his desire to win was stronger than Dressen's. Sure, they overmanaged and tried to show each other up. I can remember both of them using the same ploy, sometimes warming up a left-hander before the game even though they had said a right-hander was going to start. They did things like that all the time."

For Pee Wee Reese, it was a matter of both managers being cut from the same mold. "I played for both of them," said the Dodger captain, "and they were great managers, a great deal alike. They both had a lot to say, were on everybody all the time. Charley felt he played a big part in the pennant we won in 1941 and I remember him helping Leo quite a bit that year."

But were the two really cut from the same mold? They were undoubtedly kindred spirits in 1941 when Pee Wee Reese observed them working together. It was true Leo was loud and combative, a guy who once said he would trip his own grandmother coming around third base if it meant winning a game. But in 1951 he was also a manager who had learned to handle his players, get the most out of each and every one of them. When he managed the Dodgers there were always players, such as Furillo and Robinson, who disliked him intensely. This wasn't the case with the Giants of 1951, although it's easy to wonder why. With the possible exception of Mays, Leo didn't coddle his players, wasn't averse to benching them, moving them from one position to another, and constantly hollering at them. Let's air it out, get it out in the open, he often said. But despite the yelling, hollering, and more than occasional outburst of anger, Durocher had the total respect of his team.

The Dodgers certainly wanted to win just as badly, but it wasn't for their manager. It was for the team. As the pressure from the onrushing Giants increased and the lead narrowed, the Dodger players began to see the real Charley Dressen. He wasn't someone they always liked. His enormous ego and towering sense of self began to irritate some players and ultimately resulted in lost ball games.

"Charley Dressen was a complete egotist," said Clem Labine, who would feel the wrath of the Dressen doghouse before the year was out. "He was quick to take credit and never ready to accept blame. Looking back, I think both Charley and Leo were basically very good managers. But managers can only do the things their players allow them to do. So a manager has to understand his ball players, relate to them, and then get the most out of them. That's what managing is all about.

"Leo certainly understood that you had to pump a player up some-times and give him confidence. I never felt that Charley could do what Leo did in terms of making a player truly confident in what he could do. In fact, he was just the opposite, which is not a very complimen-tary thing to say. But I really think he was more apt to tear a person down than build him up."

Ralph Branca, perhaps more than any other Dodger, has borne the brunt of 1951 in a very personal way. But the big righty was 12–5 going into September and on his way to a seemingly outstanding season. He also had a close-up view of Dressen that year and the memories of his manager are vivid.

"Charley was famous for taking the credit for the Dodgers' victo-ries," recalls Branca. "He was once quoted as saying, *'I* won 94 and *they* lost 60.' There was a tight game once when Jackie came up in a key situation and Charley put on the hit-and-run sign. I don't know if the other team had our signs or not, but the pitcher put the ball in the dirt, actually bounced it in front of home plate. Jackie, being the great athlete he was, went after the ball and actually hit it on the bounce, a base hit to right field, and we won the game. It was one of the best pieces of hitting I ever saw. After the game, Charley was telling anyone who'd listen that 'I put on the hit-and-run. That's why we won the game.' Here the damn ball bounced in front of home plate and Jackie still managed to hit it to right field and Dressen is taking all the credit. I've said it many times over the years and I'll say it again. Leo Durocher was the best manager I ever played for. When the Dodgers fired him, they were firing the best manager in baseball."

Dick Williams, who would later become a successful manager with Boston and Oakland, was a rookie with the 1951 Dodgers, the twenty-sixth man, a special roster allowance because of the draft and the Korean War. Though he didn't play much, Williams remembers well the first big league manager he played under.

"I was a vocal guy even then," Williams said. "Because I didn't play much, I became Dressen's DSA, which stood for designated smart ass. My job was needling. It wasn't a lost art then, the way it is now.

"Whenever we played the Giants, our big guys used to say that it wasn't really the Giants against the Dodgers, rather it was Durocher against Dressen. We were just pawns in a game, with the biggest sideshow in baseball. Dressen was very egotistical, and he could also be insensitive. "I never became a regular for the Dodgers because the ball club had so much talent, but I once dove after a ball in the outfield and heard my shoulder crack as it hit the ground. I was in intense pain and could barely move my arm, just enough to lob the ball back to the infield. Then I collapsed. The next thing I heard was Charley's voice and I still can hear it today. 'Get him up and get him out of here!' he shouted. That's the kind of guy we were dealing with."

It wasn't only the Dodger players who saw this side of Charley Dressen. Walker Cooper, the catcher Durocher traded away after he took over the Giants, was with the Braves when Dressen took over the Dodgers in 1951. From his own observations as well as talking to other players, the witty Cooper quickly got a handle on Charley. He decided to give the Dodger manager a present.

"It was in September, right around Charley's birthday," Cooper relates. "I knew about him by then, the way he said 'I won' and 'they lost.' I got a book, wrapped it up, and gave it to Charley at home plate when we were exchanging lineup cards. The title of the book was *The Dressen Book of I*. The pages of the book were all blank except for a capital *I* that I put on every page. I know the Dodgers got a kick out it."

One last picture of the Charley Dressen who would pilot the Dodgers down the home stretch: In 1947, Branch Rickey hired a young Canadian named Allen Roth to be the team's statistician. Back in those days, no one had statisticians, but the progressive, cerebral Rickey saw an advantage in having specific information on other teams. Long before computers were a household item, Roth devised an intricate system of statistics, done by hand with pencil and paper, that provided his ball club with an uncanny amount of detailed information.

"I used to give the Dodger managers a tremendous edge with the information I developed," Roth says today. "Back then, my system was unique. I would record types of pitches and location. I even had averages for players when they were ahead or behind on the count. My system showed the record for a hitter against a pitcher for the year and over his career. I even had breakdowns on where opposing batters hit the ball. It was all recorded on a card system that was easy to use. I had one for each team and would offer it to the manager before each new series.

"Yet Charley Dressen didn't want to see it. He made little or no use of the information I provided. The man didn't want help from anybody. He thought he could do it all by himself. It's always been that way with the big ego managers. They couldn't believe a statistician sitting in the stands could give them information they didn't know themselves. So Charley ignored me. Yet once he was gone and Walter Alston took over, I became known as Walter Alston's secret weapon."

With just a month left in the upcoming season both ball clubs were poised for the stretch run. The Dodgers still had the lead, but the Giants had been the hot team. It certainly appeared at this point, however, that there was still another difference in the two teams aside from their respective won-lost records. The Giants were poised and ready, rallying behind a manager who had his team together, a guy who announced that this was his team and he would sink or swim with them. Leo Durocher was right out in front, leading the charge.

The Dodgers, on the other hand, had all that natural talent but were being directed by a skipper who, according to a number of his players, was more concerned with outmaneuvering his rival and stroking his own ego while doing it. Charley Dressen must have been aware that he had a powerful ball club under him. Yet in some ways he seemed to resent that, because the Dodgers didn't give him enough opportunities to pull the strings, direct the action, and say to them, "Just hold 'em and I'll think of something."

His chance to do just that would come, however. In fact, it was not very far away.

September Showdown

On the morning of Saturday, September 1, an aura of anticipation weighed heavily in the Labor Day weekend air. The final month of the regular baseball season was about to begin in style, with the Giants and Dodgers meeting in a crucial two-game series at the Polo Grounds. A pair of Brooklyn victories and New York losses at the end of August had brought the lead back up to seven. A sweep of the two contests by the Dodgers would build the margin to a substantial nine games, but if the Giants could win both, they would pull it back to five—a bona fide pennant-race distance.

Durocher had his ace, Sal Maglie, ready to go, while Dressen planned to counter with Ralph Branca. Maglie at 17–5 was en route to another outstanding season while Branca, 12–5, was coming off a pair of consecutive shutout performances. It was a solid matchup. Before the action even began, however, two curious items appeared in the early edition of Saturday's *Brooklyn Eagle.*

The first, a short blurb in a big league roundup column, reported that Durocher was contemplating a pair of infield changes. One involved the replacement of Eddie Stanky with young Davey Williams. The second change involved "the third base spot where Bobby Thomson lacks the necessary equipment."

The blurb was intriguing because Leo had recently proclaimed that his starting lineup was "his team" for the rest of the year. Stanky was

173

still a leader and winner at second, while Thomson had been hitting extremely well, his average now approaching .260 to go with his 23 homers and 77 RBIs. Moreover, his teammates Al Dark and Whitey Lockman had expressed complete satisfaction with the way Bobby was patrolling the hot corner. Even coach Herman Franks, always a Durocher confidant, confirmed that there was no displeasure at the way Bobby took to his new position.

"Bobby was simply a good third baseman," said Franks. "But the thing that impressed us was that he continued to improve, got even better as the season wore on."

The story seemed little more than idle gossip—or maybe wishful thinking for Brooklyn fans, who were beginning to view the Giants with incipient trepidation.

The second item in the pregame story, said that Leo Durocher admitted that "his jittery Giants must win both games against the Dodgers in order to get back into the pennant race." The story went on to say that a split wouldn't help the Jints. In fact, if the Dodgers swept, they should begin printing World Series tickets.

Every game between the two ball clubs was certainly important. But for Durocher to make this a must-sweep for the Giants seemed to put unnecessary pressure on the team. The Giants had already shown there was no such thing as a safe lead in 1951. In retrospect, it's extremely doubtful that Leo Durocher would put a make-or-break label on sweeping the series. Leo knew enough not to pressure his team that way. One game at a time. That's what he had said and that's the way the Giants continued to operate.

The two-game series turned into pure delight for Giants fans. The Giants not only beat the Dodgers, they destroyed them, winning the two games by 8–1 and 11–2 scores. More to the point, the two games were chock-full of the things that made the rivalry intense, controversial, bitter, and personal.

There was no question about the outcome of either game. In the opener, nearly 41,000 rabid fans showed up at the old, horseshoe-shaped ballpark. Missing, however, was Charley Dressen. The Dodger manager was a no-show, home in bed with the flu. Coach Cookie Lavagetto ran the team and failed to emerge as a candidate for substitute manager of the year. The Giants jumped all over Branca and staked Maglie to a 5–1 lead after just three innings. With Sal the Barber pitching, the game was money in the bank.

Don Mueller started things off in the last of the first inning, blasting a long home run into the upper deck in right field. Then, in the second, Lockman singled and up came Bobby Thomson. Despite a strong wind blowing in from left, Bobby stepped into a Branca fastball and drove it 400 feet into the upper left field stands, a titanic shot and the third sacker's twenty-fourth of the year. Looking back, Bobby could well have been sending a message to Branca and the Dodgers. As it turned out, they didn't receive it.

In the third, the Dodgers mounted a threat, loading the bases with one out. The batter was Jackie Robinson. Maglie's first pitch was a high inside curve that didn't break. Instead, it struck Jackie on the left wrist as he threw up his hand to protect his head. Not only did the play force in a run, but it raised already high tensions between the two ball clubs. While Maglie insisted that the ball hit Jackie's bat, not his wrist, umpire Lee Ballanfant called Durocher and Lavagetto out to tell then to cut the nonsense right then and there. No more brushbacks, no payback. Cool it.

It seems unlikely that Maglie would be throwing at Robby with the sacks full and just a 3–0 lead. Despite his animosity toward Jackie, Sal thought about winning first and proved it by bearing down and getting out of the inning with just the single tally. In the Giant third, Mueller did it again, hitting his second homer of the game, this one with Dark on first. The blast made the score 5–1.

The Dodgers stirred things up again in the fifth. Cal Abrams batted for Branca and reached first on an error by Thomson. Furillo followed with a single and the Brooks had something going. Now Pee Wee Reese was up. The Dodger shortstop timed a Maglie curve and hit a sharp liner to the left of Alvin Dark. Both Abrams and Furillo thought the ball was headed to left-center for a hit and were off and running. But so was Dark. He moved quickly to his left and speared the ball in his gloved hand. One out. He then flipped to Stanky at second, forcing Abrams. Two outs. Stanky then turned and simply tagged the shocked Furillo who was bearing down on second and knew he was a dead duck.

The New Yorkers had pulled off a rare triple play as the Polo Grounds crowd went wild. The final blow came in the seventh when Mueller, who had hit just 10 homers prior to the game, whacked his third round-tripper of the game, another two-run shot off reliever Phil Haugstad. Maglie coasted to win number 18 and the Giants had their fourth straight victory over the Dodgers since dropping 12 of the first 15 between the two teams.

More than 37,000 fans were on hand the next day as the Giants did it again. Dressen was back at the helm but his presence didn't help. The Giants got seven runs off Don Newcombe in six innings, then coasted to an 11–2 victory, with Don Mueller again doing the brunt of the damage. The Giants' right fielder had two more homers and five RBIs, and in doing so tied a major league record with five home runs in two games. Hearn coasted to his fourteenth victory, while big Newk lost for the eighth time.

But that wasn't the whole story. In the fifth inning there was an incident that did nothing to dignify a first-place team like the Dodgers. Al Barlick was the plate umpire and when he called a strike on Pee Wee Reese, trouble erupted. The Dodger bench exploded in catcalls directed at the ump. Barlick whirled around and promptly thumbed out Branca and young Dick Williams.

In the sixth it started again as Barlick called a Newcombe pitch a ball when Eddie Stanky was up. Barlick chased a fuming Newk off the mound, then banished Clem Labine and Jackie Robinson from the bench. As if on cue, Dressen came forth, called time, and ordered his remaining players from the bench to the clubhouse, allegedly to protect them from Barlick.

The clubhouse at the Polo Grounds, of course, was in dead center. The Dodgers walked slowly across the outfield, delaying the game for several minutes. Dressen would delay it again each time he had to call a player forth to pinch hit. All in all, Dressen stalled and played his little game for more than half an hour. Funny at first; ridiculous a short time later. Dressen would be fined another $100 for "failure to control his bench." It was the third time during the season that he had pulled similar stunts, antagonizing umpiring crews along the way.

By this time, people were beginning to wonder what made Charley Dressen tick. Red Smith, who would become the dean of New York sportswriters, pulled no punches when he characterized the Dodger manager's antics in his *New York Herald Tribune* column of September 12.

"Charley Dressen, manager of the best National League club in years, has been making a spectacular fool of himself," Smith wrote. "Three times this summer he has cleared the Dodgers' bench of reserve players and sent them to the clubhouse to 'protect' them, he says, against unfair treatment by the umpires. It is a deliberate and calculated gesture of insult to a body of honest working stiffs who are, as a group, a credit to baseball.

"When Dressen empties the Brooklyn dugout, he is saying, in effect: 'These men are not honest, impartial umpires. They've got it in for my ball club. They're always picking on us. They are so shot with bias, so governed by prejudice, so swollen with self-importance, that I dare not trust my players within range of their petty tempers.'

"He is saying all this publicly, before a grandstand full of people, but does not say it aloud in words he would be held to account for later on. He says it instead by sly indirection, employing a cheap device that is permissible under the rules. It should cease to be permissible and no written change in the rule book is necessary to put a stop to it. Ford Frick, president of the National League, can take care of it with a phone call and five words: 'Cut out the nonsense, Charley.'

"It may not have occurred to Dressen that there is a confession implicit in his unspoken charges against the umpires. If he must empty his dugout to avoid having the umpires do it, then it is an admission of his inability, or unwillingness, to control the loud-mouths of his bench."

As Smith said, it had to stop. But Charley Dressen wasn't about to stop it. The $100 fine meant nothing. When the opportunity to clear the bench came again, Dressen would do it.

The two-game sweep cut the lead back to five. But it did more than that. Mueller, who had hit the five homers in impressive style, also became a proud father during the second game. Told just before hitting his second homer in the eighth, Don circled the bases with a big grin on his face, shouting to Durocher in the third base coaching box, "It's a boy! It's a boy!"

"When Don hit those five homers in two games and we scored 19 runs, I think a lot of us knew we could beat them," Wes Westrum said. "We had a few more games left with them and by beating them we got back in it a lot faster."

After the game, Mueller's slugging feat would become the focal point of another controversy, one that would continue through the end of the season. The story was that Leo had a guy in the center field clubhouse with binoculars stealing signs. If the Giants didn't know every pitch beforehand, the story went, Mueller never could have hit five home runs.

Stealing signs, or trying to steal signs, has always been a big part of baseball. Everybody does it. Some of the methods are crude, other ingenious.

"Leo definitely had a guy in a clubhouse stealing signs with a spyglass," Dick Williams said. "He'd beep it to one of their guys in the bullpen, who would then relay it in."

The spyglass theory was also espoused by two former Giants, Willard Marshall and Walker Cooper.

"There was a lot of sign stealing going on back then," Marshall recalls. "When I was with the Giants we had Bill Rigney in the clubhouse with a spyglass. The funny part was that there were guys who still couldn't hit the ball even when they knew what was coming. I remember one game when we were stealing signs against Pittsburgh and they still shut us out."

Walker Cooper takes the story one step further. "Sure, the Giants were stealing signs from the clubhouse," said the candid Coop. "But other teams were doing it, also. I remember a game with the Cubs before I left the Giants. We were calling their signs from our clubhouse and they were stealing our signs from their clubhouse. And we lost, 6–0. The guys still didn't hit even when they knew what was coming. In Comiskey Park they used to have a guy out in the scoreboard stealing signs. The guy would use a towel to signal his team. Believe me, Leo wasn't the only manager in the league with a spotter."

Bill Rigney said it was done differently. "I used to sit on the bench and watch the pitchers and catchers," says Rig. "We stole signs quite often. The first man to get on second would watch the sequence of signs that the catcher flashed and as soon as he came back to the dugout he would give them to me. We also flashed the signs to the hitter from second base."

Bobby Thomson confirms that. "Guys like Dark and Stanky were very good at stealing signs, even on the road," Bobby recalls. "They were always especially alert when they were on second. They were both smart players and could pick up opposing teams' signs very well. Then we would talk about it in the dugout—the catcher did this or that, then threw a fastball.

"They also flashed signs from second. It can be done with the hands, but Dark and Stanky did it with their feet. If the first move off the bag is with your right foot, a fastball is coming. If you step off with your left or cross over, then it's a curve. Very simple. I'll also say this. The Dodgers had a lot of smart players like Reese and Robinson. I'm sure they did the same thing and definitely with Charley Dressen's blessing."

There has been speculation about Durocher and the spyglass for years. Leo probably stole signs any way he could. He would do anything to get an edge. But so would Dressen, Frankie Frisch, and other veteran managers of the time. Don Mueller had a hot bat for two days, walloping those five homers. If his bat was cold, all the stolen signs in the world wouldn't have helped him.

Recovering from the two-game sweep by the Giants, Brooklyn rebounded to take a pair from the Braves by identical 7–2 scores. Erskine won his fifteenth in the opener and continued to be a hot pitcher. Young Labine made it two straight with a route-going performance in the nightcap. He looked to be just what the doctor ordered, a fresh arm that could win. The Giants, in the meantime, split with the Phils. Young Al Corwin finally lost one after winning five straight. But lefty Dave Koslo was coming on, running his record to 7–9 in the second contest. At day's end, the Dodgers were at 84–47, the Giants six back at 79–54.

On September 5, the *Brooklyn Eagle*, on a gloomy note, reported that Robinson, Hodges, and Snider all looked like tired hitters, and Roe and Newcombe, despite 35 wins between them, had not been effective in August. The article also pointed out that the Dodgers did not have a particularly strong bench, an element that had gone pretty much unmentioned because of the strength of the starting lineup.

Another short blurb in the same edition of the paper said the Dodgers' president, Walter O'Malley, wasn't happy with the way Dressen and the Dodgers baited the umpires in the second game of the two-game set with the Giants. "I think we should concentrate more on the winning of ball games," O'Malley said.

On September 5, Branca beat the Phils for his thirteenth win of the season. Hodges won it with his thirty-seventh homer, a grand slam. In the Giant sweep of the Braves, Maglie won his nineteenth and Sheldon Jones went the distance for the first time all year. A rainout the next day brought rumors of dissension on the Dodgers, with an alleged fight between Newcombe and Hodges.

"Ridiculous," was the one-word answer when members of the press followed up.

Dissension might have been too strong a word at this point. Even though there's no evidence of a fight between Hodges and Newcombe, big Don admits that the Giants were causing some jangled nerves.

"When they won those 16 straight games we began to notice them and become aware of what they were doing," Newk said. "We began to play scoreboard and we'd see the way they were pulling games out in the ninth inning, coming from behind so many times. Whenever a team plays scoreboard they're in trouble. We hadn't cared about the Giants all year, unless we were playing them, and suddenly everyone always wanted to know what the Giants were doing. Like I said, that's trouble."

While Carl Erskine didn't talk of dissension, he did admit there were times when competitiveness spawned anger. "There was one game against the Giants at Ebbets," Erskine remembers, "when Maglie was pitching and Jocko Conlon was umpiring at the plate. Sal had thrown at a couple of guys already and when I was up he threw an inside pitch that came right at my face. It wasn't done on purpose, but I froze in my tracks. I wasn't accustomed to seeing pitches like that. At the last second I threw my hand up, still holding the bat, and the ball hit the knob of the bat and shot down the third base line. Luckily, the ball was foul. I just stood there, white as a sheet. But the next thing I know Robinson is screaming at Conlon, claiming the ball hit me. I was still trying to get my composure, while the argument continued to rage. Finally Jocko asked me if the ball hit me or the bat and I said it must have hit the bat because I didn't feel it hitting me. Jackie looked like he wanted to kill me."

Because the pitch had so unnerved him, Erskine didn't consider the possibility of backing up his teammate. It was just a minor thing, but perhaps a small crack indicative of a team that was starting to worry.

Outwardly, the Dodgers didn't appear concerned about the onrushing Giants. Erskine doesn't recall worrying about a team slump at that point of the season. Big Newk was so sure the Dodgers would win that he borrowed money from the ball club to buy a car.

"I bought myself a new Cadillac," Newk recalls, with a laugh. "I got it in August and was riding around in it during September. I figured I would pay the money back when I got my World Series check. Before the Giants went on that 16-game streak we all felt comfortable. Looking back, I think we felt too comfortable, because some of us began to horse around. We were so cocksure of ourselves we thought we could turn it on and turn it off whenever we wanted."

The comfort zone was receding by the first week in September. Roe won his eighteenth on September 7, an 11–6 win over the Phils, as Furillo hit a pair of homers and Pafko slammed one. But up in Boston, Bobby Thomson made news with a big, five-for-five day, including a double and triple. Irvin blasted a 500-foot homer as the Giants completed a sweep of the Braves, becoming the first National Leaguer to drive in 100 runs on the year. The Giants just weren't quitting.

Although the Dodgers certainly had to be taking the Giant run seriously, plans were afoot in Brooklyn to give manager Dressen a day on September 22. The newspapers called Charley "the type of manager, as was the Lip before him, Brooklyn fans love. He steals signs down on the third base coaching lines, barks angrily at umpires and speaks his mind upon all and sundry occasions." A day for him in late September seemed tantamount to a pennant celebration.

On Saturday, September 8, the two teams met in a two-game series at Ebbets Field. This time the Brooks got a measure of revenge as Newcombe blanked Hearn and the Giants, 9–0, throwing a powerful two-hitter. The lead was now 6½, and a victory in the second game of the series could open it up once again. But the Giants had their trump card, Maglie, and the Barber again pitched brilliantly in Brooklyn. He topped the Dodgers and Branca, winning his twentieth game of the year, 2–1, despite Dodger fans waving a cluster of white handkerchiefs at Durocher every time the manager appeared on the field. Sal had great support, notably on a brilliant fielding gem by neophyte third baseman Bobby Thomson.

It was a 2–0 game in the eighth (the result of a Monte Irvin homer) when Duke Snider, returning to the lineup after missing nearly a week with a bad back, slammed a double off the right field scoreboard. Robinson, Maglie's main antagonist, then tripled into the right center field gap to score the Duke and make it a one-run game. After Leo visited the mound and got the white hanky treatment, Andy Pafko stepped in.

Pafko promptly slammed a shot toward third that seemed ticketed for the left field line. Robinson started home, but Bobby Thomson made a brilliant backhand stop of the ball on the short hop. As Robinson dove back to third, Bobby tagged him and in the same motion fired to first, doubling Pafko. The play had saved the tying run and maybe more. It also enabled the Giants to beat Ralph Branca at Ebbets Field for the first time since August 26, 1945.

"I've always been proud of that play," Bobby recalls. "I remember the next day Dick Young started his game story in the *News* by saying—and I'm paraphrasing a bit—'If by chance the Giants go on to win this thing they won't talk about Monte Irvin's homer, rather they will remember Bobby's great double play at third.' Reading his story really made me feel good."

The hard-fought, two-game set ended the season series between the two ball clubs. Brooklyn took it by a 13–9 count, but it had been the Giants who won six of the final seven games. The New Yorkers probably wished they had more games with the Flock. Now they would have to rely on others for help while they kept winning.

The Dodgers came out of the series worried about the health of several players. Snider's bad back was still a source of concern, as was the injured right hip of Roy Campanella. Campy had hurt his right hip on Saturday when he collided with Eddie Stanky on a play at second and didn't start the Sunday game. Though just five-eight, 170 pounds, the wily Brat was no man to fool with around the keystone sack. One who tried was ex-Giant Walker Cooper.

"I was never a Stanky fan," says Coop. "He had all kinds of tricks to foul you up. He was batting one time when I was catching. The Giants had a runner on first who started to steal. Stanky put his bat right up to my face so I couldn't throw the ball. I said to him, 'You sonofabitch, the next time that happens I'll run the bat right up your butt.

"I wanted to get him in the worst way. Whenever I was on first I'd holler down to him, 'If you get in my way I'll knock you all the way into the left field fence.' I tried to get him twice and I wound up in the hospital both times. Each time I slid so hard that I went into the base and sprained my ankle. So I quit trying to do that. But that was Eddie. He really knew how to beat you."

As for Ralph Branca, he had pitched well in the 2–1 loss, giving up only a two-run homer to Irvin in the fourth. But the big right-hander was feeling the strain of the growing number of tough innings, something that would eventually affect the entire staff.

"I was the kind of guy who always wanted the ball," Branca said. "But I guess there's a limit and maybe that worked against me during September. The Dodgers had two doubleheaders back-to-back in August and I pitched a shutout on Friday night, a strong game. Then we had a doubleheader Sunday and a twilight twin bill on Monday. I pitched on Monday with two days' rest. In the third inning Mel Queen, the Pittsburgh pitcher, hit a humpback liner to right. Furillo was playing him shallow, got it on a hop, and threw him out at first. Even though it was only the third inning, a bell rang in my head. *No-hitter!* So I really started to pump the ball, really throwing hard. And I had the no-hitter until the ninth when someone got a Baltimore chop single. But I finished up and had pitched back-to-back shutouts in four days.

"In my next two games I lost to Robin Roberts, 3–2, and to Maglie, 2–1. Pitching that way with the Dodger hitters would normally mean a victory. But it seemed that whenever I pitched in September we got only one run. I also think all that throwing, trying to get the no-hitter, going on two days' rest, put some strain on my arm. It was always tougher to get loose from that point on."

By splitting the two games with the Brooks, the Giants remained 5½ games out. The Giants only had 16 games remaining, the Dodgers, 19. But to show just how far the Jints still had to come, if the Dodgers won just 10 of their remaining 19, a game over .500, the Giants would have to win 14 of 16 just to *tie*. It still appeared very unlikely.

The Dodgers got off to a good start when Clem Labine shut out the Reds, 7–0, for his third straight victory. In his three starts, the young right-hander had given up just three runs while striking out 20 hitters. "I like the way Labine has been going," Charley Dressen said. "He's a cocky young rascal."

At the same time, Durocher was praising his ace, Maglie, who was now 20–5 on the season. "Sal's a great pitcher," said Leo, "and I'll tell you why—three curves and the guts of a burglar." But that day the Giants could only split with the Cards, leaving them once again six full games back. They needed another winning streak, a Dodger losing streak, something.

Help came from the Reds, who beat the Dodgers, 6–3, on September 12. Pafko managed his twenty-third homer, but Furillo was mired in a 0 for 17 slump. The Dodgers were not the same baseball-bashing outfit they had been earlier in the season.

The Giants gained a half game by being idle, but promptly lost it back when St. Louis beat Maglie and the Jints, 6–4. It was a milestone day at old Sportsman's Park. The Giants and Cards had been rained out the night before, so they played a Thurday afternoon game. That night, the Cards played their regularly scheduled game with the Braves, losing 2–0 as Warren Spahn won his twentieth of the year. It was the first time a team had met two different rivals on the same day since 1883.

Both clubs won on the fourteenth, the Giants topping the Cubs, 7–2, behind Hearn's fifteenth win, while the Dodgers whipped the Pirates, 3–1, as Preacher Roe, steady all year, raised his record to an impressive 20–2. Roe pitched well despite having some problems with a stiff arm. Don Newcombe also complained of a sore arm and was examined by Doc Wendler, who found nothing specifically wrong. But suddenly, the big right-hander found himself coming under fire.

Newcombe was one of the few Dodgers to continually defend Charley Dressen, saying even today, "He was a great manager who made his players feel important and secure. He never let anyone from the front office into the clubhouse. He would say, 'If you want to talk to my player, you let me know and I'll send him to the office. Don't come into my clubhouse and interfere with the stability of my team.' "

But it certainly didn't seem that Dressen was promoting stability when he referred to Newk's quick exit from the 6–3 win over Cincy on September 12. The big guy lasted only an inning before coming out complaining about a sore arm.

"I never know what's with him," Dressen quipped to the press, the implication a lot stronger than the words. The curt remark was followed the next day by sportswriter Tommy Holmes's column in the *Brooklyn Eagle,* entitled, Is Newcombe Ailment Case of Imaginitis?

The column talked about big Newk's power and potential, claiming the ball players around the league felt he was close to the best and should win 30 games every year. Quite a statement considering no major league hurler had won 30 since Dizzy Dean in 1934 and wouldn't do it again until Denny McLain in 1968. Holmes went on to say that first Burt Shotton, then Dressen, said that Newk was too prone "to ask out." Burt Shotton had been so fed up with Newk's bellyaching that the "kindly old man" said he had no sympathy with pitchers who didn't want to pitch and that Newk was "jaking it."

It was both a strange column and an ill-timed attack on a pitcher who was one of the keys to the pennant race. The *Eagle* was the hometown paper, and almost an arm of the Dodgers. It's curious that Holmes's column came a day after Dressen's expressed displeasure.

Was the story a plant? Did Dressen want Holmes to come at Newk in the hope of shaking the big guy up? It's certainly a distinct possibility in view of the facts.

For example, it was just a year earlier, September 6, 1950, when Newcombe made headlines all over the baseball world. On that day he rescued a tired Dodger pitching staff by volunteering to start both ends of a doubleheader against the first-place Phillies. After throwing a brilliant, three-hit shutout in the opener, Newk went up to his manager, Burt Shotton, and volunteered to "try it again." Shotton thought of his tired pitchers and agreed.

In the second game Newk pitched his heart out, giving up just two runs on eight hits in seven innings. With a little more support from the hitters he would have won both games, becoming the first pitcher to accomplish the iron man feat since 1928 and the first Dodger since way back in 1890. Does that sound like a man prone to asking out? Not likely.

Duke Snider spoke for most of the Dodgers when he said emphatically "I never, ever heard Don Newcombe ask or beg to be taken out of a game. Never!"

Newk himself gladly addressed the problem of his arm.

"I never really had a strong arm," he said. "It has nothing to do with throwing hard. I could certainly throw the ball hard, but I had to have my regular rest. It wasn't easy for me to pitch out of turn, with two days' rest, and be effective like some other guys. I always had small, almost skinny arms for a guy my size. I never had a real sore arm due to an injury, but when I didn't get my rest, my arm became sore from overwork. By the same token, I pitched through that soreness many times. I always did whatever I was asked or told to do for the club. Always. If they wanted me to stay in a game, fine. If they wanted me out, it was okay with me."

Just how Newcombe and the other Dodgers would react to this kind of treatment from the press remained to be seen. But the merit of the Holmes story would seem questionable at best.

On September 15, with the days dwindling down to a precious few, the Dodgers lost again. Branca was shelled by the Pirates, who beat the Dodgers 11–4 in the final meeting between the two ball clubs. The Bucs were 32 games out of first, fencing with the Cubs for the bottom spot, yet they had won the season series from the Dodgers, 12 games to 10. The only bright spot was Carl Furillo breaking an 0-for-24 tailspin with a triple. One can only imagine Branch Rickey, sitting in his Forbes Field office with a knowing smile on his face. The Dodgers had a long reputation for feasting on second-division ball clubs. Had they won 15 or 18 from the Pirates, as they did in other years, the pennant race would have been no contest.

The Giants, on the other hand, got another fine pitching effort from Sheldon Jones to top the Cubs, 5–2. In that game, Bobby Thomson hit his twenty-seventh homer, Mays clubbed his twentieth, while Mueller slammed his sixteenth. Thomson, whose batting average was once lower than the Dow Jones Average after the crash, was up around the .280 mark. Bobby also had 87 RBIs to go with the 27 homers and was en route to a big season.

Though the lead was still five games, the pennant race had a strange look to it. The Giants seemed the more confident, relaxed team. They were "letting 'er rip" every game, while the Dodgers seemed more tentative. In a way, it seemed as if the first-place team was chasing the second-place team.

But plans had to be made. The Dodgers announced they would begin distributing application blanks for World Series tickets the following week. Erv Palica, the doghouse pitcher earlier in the year, wouldn't have to worry about Dressen anymore. He was ordered to report for induction into the army. But the doghouse would soon be filled again and this time it would cause people to wonder whether Dressen was beginning to lose it.

The only bad news for the Giants was the loss of Wes Westrum for three days. The rugged catcher was suspended for pushing umpire Al Barlick during a heated argument about a play at the plate. Durocher had to wrestle his catcher away from the ump and was himself eventually banished.

"It was the worse decision I ever had called against me," Wes said.

Even with the controversial call, the Giants managed to win the game. The Dodgers would be involved in a similar play a short time later. Only theirs would cost them the game—and ultimately a lot more.

The Final Two Weeks

From the time they started their run with the 16-game win streak in mid-August, the Giant players sensed something special happening.

"People today can't understand what happened to us during the last six weeks of the season," said Al Dark. "It was a real exercise in character building, to be down as far as we were and to keep going out there every day, doing our best when no one thought we had a chance. I saw how guys under tremendous pressure were able to give 100 percent every day. You start to pick up little things that bring you closer, like one of your teammates having to deal with adversity. I think everybody on the ball club was pulling for Bobby Thomson to do a good job when he was moved to third.

"Bobby was used to being in the outfield and all of a sudden he's dealing with bullets at third and he knows he can't dodge them. He's got to get in front of them. Just seeing the job Bobby did helped to bring us closer."

Bill Rigney gives Durocher credit for leading the charge and bringing everyone else with him. "I never saw anyone manage better than Leo that last month of the season," Rigney recollects. "We didn't score a lot of runs, but thanks to Leo we won a lot of one-run games. During the last weeks I remember Larry Jansen saying, 'Do you realize what we have to do even if the Dodgers only play .500 ball?' We knew it, but didn't worry about it. We just kept playing for tomorrow. Every night on the road, a bunch of us would go to my room or Stanky's room, get some club sandwiches and beer, and talk about the game the next day. We'd go over the catcher's signs and the opposing pitcher's little traits. We knew we had a chance even though it might have been a slim one. But it brought the club closer together, vocally and by action. Every time we won a game it was: Whose room are we going to now? It became routine."

Larry Jansen looked at it from a pitcher's point of view. "I've always said that the club which has the better pitching staff the last six weeks of the season is going to win. The hitters are getting tired and if the pitchers can stay sharp, they can win. In fact, if a pitcher can stay strong he will be a lot sharper at the end of the season than at the beginning. I think we all stayed basically strong.

"I didn't get tired until maybe the last two games I pitched that year. During the last two weeks I lost 10 pounds but by then, emotion and adrenaline take over. You say: gotta win just one, gotta win just one more, one more. And that keeps you going. I would tell Bobby, Whitey, and the other guys to get me two runs. That would be enough to win. I had to look at it that way. I didn't care who I pitched against because I knew if I pitched a good ball game I was going to win."

It was Jansen who got the Giants moving on September 16, winning his nineteenth game, 7–1, over the Pirates in the first of two. Maglie then went out and helped the ball club complete the sweep with a 6–4 triumph. This was the game in which Augie Donatelli thumbed Bobby for complaining about the high strikes. But Bobby helped the cause with a homer in each contest, enabling him to tie his career best of 29, the number he had reached as a rookie back in 1947.

Even though Labine won his fourth in a row by trimming the Cubs, 6–1, the Jints had cracked the five-game barrier. They now trailed by just 4½ games. Labine's presence, however, like Al Corwin's with the Giants earlier in the year, had definitely given the Dodgers a much-needed shot in the pitching arm. The *Brooklyn Eagle* of September 17 reported:

"It's highly conceivable that if Clem hadn't been recalled from the St. Paul Saints in a desperation move for pitching strength the Dodgers might have blown the flag to the never-say-die Giants, now four and a half games off the pace."

However, the double win over the Bucs enabled the never-say-die Giants to clinch second place. When the club was 2–12 after their disheartening 11-game losing streak at the outset of the year, the odds against them finishing second were probably off the board. At this point, however, news about capturing the runner-up spot was meaningless. Only a pennant would satisfy the Durochermen now.

With the Giants idle on the seventeenth, the Dodgers sent Don Newcombe against the Cubs with the chance to gain a half game. A month earlier, a half game variation would have gone virtually unnoticed. Now it loomed big, the difference between a four- and a five-game lead.

Things began going wrong for the Brooks in the second inning. Roy Campanella was up, facing Cubs right-hander Turk Lown. The Turk let loose a fastball, ticketed for the inside corner. But the ball got away and sailed up and in on the Dodger catcher. Campy tried to cover up, but was a split second too late. He went down, blood streaming from his left ear. Frightened teammates rushed to his side, fearful their all-star catcher was seriously hurt.

"I'm all right. I'm all right," Campy kept insisting as he was lifted onto a stretcher. Ralph Branca accompanied Roy to Illinois Masonic Hospital, where the injured backstop would remain for several days. It was a severe beaning, but an acknowledged accident. Though Dressen was from the two-for-one school, this was not a payback pitch and the Dodgers did not retaliate.

Walter O'Malley was in the press box that day and agreed that the beaning was accidental. What made it doubly worse for the Big O and the rest of the Dodgers was the outcome of the game. Newcombe took a 3–0 lead into the bottom of the seventh when he suddenly lost the magic. The Cubs rallied for four runs, the last two coming home when former Dodger Gene Hermanski blasted a two-run homer off reliever Clyde King. The final was 5–3 and the lead was down to four.

No one kept stats on game-winning hits back then, but the day after the eight-player deal that brought Andy Pafko to the Dodgers was made, catcher Bruce Edwards cost his former club a victory by blasting a home run. Now Hermanski did the same thing and in a pennant race where every single game would count, Edwards and Hermanski definitely put two of them in the Dodger loss column.

A day later the lead was down to three as a fatigued Branca was blasted by the Cards, 7–1, a five-run sixth inning sending Ralph to the showers. The big righty, 13–5 at one point, had now lost four straight. Meanwhile, the confident Giants topped the Reds, 6–5, behind Dave

Koslo and reliever George Spencer, who was making his fifty-fifth appearance of the year. Westrum returned from his suspension and Irvin hit his twenty-second homer.

At this point the Dodgers still had a higher team batting average than the Giants, .277 to .262, but the gap was a lot smaller than it had been earlier in the year. The surprise was in the power department. Notwithstanding the likes of Hodges, Snider, Campanella, Pafko, Robinson, and Furillo, the Giants had eased ahead of them with 173 total home runs to 171 for the Brooks.

Duke Snider admits that both he and Pee Wee Reese were bugged by September batting slumps. "When a team has it's leadoff and number-three hitter slumping at the same time it becomes a lot harder to score runs," was the way the Duke put it.

Manager Dressen saw it the same way, benching his center fielder when the Dodgers met the Cards on Wednesday. It was the Duke's twenty-fifth birthday and Dressen's present was a seat on the pine. Light hitting was the reason, though Charley made the official line a need to field an all-righty lineup against southpaw Max Lanier. Pafko moved to center and Dick Williams was inserted in left.

But the night belonged to Preacher Roe. The veteran lefty twirled a five-hit shutout for his twenty-first victory and ninth in succession. With his parents among the crowd and his mother watching him pitch for the first time, Roe was masterful, though the Cards repeatedly asked umpire Babe Pinelli to examine the baseball.

"I guess they thought I was scuffing it up," said the Preacher, with a wink.

With the lead at 3½ the flip-flopping fortunes of the two teams seemed to reverse once again. On September 20 the Dodgers whipped the Cards behind Erskine, 4–3, the Brooks again looking like a championship ball club. Hodges slammed his thirty-ninth home run, Robinson made a great leaping catch of a Red Schoendienst liner to bail Erskine out in the fifth, and Carl won his sixteenth game in a route-going performance. The victory came on Dressen's fifty-third birthday, giving the manager a considerably better present than Snider had received the day before.

When Hearn and the Giants lost a heartbreaker to the Reds, 3–1, Cincy getting all its runs in the eighth, the Dodgers had moved out to a 4½ game lead and suddenly the Brooklyn bandwagon seemed to be rolling again. One paper said the victory "virtually sewed up the flag for Flatbush delivery," while another said the Giants had "received a serious blow" to their pennant hopes. What a difference a day makes. The Dodger magic number was five and the Brooks had 10 games left to reach it. The Giants had but seven to play.

The Dodgers also handed out 12,000 applications for World Series tickets on September 20. A large crowd gathered outside the team offices at 215 Montague Street. First on line was David Lande, a 63-year-old who had been camped out since 5:10 A.M.

"Our chances for copping the World Series are very good and you couldn't keep me away," Mr. Lande said, adding, "I'd like to see the Yankees win in the American League and then we can give them a good shellacking."

It was Clem Labine, however, who took the shellacking the next day. The rookie right-hander had his first rough outing since joining the Dodgers and winning four straight. On paper, it looked as if he simply had a bad game. Clem got in trouble in the first and the Phils third sacker, Willie "Puddin' Head" Jones, tagged him for a grand slam home run, paving the way for a 9–6 Philadelphia win.

But the ramifications of the homer would be a lot more far-reaching than a simple loss. Labine lasted into the second, gave up another pair, and was yanked by Dressen. Not only was Clem yanked from the game, but he was also yanked from the rotation and almost from existence on the Dodgers. The young righty was about to enter Dressen's twilight zone, the doghouse that didn't exist. Labine relates the strange turn of events.

"There were two out when it happened," Labine recalls. "The Phils loaded the bases on a bouncing single, a bunt, a wild pickoff throw, and an intentional walk. I wasn't getting my curve over that day and felt I had better control from the stretch. So when Jones came up I began pitching from the stretch. Charley didn't want that. He yelled to me to take the full windup. I guess I was pretty cocky and thought I knew better. So I kept pitching from the stretch and he kept yelling at me to take the windup. Then, on a two-one pitch, Jones hit it out."

There's no telling what would have happened if Labine had retired Jones from the stretch. But the grand slam changed everything. Because he didn't take a full windup, a pitcher who had given up a total of four runs in winning four straight ball games suddenly didn't start again. One token relief appearance was all that was seen of Labine for the remainder of the regular season. If it was Dressen's way of teaching a lesson, it may well have been the most ill-timed lesson in Dodger history.

"Sure, I made a mistake," Labine admits. "I should have listened to Charley. He was the manager. And he let you know he was the manager. I know it today as well as I knew it then. But you don't take out one man's mistake on the rest of the ball club.

"After that he wouldn't talk to me, wouldn't even recognize I was on the team. He never asked me how I pitched certain hitters during our clubhouse meetings. I was there, but he never even asked me one question. Charley was a vindictive guy. He wanted to make sure I paid the penalty for not listening to what he said."

Pitchers know other pitchers. From the time Labine joined the team he had observed the other Dodger hurlers and soon concluded that the manager didn't realize what was happening to the staff.

"We had a very tired pitching staff in late August and through September," says Labine. "Both the starters and the guys in the pen were tired. We had pitchers whose earned run averages started around three and were slowly going up to four. They were giving up many more hits in the early innings, which was another barometer, but I don't think Dressen noticed what was going on. To be honest, I had great stuff at the time. I couldn't pitch much better than I had during those first four starts. So to sit me, not let me pitch again for the remainder of the season, well, everyone knows what happened."

As sportswriters became aware of Labine's sudden disappearance to the purgatory of the Dressen doghouse, they began asking the manager the reason. Charley replied he was holding his young pitcher for the right spot. But the right spot never came, even as the team was fighting for its pennant life.

The Dodgers' September 21 loss to the Phils was a turning point. The lead was at four, then dropped to three the next day as the Giants beat the Braves, 4–1, behind Larry Jansen's twentieth victory. Once again, the Jints did it in the late innings, breaking through against 21-game winner Warren Spahn with three in the eighth. At the same time, Newcombe failed to win his nineteenth on his third try as the Phils triumphed over the Brooks again, this time by a 7–3 count. Roy Campanella was back in the lineup, but his presence didn't change the end result.

Oddly enough, there were less than 12,000 fans at the Polo Grounds to see their team pull a step closer.

The next day both Roe and Maglie won their twenty-second games. It was the final regular season game at Ebbets Field with a little over 19,000 fans in attendance and a day later, with the Brooks idle, the Giants wound up their Polo Grounds campaign with a 4–3 win over the Braves. Incredibly, there were only some 6,000 fans there to witness this one. Didn't the Giant fans realize what was happening? Both teams would finish up on the road with just 2½ games separating them. The Dodgers still had seven to play, but the Giants were down to four.

The Dodgers headed into Boston for a four-game set, while the Giants traveled to Philadelphia for a pair against the Phils. Then the teams would reverse things for the final series of the regular season— the Giants in Beantown, the Dodgers visiting the City of Brotherly Love. It was hard to believe that the entire season had come down to just these few ball games.

The pennant race was a baseball fan's dream, especially if he lived in New York. Only they weren't alone. There were six other National League teams, each of which had to take its turn playing both the Giants and the Dodgers. It's taken for granted that each team plays to win every game, no matter who the opposition. Certainly the top players, the guys who take real pride in their performance, go all out every day, even if their team is out of the hunt.

Warren Spahn, one of the greatest pitchers of his time, never let down against anyone. "It may be an old cliché," said Spahnie, "but you always concentrated on the club you were playing. Leo, of course, rode me all the time and I hated it. The way to get back at Leo was simply to beat him. Early in '51 we considered the Dodgers the team to beat and always went hard against them. But I didn't care about the Dodgers or Giants. I was concerned about the Braves."

Stan Musial, who would take another batting title in '51, loved playing against both clubs. "It was always exciting playing in New York," said Musial. "The Cards had a great rivalry with the Dodgers throughout the 1940s, so we always played hard against them. But we battled the Giants, too. Hitting in the Polo Grounds was great because the foul lines were so short and you could pull the ball there. Plus you always knew that playing against Leo was rough, tough baseball."

But Spahn and Musial notwithstanding, many players harbored different feelings about the two ball clubs. While, in theory, players and teams should go equally hard every day, there are often personal and deep-seated emotions that control and influence on-field actions. Some are a direct reaction to what the opposition does, while others are a direct reaction to who the opposition is. There is evidence that suggests both these factors were becoming part of the pennant race during the last part of the 1951 season. In other words, the rest of the league was taking sides.

With the Giants, the focal point was almost always Durocher, with a little help from the Brat, Eddie Stanky. Everyone knew the way Leo was, his voice, his jockeying, the stick-it-in-his-ear shouts that came from the bench. But while Leo could inspire heated emotion, he was also respected as a competitor. As Spahn said, the best way to get back at Durocher was to beat him. His personality inspired teams to come at the Giants with fire and intensity.

"When you're playing a team that isn't antagonistic you're out to beat them, but you don't always have that killer instict," Bobby Thomson explains. "But against wise guys, you tend to bear down harder. Beat them and you can shut them up, at least for a game."

With the Dodgers, the focus was on a player—Jackie Robinson. Even today, it's Jackie's name that most often surfaces when players talk about the Dodgers. They equate Jackie with the team's antagonistic attitude, with the Dodgers' tendency to show up already vanquished foes. And for being the first black man in a major league uniform. Because of Robby and the seemingly invincible quality of the Brooklyn ball club, most players around the league were beginning to favor the Giants.

"The Dodgers were the team everyone loved to hate," recalls Jack Lang, present secretary of the Baseball Writers Association of America and a man who covered the Dodgers as a beat reporter in '51. "They were the dominant ball club, with a kind of swagger and arrogance that said we know we're good and we're not going to lose."

Jim Hearn, who played against both the Dodgers and Giants when he was with the Cards, felt there was always a special feeling of animosity toward the Dodgers. "When I was with the Cardinals from 1947 to 1949 all the other teams in the league hated the Dodgers," Hearn relates. "We all wanted to crush them because the Dodgers were so strong. Back then, Leo was also a factor. He was the kind of guy that you wanted to beat and beat badly. Naturally, the Cards wanted to win against everyone, but the feeling was always stronger when we played Brooklyn. When Leo went over to the Giants in '48 the Cards still hated the Dodgers. When the Giants made their move in '51, and remember I was playing for the Giants then, I had the distinct feeling that the rest of the league was rooting for us and against the Dodgers."

Willard Marshall, a former Giant who went over to the Braves, had a similar perspective. "It always seemed that the Dodgers were trying to run over you when they came into your ballpark. Because of that, they were always one team we wanted to beat and I can honestly say that we tried harder against them. I also think the rest of the league was glad to see the Giants catch up to them because of the strong feelings the Dodgers always provoked."

Andy Pafko was on the outside looking in with the Cubs before coming to the Dodgers in June of 1951. Not surprisingly, he saw things the same way as others. "The Dodgers were a sharp-nosed team," Pafko said. "If you beat them that meant you played hard and de-served to win. Not many clubs liked the Dodgers in those days, par-tially because of Robinson and also because of the way they played. When I was with the Cubs I can definitely say that we always fought harder against them."

Though a rookie in '51, Clem Labine watched everything that hap-pened within the league closely and feels that a lot of the animosity around the league stemmed from Robinson. "Jackie often put us in the position where other teams disliked us," Labine says. "He would do a lot of little things to antagonize our opponents. I've seen him get hit by a pitched ball and go limping down to first like he could hardly walk. Then on the first pitch—boom, he's gone. I always thought of it as showboating and it did make the opposition angry. But I will say this: No matter what Jackie did he was always right there with the bat in his hand ready to face anybody and everybody, and that takes courage. But because of Jackie, a lot of teams played harder against us."

Baseball writer and historian Donald Honig is another who shares the same opinion. His conclusion is based on years of research, talk-ing to players, and writing about the game. "Every team in the Na-tional League wanted to beat the Dodgers," Honig says. "Part of it was the New York factor, part was because the Dodgers were the stron-gest team in the league, and the other part was Jackie Robinson. You can't rule out the Robinson factor. Jackie antagonized a lot of people,

had a very vivid personality and was very combative. He even antagonized people on his own team. It wasn't because he was black, but
because of his aggressive style of play and his outspokenness."

But it was Walker Cooper who had the courage to say what many
others wouldn't. A member of the Braves in 1951, Cooper also felt
most teams in the league wanted to see the Giants win. "I'm not saying
that other teams let up against the Giants," Coop said. "But the feeling
most of them had was that they wanted the Giants to beat the Dodgers. Playing at Ebbets Field, with that band, those fans and that runway to the playing field wasn't easy."

The former Giant catcher felt there was another underlying reason
that National League teams wanted to see Brooklyn beaten. It dated
back four years, to 1947.

"There was also a racial feeling about the Dodgers," Cooper said
recently, choosing his words carefully. "People today tend to forget
that it was the Dodgers who had broken the so-called gentleman's
agreement that was keeping black players out of the majors. Rickey
brought in Robinson and the rest of the league formed strong feelings
about it. Those feelings—blaming the Dodgers for breaking the color
line—were still lingering in 1951."

Don Newcombe agreed with Cooper's remark citing racism as a
prime reason the Dodgers were hated in 1951. "That certainly was
true," said Newk. "There were plenty of guys in the league who
wouldn't want to share a hotel, meals, bathroom facilities, or even a
drinking fountain with a black man."

It would be difficult to argue the point. The fact that Sam Jethroe of
the Braves was the only other black player in the National League
beyond the Dodgers and Giants speaks volumes. Moreover, a large
percentage of ball players were from the Deep South, where racial
segregation still reigned supreme. In the minds of many players and
managers of the day, the Dodgers had committed two sins: Not only
did they begin to sign black ball players, but they were also able to
build a superior team around them. To many die-hard southerners
this was tantamount to an immoral act. Not only had the Dodgers
committed an unpardonable sin by bringing in black players, but they
had also profited from it, and this was an offense that demanded
retribution.

There was also the factor of job security. Anyone who could add
and subtract was able to reach the same conclusion. Every time

another black came in, another white would be going out. The fact that five of the eight National League teams didn't have a single black player in 1951 indicates that the majority of owners were still hoping it would all go away.

Brooklyn had won pennants in 1947 and 1949, just missed in 1950, and was leading again for most of 1951. With the nucleus of talent on the ball club, including the trio Stan Musial called "the three best black players in baseball," there was already talk of a National League dynasty. Add Charley Dressen with his penchant for kicking sleeping dogs, and the combative, antagonistic Robinson, and the formula for resentment was complete.

Going into their all-important series with the Braves at Boston on September 25, the Dodgers would soon prove they hadn't learned the lesson that there is a psychological side to the game as well as a physical one. Charley Dressen's yearlong battle with the umpires would also play one final time, and the last act of this drama would prove the most costly one of all.

As the ball club headed for Boston, they were given a unique send-off at Ebbets Field. Camped out in front of the bleacher gate was Samuel Maxwell, a 62-year-old lifelong Dodger fan. Maxwell vowed to remain at Ebbets until the start of the World Series, counting off the days on a large, homemade calendar which he had taped to the gate.

Though still leading by 2½ games, the Dodgers were showing signs of stress that even the newspapermen were noticing. One story referred to them as a winded ball club that looked like a "tired old fighter, a little punch drunk, who occasionally brings one up from the resin to stay in the scrap." The Giants were described as "strong, courageous and resourceful, and piling up points dangerously." Again it was that strange image of the first-place team chasing the second-place team. It almost seemed a matter of time before the positions flip-flopped.

At this point, manager Durocher was finally talking pennant. "No half way about it," Leo told a reporter. "We're shooting the works, all or nothing." In closing the gap, the Giants had won 33 of their last 40 games and were on an eight of nine run.

Branca and Erskine would be the Dodger starters in Boston. A twinight doubleheader this late in the season wouldn't be easy. The Giants had a single game at Philadelphia, with Jim Hearn set to take the hill. Durocher's advice to his troops before meeting the Phils was simple: "Keep your eyes off the scoreboard and your mind on the game."

As it turned out, the games on September 25 couldn't have gone any better for Durocher and his team. They defeated the Phils with relative ease, 5–1, beating 21-game winner Robin Roberts. But Durocher showed he was taking no chances. Hearn was hit on the thigh by a liner in the sixth, and when he seemed to weaken with one out in the seventh, the manager called Sal Maglie in from the pen. The Barber, making just his fifth relief appearance of the year, shut the door and the Giants had still another victory.

Up in Boston, the Dodgers looked anything like a front-runner. Playing before a sparse crowd on a chilly, damp, and sometimes rainy evening, the double disaster began in the first inning of the first game. The Braves jumped all over Branca, and then reliever Clyde King, knocking out both pitchers while scoring six runs. Sam Jethroe homered off Branca, and ex-Giant Buddy Kerr smacked a bases-loaded double off King to drive in three more. It was all Boston needed. Warren Spahn coasted to his twenty-second victory, 6–3.

The second game was worse. This time the Braves got one in the first, then drove Erskine from the mound with six more in the second inning. When this one ended, Boston had an easy 14–2 victory. The Dodgers made three errors, played sloppy ball throughout, and were described in *The New York Times* as looking little better than a sandlot team. What's more, they now led the Giants by just a single game. Brooklyn was 93–56, the Giants 93–58.

Manager Dressen looked at the early six-run outbursts as having real significance. "It left me without my bunting game," he told reporters. "There wasn't anything to do except hit away." As if bunting had ever been a major weapon in the Dodger arsenal. Early in the year, all the Dodgers had to do was hit away and they won. Remember, this was the most powerful offensive team in the league . . . and statistically, they still were. In a way, Dressen's comments were becoming illogical, as if he was beginning to set up his alibis . . . just in case.

The Dodgers were hearing footsteps now. It was unavoidable. Branca had been knocked out in five of his last six starts. Snider was benched again in the opener because of the presence of southpaw Spahn. Roy Campanella sounded a pessimistic note when he said, "A month ago we were a free and easy bunch breezing to an easy pennant. Now we're playing tight and nervous baseball looking back over our shoulder."

Though the team was obviously hurting, captain Pee Wee Reese tried to keep the mood upbeat. "All I know is that we're still in first place," the sparkplug shortstop said. "If we win four out of the five we've got left, we've got 'em. That's what I want to see."

So did the rest of the Dodgers as well as their loyal fans.

When the Brooks met the Braves the next afternoon, it was big Newk who got the call to make another try for that elusive nineteenth victory. The Giants, who seemed to be getting a strong pitching performance every day, sent Larry Jansen to the mound against Philly. As it turned out, both ball clubs won their games handily. Each game turned into a laugher, but for the Dodgers, the laughter would backfire. The last laugh, in fact, would belong to the Braves.

Jansen and the Giants rolled to a 10–1 victory, four runs in the first and three more in the third putting the game on ice early. Irvin led the way with a homer, triple, double, and four RBIs. The Giants now had two days to relax and watch the Dodgers in action. Manager Durocher, knowing it was still anybody's flag for the taking, was full of praise for his players.

"There are 25 men here who have hustled their hearts out," the Lip said, "and they're still hustling. You can give them the credit for what we've done in the last weeks."

As for the Dodgers, they made it look just as easy, jumping out to an 8–0 lead and winning their game by a 15–5 count, one of their biggest offensive explosions in recent weeks. But the game ended with controversy and hard feelings which, as usual, were directed at the men from Flatbush.

It happened in the eighth inning. The Brooks had an 8–3 lead and were piling it on once more. Five more runs had already crossed the plate, upping the margin to 13–3. Robinson was on third as the Braves' Dave Cole got ready to pitch to Snider. Suddenly Jackie broke for home, digging hard in that pigeon-toed running style of his and sliding under the tag of catcher Walker Cooper. It was the fourteenth run, but one that the Dodgers would have been better off not scoring. For the aggressive Robinson had just violated one of baseball's most solemn unwritten rules: Don't show the other team up when you have a big lead. Ironically, it was Jackie's first steal of home that season.

Braves manager Tommy Holmes called Robby's theft humiliating to his team, especially in front of the hometown fans.

"They may be sorry for that," he threatened. They needed that run like a hole in the head. All I know is it made my guys mad and they're really gunning for them now. They wanted to show us up? Well, maybe we can fix their wagon for good."

Ralph Branca remembers the moment well. He feels it was an instinctive play on Robinson's part that developed into something more. "I know the kind of player Jackie was," Branca said. "I doubt he was thinking about the score. He just saw the opportunity to steal home and did it. Right afterward there were words between Holmes and Dressen and some of the Braves got on Jackie pretty good. Well, he turned around and just patted his behind, as if to say, 'Kiss my ass,' and that really got them mad."

Dick Williams was another Dodger who saw the by-product of Robinson's slick baserunning. "Tommy Holmes and the entire Boston team were outraged by Jackie's steal," said Williams. "We went into Philly after we finished with the Braves and the Giants came to Boston. We heard stories that when one of the Giants slid into a base, a Braves player would help him up. I'm sure the Braves weren't laying down and dying for the Giants, but they certainly weren't giving as good an effort against the Giants as they did against us—especially after Jackie stole home."

Several days later, Braves manager Holmes, who made his home in the Bay Ridge section of Brooklyn, reported that his family was beginning to receive threatening letters in answer to Holmes's threat of revenge. Dodger fans, already living with the dreaded thought that the Giants would win it, took out their wrath on a Brooklyn neighbor.

"Letters and telegrams from cranks is one thing," said Holmes, "but when they threaten your family, that's something else."

The lead was still one game and the Giants were idle when the Dodgers and Braves squared off for the fourth and final contest of their series on September 27. Dressen had Preacher Roe and his brilliant 22–2 record on the mound. The Braves countered with 20-year-old rookie southpaw Chet Nichols, who was 10–8 with the best earned run average in the league. Barely 2,000 fans were at old Braves Field, but the players couldn't have cared less. It was obvious from the start that both teams wanted to win.

The Dodgers scored a run in the first when Furillo doubled, went to third on a Reese sacrifice, and scored on Robinson's infield out. They got a second tally in the fourth when Roe squeezed Snider home. A Sam Jethroe homer followed by a pair of singles and a wild pitch enabled the Braves to tie it in the fourth. Both teams scored single runs in the sixth, making it 3–3. Then in the bottom of the eighth came the play that turned the game around—and the Dodgers' season.

Left fielder Bob Addis, a former Dodger farmhand, opened the Braves' half of the inning with a single. When Jethroe followed with his third hit of the game, Addis motored around to third. As first sacker Earl Torgeson stepped in, Roe rubbed up the baseball and pawed at the rubber. Manager Dressen waved his infield closer, hoping to keep Addis from scoring on a grounder. Sure enough, the left-handed–swinging Torgy smacked a slow bouncer toward second. Addis broke for home and Robinson broke for the ball.

Jackie fielded it cleanly and fired the ball toward the plate. Campanella stepped out to block the dish and Addis started his slide. The ball and runner arrived at the same time. There was a cloud of dust as Campanella applied the tag before falling over to his right. For a split second everything stopped. Then umpire Frank Dascoli, stationed just on the third base side of home plate, threw his arms straight out to each side. *Safe!*

Within seconds, the Dodgers blew sky high. Campanella went berserk at home plate, joined by Roe, then Dressen and the other infielders. Within seconds, Dascoli thumbed Campy out of the game. Then coach Cookie Lavagetto was thumbed for the first time in his career. The Dodgers would have argued the call in any game, but with the go-ahead run scoring in the eighth inning at this stage of a tight pennant race, the call loomed as potentially huge.

"I didn't call him any names," Campanella insisted afterward. "I never called an umpire names in my life. I just said 'No, no, no, no, I had him!' I asked him how he could call Addis safe when I had the plate blocked—and he threw me out of the game."

Dascoli claimed that Campy threw his glove in the air, an act that "calls for an automatic ejection."

Once the game resumed, Sid Gordon grounded into a double play. Then, with Walker Cooper at bat, Dascoli whirled around and ordered the Dodger bench cleared to stop the jockeying, so when the game resumed again only manager Dressen and coach Jake Pitler were in the dugout. The players weren't banished, just removed from the dugout so some semblance of order could be restored.

The Dodgers, to a man, felt that Campanella had tagged Addis out. "Addis tried to hook the plate but never got there," Ralph Branca recalls. "To me, the pictures have always shown that Campy had the ball and blocked the plate. I remember Campy throwing his glove in the air and Dascoli thumbing him."

The prevalent opinion at the ballpark was that Dascoli had been too hasty in his banishment of Campy. Even the Boston writers agreed that because of the catcher's importance to the team and the magnitude of the game to the pennant race, the ump should have allowed Campy to remain. His absence would be sorely felt in the Dodger ninth.

That's when Reese doubled and was still on second when Campy's spot in the order came up. Instead of the slugging catcher, Dressen was forced to send up the light-hitting Wayne Terwilliger to bat for sub catcher Rube Walker. All the Twig could manage was a weak ground out to third. Then Nichols fanned Andy Pafko and the Dodgers had lost it. Now the Dodger lead was down to just a half game. Both clubs had won 94, the Giants had one more defeat.

The fallout continued after the game. Dascoli was an umpire who had clashed with the Dodgers repeatedly during the season. Dressen pulled no punches when he said, "Dascoli is just imcompetent. We've been in five incidents with him this year."

Robinson, the ultimate competitor, continued to ride the umpire. "I gave it to him good while we were leaving the field and everything I said still goes," Robby told the press. "He chokes up worse than the players."

Some of the Dodgers began kicking at the door to the umpires' room, which was right next to the door to the visitors' clubhouse, doing considerable damage.

Dascoli insisted he had made a correct call. "Addis was definitely safe," he said. "He slid right under Campanella and his foot was all the way across the plate before Campanella could put the tag on him. Robinson's throw was just a little wide and that gave Addis the chance to hook in there."

The fallout included $100 fines for both Robinson and Campanella, and a $50 assessment against Roe. Ford Frick, newly elected commissioner of baseball, levied the fines in his capacity as outgoing National

League president. "These fines are not for actions on the field, but rather for those in the runway on the way to the clubhouse," he said. The Dascoli call wouldn't be forgotten. Looking back over a 40-year span, Duke Snider still insists that "Dascoli completely blew the call. It cost us the game and ultimately forced us into the playoffs."

On the other side of the coin, it wasn't Dascoli who caused Duke Snider to strike out with the bases loaded in the seventh, or Pafko to fan with the tying run in scoring position in the ninth. Along with their other problems, the Dodgers were not delivering in the clutch.

But the Giants were riding high. Caught up in their own momentum, they were gaining power and confidence as they rolled on. Though idle on the twenty-seventh, Al Dark approached manager Durocher and asked if the club could work out on what was supposed to be a day off. Leo said sure, if you want to work out, then work out.

There was one other scenario taking place on that fateful Thursday, September 27. No one could deny the possibility of a tie between the two ball clubs, and provisions had to be made if a best-of-three playoff series was needed. A coin toss was held in Commissioner Frick's office. Giants' owner Horace Stoneham called the toss, but lost. Representing the Dodgers was business manager Jack Collins, who said his club wanted the first game played at Ebbets Field, the next two (if a third was necessary) at the Polo Grounds.

Over the years there have been stories that the Dodgers made a colossal error in choosing Ebbets for the first game and by not having a more knowledgeable club official at the coin toss. But evidence suggests that Collins was acting on orders from Dressen. Charley wanted to open at home because the Brooks had beaten the Giants 9 of 11 times at Ebbets during the regular season. Winning the first one, he felt, was a huge advantage in a best-of-three series.

Leo, too, was satisfied with the choice. If there was a playoff, he was only too happy to have the second and third games at the friendly Polo Grounds.

The Giants had a second consecutive off day to rest and regain their strength. Even the schedule seemed to favor the New Yorkers. Brooklyn had a Friday contest with the Phils that would finally pull them even with the Giants in total games played.

Erskine was on the hill for the Dodgers and for most of the game seemed to have things well in hand. Brooklyn had a 3–1 lead going into the last of the eighth, but Lady Luck didn't seem to be shining any kind of light on the Dodgers. Phils catcher Andy Seminick slammed a two-run homer off Ersk to tie the game. When the Dodgers failed to score in the top of the ninth, the Phils had a chance to win it.

Richie Ashburn opened with a bloop single to left. Dick Sisler sacrificed him to second and Bill Nicholson was walked intentionally. Then Willie Jones, who had hit the grand slammer off Labine a week earlier, slashed a sharp single under the glove of Billy Cox at third and Ashburn sped home with the winning run. Not only were the Dodgers beaten in another late-inning heartbreaker, but the impossible had finally happened.

The lead was gone.

The Giants and Dodgers were dead even with 94–58 records.

Each team had two games left.

It was perhaps Roy Campanella who best caught the mood of the Brooklyn ball club. It didn't sound as if the Dodgers relished the upcoming showdown in quite the same way Durocher and the Giants did. "During the last week we fought desperately to keep the pennant from slipping through our fingers," Campy would say later. "Everybody was grim and silent. There was no horseplay going on. Tempers were short. We stayed out of each other's way."

That feeling could be seen as the Dodgers left the field in Philadelphia. The team appeared disconsolate. They had been booed all afternoon by the Philadelphia fans, with Robinson again the primary target. Jackie had never been a favorite of the fans in Philly, not since the problems with Chapman his rookie year. As rookie Dick Williams said, recalling the feeling around the league that year: "The only people rooting for the Dodgers down the homestretch were intimate friends, family, and, of course, their fans."

The Giants, on the other hand, were enjoying every minute of the Dodger collapse. Durocher's ball club was quartered in a Back Bay hotel in Boston, awaiting their Saturday game with the Braves, when they heard the Dodgers had lost once more.

"If I make a move I'll explode with happiness," Leo told the inquisitive press. "I'm so happy for my players. They never gave up and never will. This is the greatest team I ever managed and it will be the biggest thrill of my life when we clinch the pennant here on Sunday. The other teams have done all they can for us. Now it's between the Dodgers and us. Down on the mat. We like it that way. Let's see if they do."

With two games left, they were dead even. The Giants' game with the Braves was set for Saturday afternoon, while the Dodgers would play the Phils at night. So, with a victory, the New Yorkers could move into first place and put the pressure directly on the Dodgers.

That's just what happened. With Sal Maglie pitching every bit as well as he had early in the year, the Giants defeated Warren Spahn and the Braves, 3–0. Spahnie had come into the game with 22 victories and was the major league leader in complete games and strikeouts, yet the Giants whipped the future Hall-of-Famer for the sixth time.

Bobby Thomson had a pair of hits, Mays was electrifying on the bases, while Mueller, Dark, and Westrum produced the RBIs. Meanwhile, the Barber scattered five hits en route to his twenty-third win of the year. When he closed the Braves down in the last of the ninth the Giants players erupted in joy. After 153 games of baseball, the ball club had moved into first place, one half game in front of the Dodgers.

"These guys have been great," Durocher said after the game. "You can't put your finger on any one guy and say he did it. It has been a team job, and each and every one of them is entitled to the credit. If there's any justice at all they'll win it because they deserve it." Looking back over his long big league career that reached back 26 years to 1925, Leo the Lip put 1951 at the head of the class. "I never in my life got such a bang out of baseball as I have had this year. It's a real pleasure to manage a team like this."

Asked about a turning point, Leo said it was July 20, the day he made his final move and brought Bobby Thomson in to play third base. Then he laughed. "I'm still second-guessing myself," he said. "If I had brought Bobby in a month earlier, perhaps the race would have been over by now."

Thomson had indeed been magnificent. His average was close to the .290 mark, he had 29 homers, and still had a shot at 100 RBIs. Perhaps more important had been his play at third. He surprised almost everyone with the way he had taken to his new position; some said he was the best third sacker in the league after Billy Cox.

But there still was no time for celebration. The Dodgers were getting ready to take center stage and Dressen had Don Newcombe ready to go against another of the National League's best, Robin Roberts. Big Newk would be gunning for his twentieth victory and the Dodgers would like nothing better than for their ace right-hander to find the groove.

They gave him some real incentive in the second inning. Campanella started it with a ringing double off the left field wall. Andy Pafko promptly whacked his twenty-eighth home run into the upper deck in left, his sixteenth circuit as a Dodger. The Brooks got a third run in the inning, then picked up another pair while Newk breezed.

Don scattered seven hits for his third shutout of the year. When he got the final out in the ninth, covering first to take Gil Hodges's toss on a Granny Hamner grounder, hundreds of Brooklyn fans who had traveled to Philly swarmed out on the field in celebration. It was an ironic moment. After being in first place virtually all year, cheering Dodger fans were celebrating a victory that had pulled their beloved Bums even with the Giants. Suddenly, it was the Dodgers doing the chasing. Now there was just one game in the regular season remaining for each club.

While Leo Durocher had spent the last weeks of the season in constant praise of his team, telling them over and over again how important they were, Charley Dressen mouthed no similar sentiments. On the contrary, the man who had made a practice out of kicking sleeping dogs was at it again.

This time he used the *Brooklyn Eagle* as his forum. The story appeared in the September 30 edition. There was a picture of Charley, a smile on his face, winking at the camera, fingers crossed on both hands. But the accompanying words bordered on the bizarre. Was the story tongue-in-cheek, an ill-timed attempt at humor? Was he trying to use a kind of psychological ploy, getting the Giants so angry at the Dodger manager they would forget about the business at hand? Or was Charley Dressen simply starting to lose it?

"The Giants can't hurt us," was the way the story, written in the form of a monologue, began. "Let me explain about the Giants. They are a flash in the pan. You'll see, when they come down the stretch, they'll crack. It isn't that I have anything against the Giants personally. I admire the Giants, in a way. They are so lucky. For a team that has no class, they have been very lucky. But in the long run, you know yourself, class will tell."

The Dressen dialogue continued. "It is not their fault if they have no class, no ability, no—talent. People without talent, you know yourself, would *like* to have talent, but where are they going to get it? Now about the Giants, you mark my words—from now on, the pressure is on them. The way to tell about a club is what happens when the pressure is on. When a club is a flash in the pan, like the Giants, what happens? It tightens up. It gets jitters. It makes mistakes. It can't stand the gaff. That's the Giants for you."

The story and Dressen quotes almost seem like a put-on. The Giants were going to crack down the *stretch!* There was one game left. Could the story have been a put-on? If so, why?

Even today, the actions of the two managers is a fascinating study in contrasts. Leo Durocher and Charley Dressen were dead even in the standings, but not in the way they handled their teams and players. This relationship was explored by Dr. Ted Saretsky, a practicing psychologist and clinical professor of psychology at Adelphi University. Besides being a lifelong sports fan, Dr. Saretsky has been called upon many times to speak and write about the psychology of athletics. He also remembers the Giant-Dodger rivalry and the machinations of the two managers.

"Leo Durocher had the ability to mold a collection of individual players and create a sense of cohesiveness and unity," Dr. Saretsky said recently. "He established a 'collective ego' that stressed 'we' and 'us' as opposed to the individual 'I.' Durocher's positive attitude and almost daily team meetings held during the last month of the pennant drive created a sense of solidarity that was synergetic in its effect. The whole became greater than the sum of its parts."

It wasn't that way with Charley Dressen. "There are certain personality types who, even at the pinnacle of their success, still manage to self-destruct," continued Dr. Saretsky. "Supreme egotists like Charley Dressen are notorious for letting their vanity and self-centeredness interfere with sound judgment. Dressen wasn't satisfied with having a comfortable, 13½ game lead and a winning team. He felt that the beat writers were crediting his all-star lineup and not him for the Dodgers' success. His colossal 'The Giants is dead' blunder, and the taunting through the locker room door, are classic examples of snatching defeat from the jaws of victory.

"In addition, Dressen's insatiable need for recognition made him chafe to get out from under the shadow of Leo Durocher. And his rigid need to be in control made him prone to impulsive decisions that didn't work. As the Dodgers unraveled down the stretch, they needed a calm yet inspirational leader. Yet Dressen's deteriorating relationship with his players, his tendency to place blame and responsibility, and to publicly chastise individuals, were symptoms of a rattled man who couldn't effectively deal with stress."

This was a large part of the difference in the two as the season reached its now classic climax. Mark Twain once said, "Praise is well, compliment is well, but affection—that is the last and most precious reward that any man can win, whether by character or achievement."

Leo Durocher had that affection from every member of his team.

The Final Years

There was a poll taken back in 1969 and Hank Aaron's 715th home run was named the most memorable event in baseball. I always thought Bobby's should have been. When Hank got to 714 everyone knew it was just a matter of time before he got another. Bobby's home run was so much more dramatic because no one expected it. It was spontaneous, and that, to me, makes it the most memorable.

—Monte Irvin

I was about three weeks away from my twenty-eighth birthday on October 3, 1951. Much of my career was still ahead of me and I've talked about some of it already. But before getting into the complete story of the playoffs, this might be a good place to tie up the loose ends, especially about my final years in the big leagues.

I've already talked about my trade to Milwaukee and the broken ankle I suffered that spring. Being on a good team and not contributing the way you know you can is a tough thing to take. I came back to play about 100 games in 1955, the year after my injury, although there were still nagging problems stemming from my ankle. It wasn't until 1956 that I felt I was all the way back physically and ready to produce.

Milwaukee came close to beating the Dodgers that season and in the final weekend I had a chance to make a difference in a game at St. Louis. I was facing a pitcher named Herm Wehmeier with an opportunity to knock in a few runs. I did my best, but grounded out. It bothered me quite a bit, especially when we lost and finished a game behind the Dodgers. Spahnie had pitched his heart out and shed a tear or two in the clubhouse afterward. And I felt just as badly as he did.

I had 20 homers and 74 RBIs in 1956, not the kind of numbers that really made me happy. Maybe it shouldn't have come as a surprise when I found myself in an unfamiliar position the next year. I was healthy, but sitting the bench. That was the year the Braves finally broke through and won the pennant and the World Series. But I wasn't around at the finish. I had played just 41 games for the Braves through June 15 and that's when I got the news. Believe it or not, I was traded back to the Giants.

The Braves traded me along with second baseman Danny O'Connell and a pitcher named Ray Crone for Red Schoendienst. Red was a real pro, the glue the Braves needed to anchor their infield and the final link that made it possible for them to win the pennant. You might say there are a lot of guys on the '54 Giants and '57 Braves who can thank me for their World Series checks. John Antonelli, who came to the Giants when I left, won 21 games and was the ace of their staff. Then Schoendienst went to the Braves and they won.

Going back to New York wasn't easy. Talk about mixed emotions. Leo was gone and Bill Rigney, one of my old teammates, was the manager. Some of the old guys were still there—Whitey, Don Mueller, Mays—but there were also a lot of new faces. They weren't the old Giants and I wasn't the old Thomson.

What's that old saying? You can't go home again. That's the way it was for me and the Giants. I felt my days there were over. In addition, the team just wasn't doing that well. Willie was a superstar by then and guys like Whitey and Don still made the plays. But it wasn't enough.

In August, we learned the ball club would be moving west. It was a jolt, even though we realized the team wasn't drawing and the ballpark was ancient. It's not difficult to remember the last days at the Polo Grounds. I found myself looking around the old place now and then, and letting the memories run through my mind. I remembered the early years, playing alongside guys like Mel Ott, Johnny Mize, Walker Cooper, and Willard Marshall—even back to Bill Terry, who was in the front office when I first signed.

On the last day, Rigney played me at third for the only time all year. I'm sure he did it for sentimental reasons. After the game I went back onto the field and took pictures of Wink and my four-year-old daughter, Nancy, sitting in the Giant dugout. Then I took a shot of Nancy running around the bases. And finally, I snapped one of the clubhouse in dead center, with the Chesterfield sign over it. Tough as it was to go back to the Giants, I enjoyed being part of that final farewell.

I was really looking forward to playing on the West Coast, but I never got there. The ball club had a slew of young players in 1958, guys like Orlando Cepeda, Willie Kirkland, Leon Wagner, and Felipe Alou, and I did not figure in their future plans. On April 3, I was traded to the Cubs for a pitcher named Bob Speake, a guy I'd never heard of.

The Cubs were a last-place team and I thought about quitting. I even said it to Wink, but in my heart I knew I wasn't serious. I needed a job and always enjoyed playing in Wrigley Field. Day baseball. Why not! Chicago was great and I spent two enjoyable years there. Al Dark also joined the team and it felt good to be with an old Giant again. As far as I was concerned, it was just what the Cubs needed, a couple of Durocher-type players to get them out of last place.

Day baseball also gave me more of a semblance of a normal life. Home games in Chicago meant being at home with the family at night. Maybe that was a sign. I was starting to gravitate toward a nine-to-five routine. Pretty soon the road trips and night games were getting more difficult.

I played in 152 ball games in 1958 and I put up some Thomson-like numbers: .283 batting average, 21 homers, 83 RBIs. I enjoyed playing alongside Ernie Banks, who had 47 homers and was the MVP that year. When I think of Ernie, I think of a guy who hit more three-run homers than anyone I played with.

In 1959 I played in only 122 games and my production was down across the board. After the season the Cubs said they wanted me back, but ended up trading me to Boston during the off-season. The year 1960 with the Red Sox and Orioles marked the end of my baseball career and enough has been said about that already.

So let's get back to happier days, those final three games of the 1951 pennant race, probably the three most exciting and important games of my life.

On to the Playoffs

There was a feeling of anticipation in both Boston and Philadelphia as the teams got set for the final regular season game. The early autumn weather was chilly and in Boston heavily overcast. The lights at Braves Field were turned on from the beginning. Neither game would be easy and the way each contest unfolded would only add to the growing tension and drama.

There were just over 13,000 fans in Boston to watch the Giants and Brave battle. But some 31,755 fans nearly filled Shibe Park in Philly, with thousands of them traveling down from Brooklyn. They would witness an epic battle that proved all over again that Jackie Robinson was one of the greatest competitors ever to play the game.

Larry Jansen was the Giants' starter and would be gunning for his twenty-second victory of the year. He was opposed by journeyman right-hander Jim Wilson, who had just a 7–7 record. With that matchup the New Yorkers had to be considered solid favorites. The Giants were also coming into the contest having won their last six games in succession.

Yet it was the Braves who broke on top first. Bob Addis, the centerpiece in the Dascoli-disputed run against the Dodgers, opened the frame with a double, went to third on a one-out grounder to second, then came home on a base hit by old friend Sid Gordon. But Jansen bore down, got out of the jam without further damage, and then began pitching like the 20-game winner he was.

The Giants, in the meantime, began chipping away at Wilson. With one out in the second, Bobby Thomson came up. The Scot worked the count to to three and one, then caught a Wilson fastball and drove it high and deep off the scoreboard above the left field fence. It was Bobby's thirtieth home run of the year and perhaps his biggest one yet. The New Yorkers had pulled even.

In the third they took the lead. Jansen started it with a single, followed by a Stanky base hit. Sibby Sisti made a sparkling play to knock down Dark's shot up the middle and forced Stanky at second, Jansen moving to third. Then Don Mueller waved his magic wand and sent a run-scoring single to right. The Giant bench erupted in shouts and screams. The New Yorkers had pulled in front, 2–1, and losing leads wasn't something the Giants had done very often in the last month and a half.

There was more reason for the Giants to cheer. Things weren't going well for the Dodgers. Dressen had started Preacher Roe on just two days' rest and despite his brilliant 22–3 record, the Preacher didn't have it. The veteran southpaw failed to survive the second inning as the Phils scored four times to jump on top. When the score was posted in Boston, a huge roar went up from the crowd, as well as from the Giant bench.

Al Dark and Monte Irvin combined to give the Giants a third run in the fifth. Dark singled, swiped second, and rode home on an Irvin single. The way Jansen was pitching, the 3–1 margin appeared secure. And it looked even better moments later when the scoreboard updated the Dodger game. Though the Brooks had gotten a run in the third, the Phils came back with a pair of their own and suddenly had a sizable 6–1 margin. It began to look as if the Giants were just a couple of hours away from celebrating a pennant.

The Giant game was breezing along. Jansen and Boston relievers Max Surkont and Vern Bickford matched goose eggs right into the ninth inning. In Philly, however, an old-fashioned slugfest, complete with a slew of pitching changes and delays, was slowing everything down.

The Dodgers had bounced back to score another run in the fourth, then three in the fifth, making it a 6–5 game. Robinson had tripled home one run in that frame, partially redeeming himself from a bad start that saw him hit into a double play in the first and look at a third strike in the third. Robby had also failed to grab an Ashburn grounder in the second which went through for a two-run single.

With Clyde King pitching, the Dodgers hoped to stay in it, but King didn't have any more luck than Roe or Ralph Branca, who had followed the Preacher. Ralph had thrown an inning and a third before King took over. But a triple by Granny Hamner in the last of the fifth drove King from the mound and two more runs across the plate. The Phils led 8–5 after five. An inning later, at 3:35 P.M., the Dodgers would learn the result of the Giants game.

It was already the ninth inning in Boston as the Dodgers moved into the sixth. Jansen had been brilliant since the first inning, facing just 22 hitters from the second through the eighth, and the score was still 3–1 with the Braves coming up for their final turn at bat. But the last three outs didn't come easy.

Addis started things with his second double of the game. Jethroe followed with a bloop single that allowed Addis to go to third. When Earl Torgeson grounded into a force play, Addis scored the second Boston run. Jethroe, coming hard into second, spiked Stanky accidentally but the Brat held on for the putout, and after being checked by team trainer Doc Bowman, remained in the game. Then Jansen got Sid Gordon for the second out, but Walker Cooper scratched a single, putting both the tying and winning runs on base. Now Durocher had to make a big decision. Should he stay with his obviously tiring right-hander?

Former Giant Willard Marshall was up, a power hitter who could destroy his former teammates with one big swing. Leo started out of the dugout. The passage of four decades can sometimes alter memories, but Bill Rigney, who was watching from the dugout, recalls what happened next.

"When Leo went out I knew Larry was gone," Rigney related. "I remember Larry standing on the mound and when Leo crossed the first base foul line Larry walked off the mound and said something to him. Leo never reached the mound. He turned around and walked back to the dugout.

"Later, I couldn't wait to ask Larry what he said. He told me, 'Rig, I never did this before in my life, but I told Leo that I had come too far, that I wanted to get the last out.' Larry said Leo didn't say a thing, just turned around and went back to the dugout. I guess Leo had seen the dedication on the team and knew what they had gone through. This is probably a side of Leo that no one saw. He had enough respect for Larry to let him either win or lose. The game was his."

Jansen's version varies slightly. "I think Leo came out to make sure Stanky was all right because Eddie had been spiked when he forced Jethroe at second," said Larry. "He didn't say anything to me at first, but I had come off the mound to check on Eddie, too, and as we walked back we were pretty close. Leo said something like, 'Well, are you all right?' I said, 'Hell, yes.' And that's all I remember."

Either way, Leo decided to stay with his right-hander, and Jansen came through. He got Marshall to hit a fly to Irvin in left. Monte trotted over, made the catch, and the Giants had closed out the regular season with a huge win. The players went berserk, forgetting for the moment that the Dodger game was still in progress, and carried Jansen off the field.

"What a game! What a game!" Durocher shouted as he leaped on Jansen's back. "I knew you could do it," he told his pitcher. "I told these guys as far back as May that the only way we could lose would be by running out of games."

The score of the Dodger game was 8–5, Phils, at the time. There was no locker room party for the Giants. They showered quickly and headed for the railroad station to grab the train back to New York. Once on the train the Giants began their celebration.

"We really thought we had won the pennant," Bobby Thomson remembers. "So things were pretty wild on the train. Someone managed to bring some champagne. During the ride back to New York we kept getting reports from Philadelphia. It must have been one helluva game."

Bill Rigney was one who refused to count any chickens where the Dodgers were concerned. "I had said all along that Pee Wee and Jackie wouldn't let that team die," said Rig. "And that's just what happened in that final game with Philadelphia. Jackie Robinson simply refused to lose."

After taking the 8–5 lead after five, the Phillies stopped scoring. Dressen would bring in a parade of pitchers, including starters Erskine and Newcombe. In fact, big Newk would throw five and two-thirds innings just a day after hurling his shutout. Even doghouse-bound Clem Labine got into this one for an inning, his only appearance after giving up the grand slam to Willie Jones.

In the Dodger eighth, Hodges and Cox singled, then rode home on a pinch double by Rube Walker off the Phils' Carl Drews. Robin Roberts was called in to pitch and Furillo greeted him with a single that drove in pinch runner Don Thompson with the tying run. At 8–8, the game became a stalemate, a battle of attrition. At the end of nine it was still deadlocked. Then, in the twelfth inning, the Phils made a bid to win it and the Dodgers must have seen the entire season flashing before their eyes.

Newcombe was still on the mound and tiring. This time the Phils loaded the bases with just one out. Newk dug down deep and got Del Ennis on strikes. Now the lefty-hitting Eddie Waitkus was up. Waitkus slammed a low liner to the right of Robinson at second. It appeared ticketed for the outfield, the pennant-deciding hit. But Jackie raced over and at the last second dove headfirst after the ball. He made a sensational catch, his entire body outstretched in the air as the ball lodged in his glove. When he came down he landed hard, his right elbow jamming into his stomach. He lay on the ground, dazed, maybe even unconscious for a couple of seconds.

But he had made the catch and saved the game. On the train to New York, the Giants groaned when they heard the report. The flag wasn't theirs yet. Jackie slowly got to his feet and walked unsteadily to the dugout. Dizzy and feeling sick to his stomach, he refused to come out of the game.

With the game still knotted at 8–8 in the top of the fourteenth and well over four hours old, Jackie stepped to the plate. Roberts was still on the hill and had already retired Reese and Snider. Jackie worked the count to one and one and then on the next pitch swung from the heels. He sent a long drive over the left field wall for a home run. The Dodgers and their fans went wild as Robinson, still a bit unsteady from his diving catch, slowly circled the bases. It was now a 9–8 game.

Bud Podbielan, the Dodgers' seventh pitcher of the afternoon, retired the Phils in the bottom of the inning, leaving the tying run stranded on second base. In what had been the most gut-wrenching game of the year, the Dodgers had won . . . and had forced only the second pennant playoff in National League history.

"We were on the train when the news came in that the Dodgers had won their game," Jim Hearn remembers. "Leo walked over to me and with very little emotion said, 'Okay, Hearn. You pitch tomorrow.' Leo was that way and I loved him."

Bobby Thomson remembers the same scene. "Leo was very calm,

almost matter-of-fact about it," says Bobby. "He told Hearn he was pitching and tried to keep everything low-key. But I can remember thinking that, hell, we've got to play those Dodgers again and I wasn't looking forward to it. Part of the reason, I think, is that we all began feeling we had it won when they were so far behind early in the game. When they came from behind like that and won, well, it was quite a blow."

Needless to say, the Dodgers were elated. They had just taken their turn at coming back from the land of the dead. The emotion of the final games was so exhausting that some of the Dodgers had the same feeling as Thomson had—the reluctance to have to play more baseball against their archrivals.

"I sure remember the last game in Philly," said Pee Wee Reese. "Campy came up to me at one point and said, 'You know, if we win this today and the Giants win, we'll have to face that damned Maglie again.' "

By the time the Dodgers had beaten the Phils in their 14-inning marathon, Campanella had something else to worry about. The hard-hitting catcher had pulled a muscle in his right leg while running out a fourth-inning triple. The fact was, there would be no time for anyone to rest. The playoff would begin at Ebbets the next day, Monday, October 1. If it went three games through Wednesday, the winning team would then have a Thursday date at Yankee Stadium to begin the World Series.

For a team that had been in front by 13½ games on August 11, the Dodgers had barely made it, getting up off the canvas just as the count was reaching ten. In fact, Walter O'Malley admitted that he was just a whisker away from conceding the pennant to the Giants when his team trailed the Phils early in the game.

"When the Phillies were beating us by five runs yesterday I began to lose a little hope," O'Malley confessed. "In my mind I was going over the phrasing for the wire of congratulations I would send Horace. Then I said to myself, 'Wait, you're being a traitor.' So I put the idea out of my head. That's one wire I'm glad I never had to send."

The First Two Games

The playoffs meant a fresh start. Rule number one: Forget everything that happened before. Just concentrate on winning two games before they do. That's all there was to it. Neither team had an advantage. Or did they? Not only had the Giants come from way back, winning an amazing 37 of their final 44 games, but they had finished with the proverbial flourish, riding the crest of a 12-of-13 string and 7 in a row. The Dodgers had won only 6 of their last 13, though they did take the Phils twice under extremely trying circumstances to keep pace.

Still, the Dodgers had to be the more tired club. They didn't have those precious off days the last week. They were also a team acutely aware of being acclaimed the best ball club in years just before commencing to blow a big lead in an inordinately short amount of time. In addition, the boys from Flatbush had to deal with a manager who was a good baseball man, but for all intents and purposes not the kind of manager a team could rally around.

On the other hand, Durocher—the former raging bull, the man suspended from baseball for a year, the guy who hung out with George Raft, fought with umpires, and yelled, "Stick it in his ear!"— had a team that would follow him into an inferno, even if there was no way out.

Jim Hearn was the most rested of the Giant starters, and more rested than Dodger starter Ralph Branca, who had thrown one and a third innings the day before in Philadelphia. But neither manager really had a choice. Each had beaten his rivals twice during the year, but an exhausted Branca had lost five straight and was now 13–10. Hearn was at 16–9 and had come on strong in the second half.

However, unbeknownst to manager Durocher and most of the other Giants, all was not well with Jim Hearn. "I had a strained ligament in my left side," Hearn recalls. "It was pressing against a nerve that went down into my leg. I had almost been called on to pitch the final game in Boston. Leo told me Jansen had some stiffness in his shoulder and if he couldn't go, I was next in line. Larry ended up pitching a great game and it gave me an extra day to rest. The only people who knew about my ligament pull were Wes Westrum and the team trainer, Doc Bowman. In those days, you didn't complain about that kind of thing. You went out and pitched. Before I started to warm up, Doc Bowman and I went down the passageway behind the dugout and he rubbed my entire side with some hot salve. It felt great and helped to kill the pain. I knew I wasn't quite 100 percent, but I wanted to pitch. *I had to pitch."*

Wes Westrum rode to the park with Hearn that day. Leo had told his catcher early in the year to stay close to the pitching staff, talk to them, work with them, get to know them, baby them if necessary.

"Because of that I called 99 percent of the pitches thrown," said Westrum. "Leo would say, 'You're my catcher. You call it. If you get in trouble, look around for me behind you.'

"So Jim and I rode to the ballpark together that day, all the way into Brooklyn. During the entire ride we talked about how to pitch the Dodgers and what we had to do in certain situations. I knew Jim had a pull in his side and we agreed not to tell Leo about it. You simply played hurt back then.

"I know our talk helped Jim a lot. My job was to instill a sense of confidence in my pitchers and that day in Brooklyn Jim had a high sense of confidence which showed in the game. His only concern was the pain in his side, but Doc Bowman's salve managed to control it."

There were 30,707 screaming fans at Ebbets Field to watch the opener. The weather was warm, over 70 Indian summer degrees, as Hearn and Branca warmed up. The lineups were pretty much what they had been over the last month of the season. Stanky, Dark, Mueller, Irvin, Lockman, Thomson, Mays, and Westrum for the Giants.

Furillo, Reese, Snider, Robinson, Campanella, Pafko, Hodges, and Cox for the Dodgers.

Neither team scored in the first as both right-handers appeared loose and threw easily. There were no signs of weariness in Branca, while Hearn didn't look like a man pitching with a strained ligament. Then, in the bottom of the second, Hearn faltered, if only for a second. With two out, Andy Pafko, the man who was supposed to assure the Dodgers a pennant, did his piece by whacking a Hearn offering into the left field seats, his twenty-ninth home run of the year.

There hadn't been much for Dodger fans to cheer about during the last month, and when the ball disappeared into the seats, the crowd nearly tore the roof off the old ballpark. But the signs that all was not well with the Dodger world began to show in the next inning. With two out in the bottom of the third, Furillo hit a screamer down the third base line. Bobby Thomson lunged for the ball and made an electrifying catch. But the grab wouldn't match what Thomson would do in the top of the fourth.

In that frame, Monte Irvin was nicked on the left arm by a Branca fastball between fly outs by Mueller and Lockman. With two down, Bobby stepped up. Branca had two strikes on the Scot when he tried to come inside with a fastball. He got the pitch a little too far out over the plate and Thomson stepped into it, sending a drive over the wall in left center. Irvin trotted home in front of Bobby and his thirty-first homer of the year. More importantly, the blast gave the Giants a 2–1 lead.

"I hit a fastball and it was a great feeling to see it traveling into the stands," Bobby said. It was a 385–foot home run over the 375–foot spot in left-center. The blast would have been an easy out in the Polo Grounds. But who cared? It turned out to be the game winner and that's the only thing that mattered."

But it wasn't only the home run that Bobby thinks about when he recollects that first game. People expected Bobby to hit home runs. What they didn't know was how he would hold up at third when the chips were down. He showed them in the sixth inning.

"Before the game I was thinking about being in the playoffs and wondering how I would react," recalls Bobby. I had grabbed the Furillo liner earlier, but that was just a reflex thing. The home run, of course, was a great feeling. We still had that 2–1 lead in the sixth when Furillo came up again. This was the play that I always remembered.

"Carl topped one down the third base line. I came running in and
. . . boom . . . scoop . . . one motion. It's a do-or-die play and I made
it, threw him out. I didn't think about it at the time, but later I said,
'Hey, you sonofagun, that was a helluva play you made.' "

Bobby was on his way to becoming one of the heroes of the game
with the two outstanding fielding plays and his home run. But he had
help. In the eighth, Monte Irvin caught a Branca slider and put it out
of the park for a 3–1 lead. Jim Hearn kept throwing that sinker, the one
he discovered when the Giant coaches brought his delivery down
from straight overhand to three-quarters. On occasions when he got
in a little trouble, he was bailed out by four Giant double plays.

In the ninth, Reese walked with one out, giving Dodger fans one last
glimmer of hope. Durocher had Koslo and Spencer in the pen and said
he would have gone to one of them if Snider had gotten a hit. But
Hearn retired the Duke, then closed it out to complete his five-hit gem.
The Giants had won their eighth straight victory, and were just a game
away from winning it all. In addition, Dressen's strategy of choosing
Ebbets to open the playoffs hadn't worked. Down a game, Charley
now had to lead his club into enemy territory, the Polo Grounds.

After the game, the Giant clubhouse was delirious. The New Yorkers had won on enemy turf, clearing a major hurdle to the title.

"It's hard to explain how I felt," Jim Hearn said. "You wait so long
and then suddenly you're in the big game of your life. I waited five
years for this and now I was the happiest guy in the world because it
went so well."

It did. Hearn had scattered just five hits, shackling the Dodger
hitters with his sinking fastball. Durocher said he was hoarse from
yelling and refused to pose for pictures because of a superstition.

"I hadn't posed for a picture in two weeks," the manager said. "I
finally gave in up in Boston after Saturday's game and look what
happened. There'll be no pictures of me while this is on."

Leo had other urgent business to take care of. Mays had been
hitless in the first playoff game and battling a slump. A strikeout in the
sixth with two on had really shaken the youngster. He was having
another confidence crisis and, as usual, his manager was right there.

"You're my man," said Leo, as members of the press picked up on
the dialogue. "You're gonna stay in there all the way, Willie. Don't
worry about nothin'."

Dressen, meanwhile, was carping. "That Jim Hearn was just asking to be knocked out. But the worst break we got all afternoon was in the fourth inning when Campanella hit into a double play. If he doesn't have a bad leg they don't get him. The run would have scored if Campanella hadn't been limping. I know something else. A hit by Campanella and Hearn would have been out of there."

That might not have been the only thing Dressen had to worry about. A *Brooklyn Eagle* story said the manager might well be fighting for his job. "Should Dressen lose out," the story said "it would not be primarily because the Dodgers lost, but because Charley claimed their victory too early in the season—and also claimed most of the credit for it."

The inner man of Charles Dressen was a secret no longer. It seems as if everyone had finally realized how he operated. But that would have to be forgotten for at least another day or two. Nothing could usurp the importance of the upcoming game.

Neither manager would commit on his pitcher for the Tuesday tilt. Durocher said he was deciding between Maglie and Sheldon Jones. Had the Dodgers won the opener, Maglie would surely have gotten the call, tired or not. But with the one-game cushion and the return to the Polo Grounds, Leo had room to maneuver. He could gamble with Jones and if it didn't work out, have Maglie ready for the final game on an extra day's rest.

Dressen indicated that it would be either the veteran Erskine or the rookie Labine. Even the mention of Labine's name must have been a small embarrassment for Charley. But Charley really didn't have much of a choice. Erskine had thrown two innings in the marathon game against Philadelphia and although Labine also pitched an inning in that one, he was definitely the fresher pitcher thanks to his days in the Dressen doghouse.

The announcements of both starting pitchers were made on game day, but in different ways. "Charley was from the old school and didn't believe in pitching coaches," Carl Erskine recalls. "It's hard for me to remember our coaches in '51, but I do recall Ted Lyons coming over as pitching coach for a stretch with us and Charley just ignored him. Even though I had a pretty good year in '51 I remember not really feeling secure about my spot on the team. Clem was a rookie, so he was also trying to establish himself. When Clem and I were heading to the Polo Grounds for the second game we both knew one of us would be pitching, but Charley wouldn't tell us which one. It wasn't until we got there that Charley picked Clem."

Labine remembers a similar set of circumstances before the crucial second game. "I wasn't sure if I was going to pitch," Clem says. "It was between Carl and myself and we had both pitched briefly in the last game in Philly. Charley didn't tell us until we reached the ballpark.

"I can recall feeling pressure when I found out I was pitching, but it was a nice pressure. I don't know if a statement like that can be appreciated by everyone, but if you like to play the game it's the kind of pressure you like. You want the ball. That's just how I felt on October 2. I wanted to pitch that ball game."

Labine's recollections jibe with those of Irving Rudd, the Dodger publicist in 1951. The team had its own bus traveling from Brooklyn to the Polo Grounds the morning of the game. Rudd remembers picking up Labine with a few of the other ball players at the St. George Hotel. The youngster sat down next to the veteran PR man.

"Clem knew he might be pitching that day and I remember him being very quiet and reserved on the ride to the Polo Grounds," Rudd said. "The rookies didn't say too much back then and Clem was kind of keeping his place. But he also had to know that his team's entire season could be riding on his shoulders. That would be a big responsibility for a rookie and I remember Clem having a very determined, very businesslike expression on his face. He looked like a guy who was ready to pitch."

Unlike Dressen, Leo Durocher didn't make a solitary decision. Leo had been consulting with both his players and coaches all year long and the second game of the playoffs was no exception.

"When Sal Maglie and I got to the ballpark that morning Leo called us into his office," Larry Jansen said. "The three of us then sat down and discussed what we should do. Leo came right out and said, 'Boys, I want your help and suggestions.' He said one of his options was pitching Sal with two days' rest and then, if a third game was necessary, I would go on two days' rest. The other option was to gamble with Jones and have the both of us ready for a third game.

"Sal came right out and told Leo he'd feel better with the extra day of rest and I said I would feel better not having to go Wednesday on two days' rest, but that I'd pitch any time Leo wanted me to. Sal felt that way, too, but we both said we'd definitely feel better with the extra day of rest.

"Leo just looked at us and said, 'Okay, I'll save you both for tomorrow and we'll go with Jones today.' Leo didn't always take our advice, but he always listened to what his players had to say. From everything I've heard, Dressen was just the opposite."

So it was Labine, at 4–1, facing right-hander Sheldon Jones, who had pitched some fine ball games during the stretch run despite his 6–10 record. There were 38,609 fans in the stadium beneath Coogan's Bluff. Even though the ancient park was known as the Polo Grounds, the sport of polo was never played there. The horse and mallet game had been played at an even older field of the same name. This version of the Polo Grounds, in existence before the turn of the century, could hold nearly 55,000 fans and had been the scene of many historic baseball games.

The only lineup change for the second contest was a significant one. Roy Campanella's leg had tightened up, forcing manager Dressen to start Rube Walker, who was a fine defensive catcher but not nearly the hitter Campy was. The weather was much cooler than it had been the day before, temperature in the 50s, the sky overcast.

Pee Wee Reese started things off for the Dodgers in the first inning by swatting a one-out single. Jones then fanned Duke Snider and out came Dressen, who promptly engaged plate umpire Larry Goetz in a heated discussion. It was discovered later that Charley felt Jones was throwing a spitter, though the ump disagreed.

"Jones was wetting his fingers and not drying them off," Dressen said later. "I told Goetz about it, but he said it was only a spinner."

Perhaps Dressen would have pressed the point further had Robinson not picked out Jones's first offering and driven a line drive over the 315-foot sign in left. Just like that, the Dodgers had a 2–0 lead. Meanwhile, Labine was keeping the Giants off-balance with his assortment of sinkers and curves.

In the top of the third, the Dodgers threatened again, and while they didn't score, Durocher replaced Jones with George Spencer, the workhorse reliever who was making his fifty-seventh appearance of the year. Spencer shut the door on the Dodgers in the third, then the Giants started a rally of their own in the bottom of the inning.

It would be the biggest crisis of the game for Labine. The Giants loaded the bases with two out and had their hottest hitter, Bobby Thomson, at the plate. A hit and the game was tied, an extra base hit and the Giants could well take the lead. Labine bore down. Thomson had been the hitting and fielding star of the first game and he was the guy the Giants wanted up there.

In what was a major turning point in the game, Labine fanned Thomson on a curve and the Giants' biggest threat went by the boards. After that, the Dodgers began climbing all over the New York relievers. They got a run in the fifth on a Snider double and Robinson single, then broke through for three more in the sixth.

With the lights turned on to compensate for the increasing darkness of the day, Hodges started the inning with a homer. Then the Giants got sloppy. Thomson made a throwing error, the infield botched a rundown, Spencer gave up a walk and a couple of singles. When the inning ended the Dodgers had three more runs and a 6–0 lead, virtually wrapping up the ball game. Even a 41-minute rain delay didn't cause Labine to lose either his stuff or his rhythm. The Giant hitters were helpless before the rookie's repertoire, fastballs mixed with sinkers and curves. Al Corwin pitched the final three innings for the Giants and allowed the Dodgers another four runs.

When it was over, the Dodgers had a 10–0 victory to even the playoff series at a game apiece. Instead of a close, hard-fought contest between bitter rivals, this one resembled the proverbial laugher. Labine had thrown a six-hitter and the entire day seemed to renew the spirit of the Dodgers. The gloom and doom that had settled over the team the day before had disappeared. They hoped the home runs by Robinson, Hodges, Pafko, and Walker meant that their bats were back. Now, the Dodgers were not only alive again, but were within one game of the championship. Better yet, their one-sided triumph had come at the Polo Grounds.

After the game, young Labine was both gracious and appreciative. "I wasn't tired, but I was lucky," he told the press. "You have to be lucky when you pitch a shutout anywhere. I used mostly a curve and a fastball sinker. But it's not so much what you throw but what you can get over the plate."

Labine said his strikeout pitch to Thomson was a curve out of the strike zone. At that point, Dressen, who was standing nearby, jumped into the conversation.

"You think I am going to have him throw a fast one in there?" said Charley. "Heck with that. If Labine doesn't get it over or Thomson doesn't swing, one run is better than four. That guy wasn't going to get a chance to hit one into the stands."

Dressen may have been too happy at that moment to realize that the fallout from Labine's brilliant performance would be dropping directly on him. To see the way Labine took charge in the biggest must game of the year presented the obvious question: Where did Clem go after giving up the grand slammer to Willie Jones on September 21? When the question was asked, Charley answered quickly and with a smile.

"There were some stories written that I had given up on this kid after he lost one to the Phillies following four straight wins," the manager said. "Please believe me when I say I'm not trying to criticize fellows who criticize me. But that simply isn't true. He's been in the bullpen almost every day, but I never was in a spot to use him. I wanted him in there in a close one if I needed a relief pitcher. But we either were too far ahead or too far behind. This was the clutch game and he was wonderful. I'm pleased but not too greatly surprised."

To all the knowing scribes in the room, Dressen's story just didn't wash. Labine was a kid who gave up only four runs in his first four starts. With Branca tiring badly, Erskine fatigued, Roe with a stiff arm, how could the Dodger manager not find a place for a kid like Labine? An interesting comparison can be made between Labine's season and that of Al Corwin, the young pitcher the Giants brought up in midyear. Both hurlers finished the year with identical 5–1 records, but Labine had a 2.20 earned run average to 3.66 for Corwin. Clem completed five of his six starts, while Corwin finished just three of eight. On paper, Labine was the more effective pitcher. Yet he ended up missing one or two crucial starts because he was doghoused for an order he didn't follow. Durocher, on the other hand, fully appreciated Corwin's contribution to the Giant cause.

"The kid's part in the pennant race may be too quickly overlooked," Leo said late in the season. "But I don't think we'd have even come close without him. He gave the whole staff a breathing spell and the fact that he was able to step in there and win for even a brief while enabled me to rest Maglie and Jansen more than I could have if he hadn't been around."

The two managers had traveled different roads down the homestretch. But after the second game of the playoffs Labine's tenure in the doghouse was over. The Dodgers had finally stopped the Giants' runaway train. The New Yorkers came in riding the crest of eight straight wins and hadn't lost a game since September 20.

One Dodger who wasn't celebrating, however, was Jackie Robinson. He knew that the whole season was still riding on tomorrow's game.

"What have we accomplished?" he asked reporters. "As far as I can see, we haven't done a darn thing. It's just as if the season were beginning. No lead, no nothing. If we don't take the Giants tomorrow, I will still say we haven't done one darn thing."

Looking back four decades, Clem Labine still has memories of that do-or-die ball game. "Most of the guys had butterflies before the game began," says Labine. "But once I got the ball, they disappeared. I also had the benefit of starting the game right. Eddie Stanky, who led off, was always a good contact hitter, and I wasn't a strikeout pitcher. But I fanned Eddie on three pitches and I can remember saying, 'Boy, if I can strike out this guy on three pitches I must really have something going for me today.' And I did. After that it was pretty easy."

As for Leo and the Giants, they simply had to regroup. The blowout undoubtedly surprised them. "They just beat us, that's all," a subdued Durocher said. "There's nothing you can do about a game like that. If you gotta lose one, that's the way to do it—big."

Bobby was also low-keying his strikeout. When reporters asked him about it he simply said, "Labine made a very good pitch, his typical sinker, always a tough pitch to hit. It might have been out of the strike zone, but with two strikes, I had to protect the plate and I swung."

Now, after 156 games, the ball clubs were still deadlocked and it was all coming down to one final game for the pennant.

One Game to Go

The turning point was definitely striking out Bobby with the bases full. He was the hot hitter, the guy who had hit a big home run off Ralph the day before. To strike him out and hear the roar of the crowd, even the Giant fans, kind of gives you a real boost. After that it was all pretty easy.

—Clem Labine

The ball I hit off Branca for a homer in the first game was out over the plate, a good pitch. Big game and it's just sheer excitement. You hit a big home run like that and then wonder how it happened. After the game they whisked me onto the "Happy Felton Show." Happy was a big guy with dark-rimmed glasses and a wide grin. He would wear a Dodger uniform when he did his pre- and postgame shows. He had his "Knot Hole Gang Show" before all the games at Ebbet Field, and after the game he'd have "Talk to the Stars," with a member of each team as the guests. So I was on Talk to the Stars and when I got back to the locker room it was pretty empty.

Stanky was about the only one still there and I remember finding it odd, because he never said anything to me, just gave me a look. It ran through my mind that it was a funny way for him to act after we had just won a such a big game. But Eddie was a great competitor and maybe he felt we hadn't really won anything yet, that we still had to win another game before we could start counting chickens. He might have already been thinking about the next game, which, of course, didn't turn out so well.

Labine really did a job on us. I always had trouble hitting Clem. He had that good sinkerball and kept it low. He fanned me with two outs and the bases loaded in the third. You don't forget situations like that overnight. I wasn't a guess hitter. I had to see the ball. I looked at it and just didn't get it. Then our relievers got hit hard and they buried us. So we were all even.

When I got to the parking lot after the game my intentions were to go home and have dinner with my mother. But I didn't look forward to sitting around all night and brooding about the ball game.

It was then that some friends of mine approached. One of them was Dee Coppetelli, who owned the Tavern on the Green on Staten Island. They talked me into having dinner with them at the Downtown Athletic Club. They felt it would be the best thing for me so I could enjoy the evening, relax, and forget about the ball game for a few hours. For me, it turned out to be the greatest tonic in the world. When I got home, I was able to get a good night's sleep, even though we were facing the biggest game of our lives the next day.

I always drove to the ballpark when the team was at home, heading up West Side Drive about 10:00 in the morning and getting to the park by 11:00. I was the only guy on the team who lived on Staten Island, so I usually drove by myself, unless a friend like Al Corbin came along. I never thought about the car breaking down, or getting caught in a traffic jam, but I do recall getting stopped by a cop one day. Maybe I was too anxious to get to the park, or running a little late. Anyway, this officer has me pulled over somewhere on West Side Drive and suddenly who should show up but Stanky. He was driving by and when he saw the cop standing by my car he got a big grin on his face and pulled up in front of us. Eddie loved this kind of stuff and he started in with the cop right away.

"You know who this man is?" he said. "He's Bobby Thomson and he's gonna be late for his meeting with Durocher. Leo will fine him for sure."

Eddie went on and on about it, nonstop, almost like he was arguing with an umpire. Heck, I hadn't even gotten out of the car, never had a chance to open my mouth.

"This man is gonna get fined $50 if he misses the team meeting," Eddie kept saying. "Can't he get you a couple of tickets and we can all forget about this? We got a big game today and he was probably worried about it."

And that's just what happened. I ended up getting the cop a couple of tickets and he let me off. That was Eddie, the Brat. Always ready to put his two cents in.

No one stopped me on the way to the park the day of the final game. But there were a lot of thoughts going through my mind. I had the distinct feeling that if I could only get three hits today it could be a big factor in our winning. It also ran through my mind that this was a special day, a once-in-a-lifetime day, the most important game of my life. I had never approached a game that way before.

I got to the park in plenty of time. We all knew that Big Newk would be in there for the Dodgers. There was a kind of nervousness in the clubhouse. We were nervous, yes, but looking forward to the day. It was exciting and nerve-wracking at the same time.

Warming up before the game, a different kind of feeling went through me. I remember this clearly because it was such an unusual thing for me to do. I suddenly found myself looking at all our guys, at each one, and this thought went flooding into my head: "Hey, I'm glad that Al Dark's on my side. There's Whitey Lockman, glad he's on my team. And Stanky, Irvin, Mueller, and all of them."

As I looked around I found myself gaining comfort, knowing they would be going out onto the field with me. I was proud of all those guys, proud of what we had done and having them there with me really made me feel good.

It was Stanky who finally broke the ice. Eddie had a way of doing that. At one point before the game started he looked at all of us, smiled, and said, "Come on, we're not playing for our lives. Let's go out and have some fun."

The Moment of Truth

The air hung heavy over New York City on the morning of October 3. With the temperature once again unseasonably warm, heading into the 70s, it felt more like late summer than early fall. There was also the threat of rain in the air and some say that's one reason the crowd was so amazingly small for a game of this magnitude. Just 34,320 fans paid their way into the Polo Grounds to witness the historic contest. There are other theories, such as people anticipating a sellout and feeling tickets wouldn't be available or that it was difficult for people to leave work for an afternoon game back then.

Whatever the reason, the relatively modest crowd was surprising. When the players are reminded today about the size of the crowd, to a man they express surprise. In everyone's mind, the enormity of the moment dictated a packed house. Today, a game like that played in a metropolitan area such as New York would have enough people clamoring for tickets to fill the equivalent of four Polo Grounds. Yet there were close to 20,000 seats begging to be filled when the game began.

That didn't dampen the enthusiasm of the players. Each and every one of them knew exactly what was at stake. As promised, Durocher had Sal Maglie ready to go. The Barber had won five of six from the Dodgers during the season and would be putting his 23–6 record on the line. Facing Sal would be Don Newcombe, who, at 20–9 on the year, was still a disappointment to those with the wild notion that he was talented enough to win 30. Newk had been a hot pitcher, however, throwing 14 2/3 innings on Saturday and Sunday, and playing an instrumental role in getting the Dodgers into the playoffs. He had topped the Giants five times in '51, losing just twice.

As the crowd poured into the ballpark, preparations were being made in the broadcast booth. Ernie Harwell, who teamed with Russ Hodges to call all the Giant games on radio and television that year, recalls one reason why the event was so special.

"The 1951 playoffs were the first sports event televised live from coast to coast," Harwell explained recently. "The coaxial cable that enabled the transmission to go live was installed just a few months earlier. Prior to that, programs aired in New York had to be filmed and the film flown to the West Coast. They used to do that with the "Ed Sullivan Show"—film the live show in New York on Sunday night, then fly the film to California the next day.

"Since we had both radio and television coverage, Russ and I would alternate every three innings. For the final game, I was slated to do the first three and last three innings on the television side, with the middle three on radio. Russ, of course, did the opposite. They didn't record the TV broadcast or do playbacks then, so unfortunately there was no video record of the game."

Soon the players began to appear on the field. Because his leg was still in bad shape, Campanella was again a scratch, the only regular on both teams who couldn't play. Rube Walker would be catching Newk. Campy's counterpart, Giant catcher Wes Westrum, who had played hurt for much of the year, probably didn't know it when he arrived at the ballpark, but he was the man who inadvertently set the theme for the ball game before even leaving his home.

While eating breakfast and almost without thinking, Wes scribbled four words on a notepad that was sitting before him on the kitchen table. When his wife came in she saw the words and would remind her husband about them later.

The four words were: "Today is the day."

Perhaps the biggest game in the history of both franchises began with Maglie on the mound and Carl Furillo at the plate. As usual, the veteran right-hander was unshaven, his surly countenance staring in at Furillo. From the dugout, Leo Durocher began warming up with his own brand of baseball rhetoric.

"Stick it in his ear!" the Lip yelled in his sharp, cutting voice. Furillo was always one of his favorite targets. "Come on, Sal, stick it in his ear!"

In the stands, Leo's actress wife Laraine Day sat alongside Mrs. John McGraw, wife of the most successful manager in Giants history and a man whose fighting spirit lived on in Durocher. It was as if the two women were hoping that by joining forces, the best qualities from both their husbands would filter down to the field and help Leo's troops.

Maglie opened the game by striking out Furillo, but only after he had run the count to two and two. Then he seemed to falter, walking Reese on five pitches and Snider on just four. Trouble already. The game was barely under way, the Dodgers had a pair of runners, and the Barber couldn't find the plate. Maglie was known as a slow starter, often working through a shaky inning or two before finding the groove. Only this time catcher Wes Westrum noticed that it was something more and it had the veteran catcher worried.

"Sal was exhausted from all the pitching he had done over the last month," Westrum said. "Remember, he wasn't a young kid and as soon as the game started I could see how tired he was by the way his curveball was acting. It was coming in high and hanging. Sal probably knew it, too. But he was a guy who knew how to pitch. If he didn't have the real sharp curve then he would have to rely on keeping the hitters off balance and not allowing them to dig in."

Robinson was up next and the ultimate competitor did his thing again, smacking a first-pitch single to left and driving in the first run of the ball game. The Dodger bench erupted, as did nearly the entire borough of Brooklyn—in taverns, on street corners, in all the apartments, houses, bars, restaurants, and businesses, wherever people were able to find the nearest radio or television. Wouldn't it be great if the Dodgers could make quick work of Maglie and cruise to the pennant in another laugher? Then the celebration in Flatbush could begin early.

In the Giant bullpen, Larry Jansen began throwing easily, glancing nervously at the field and hoping his friend and teammate would settle down. "The tip-off on Sal was whether he was high in the first inning," Jansen would say later. "As Wes said, he was coming in high. The curve was hanging. That's probably why Leo had me throwing early. Sal and I were both low ball pitchers and when we couldn't keep the ball down we got in trouble. But the thing with Sal was his toughness. He was so tough and gritty out there that he could settle down in a hurry, a lot faster than the rest of us."

Jansen was right. Maglie wasn't about to let this one get away in the first inning. He reached back and got Pafko and Hodges, on a force-out and pop-up, to escape the inning without further damage. A 1–0 lead was significant—any lead would be in a game to decide it all—but the Giants had been overcoming leads and obstacles for the last six weeks. They kept up the chatter as if they knew they would be back in it before long.

"Let 'er rip!"

"Let's go get 'em!"

"Let 'er rip!"

On the Dodger side of the ledger there was Newcombe. The big guy looked overpowering in the first inning, pumping that explosive fastball, the same one that had shut out the Phils four days earlier. It was no surprise that Newk started so strongly. The combination of adrenaline and the competitive spirit just added to the enormous nature of the game. The Giants could only hope he wouldn't throw like this for all nine innings. Newk felt he could.

"I always had a theory throughout my career," Newk would say. "If you don't get me in the first seven innings you're gonna have to play like hell to get me in the eighth and ninth. I felt I became stronger because of my conditioning. I ran a great deal back then and I didn't care if it was 95 degrees in St. Louis. My body seemed to respond to my need to get stronger in the eighth and ninth innings."

Newk zipped through the Giants in the first, then Maglie went out and did what Westrum said he would. The Barber compensated for his fatigue and the lack of his best curve by mixing his pitches, moving the ball in and out, and keeping the Dodgers off-balance. It was hard for power hitters to get a good rip when Maglie moved the ball like that, often letting that big curve dance right under their chins.

In the bottom of the second, the Giants showed signs of life. With one out, Lockman singled and Bobby Thomson came up for his first at bat of the day. Still on the hitting tear that had coincided with his move to third base on July 20, Bobby sprang out of his crouch and whistled a Newcombe fastball down the left field line. In Bobby's mind, the ball had double written all over it. He put his head down, pumped his arms, and got that long stride going. As he flashed around first and headed for second he could already envision the go-ahead runs in scoring position with just one out.

What he didn't see, however, was Whitey Lockman. His teammate had rounded second as the strong-armed Pafko fielded the ball in the corner, then thought twice about trying for third. With the Giants down by just a single run early in the game, Lockman decided to play it safe. He retreated to second, only to see the flying Scot, head down, bearing in on him.

Billy Cox saw it, too. The Dodger third sacker took the throw from Pafko, whirled, and fired to Robinson at second. Bobby was a sitting duck. Realizing his mistake, he took a few steps back toward first, but Jackie quickly put the tag on him. Embarrassed, Bobby walked off the field slowly. There wasn't anyone watching who didn't realize he had pulled a real baserunning rock that became even more significant when Newcombe got Mays on a fly out to end the inning without further damage.

"It was my mistake all the way," Bobby would admit. "When I hit the ball I knew it was a double, knew I could be sitting on second. I also figured that, with a running start, Whitey could have made third. I was so determined to get to second that I didn't watch him. I got there, all right, but Whitey hadn't left.

"I felt silly, but I didn't get down on myself. I was a player in a very tense ball game where *every* little thing was important. I couldn't be thinking, Hey, stupid, you made a mistake, don't make another one. I've read other accounts that say I was down on myself then. Never happened. If anything, I felt a very special kind of presence that day. I won't say it was a premonition. But it was a very positive feeling and it stayed with me until the end of the game."

After the Giant threat in the second, both right-handers found the groove. They might have had an assist from the weather. With the overcast becoming lower and thicker, the lights were turned on in the third inning. Newcombe looked powerful and almost unhittable. Maglie, still hanging the curve and still pitching higher than he would have liked, continued to use all the guile learned from his years of struggle to keep the Dodger hitters off-balance.

As usual, the Barber didn't hesitate about pitching close, backing hitters off the plate, coming back low and outside, then high, low, in, out. For a guy who wasn't at his sharpest, Maglie was pitching a brilliant baseball game. The Dodgers were mounting no serious threats against him.

In the fifth inning the Dodgers still held a 1–0 lead when Thomson came up with one out. Once again, Bobby got in that crouch that had helped turn his season around at the plate. He waited and then stepped into a Newcombe fastball. Once again, he hit a shot into the left field corner and this time showed his long stride and great speed in legging out a double, his second hit of the game.

But Newcombe wasn't ready to concede anything. He reached back to fan the rookie Mays for the second out. With Maglie on deck, Newk pitched carefully to the always dangerous Westrum and walked the Giant catcher. Since it was still a one-run game and only the fifth inning, Durocher allowed his pitcher to hit, and Newk promptly struck out the Barber to retire the side.

"Up to that point Newcombe was really firing the ball, looking strong and confident," Bobby recalls. "No one had to say it. Everyone on the ball club was aware of the way he was pitching. But we just kept hollerin' anyway. Our guys were brought up to holler, to root for the guys who were playing. That was Leo's way and it didn't change against Newcombe that day. We were out there trying to do our best, but for the first six innings it wasn't a helluva lot."

The score remained 1–0 as the game moved through the fifth inning and into the sixth. Neither pitcher was showing signs of losing his grip on the ball game. Newcombe may have had the better stuff at this point, but Maglie continued to pitch a brilliant tactical game.

In the sixth inning, and without any word from the dugout, a big right-hander with the number 13 on his back got up in the Brooklyn bullpen. Ralph Branca began to throw. He looked like an old man trying to get rid of the kinks.

"My arm was tight," Branca says. "I had thrown a lot of pitches on Monday and I couldn't even throw the ball the full 60 feet at first. So I just started lobbing the ball. I kept throwing from the sixth inning on, just to get loose. I knew then if they needed me there was no way I could get loose in a hurry."

But it didn't seem the Dodgers would need anyone the way Newk was going. The sixth inning went into the books, the score still 1–0. By this time the partisan crowd was growing restless. Everyone knew that one swing of the bat could equal one run, but by the bottom of the seventh, reality was beginning to sink in. The Giants had just nine outs left to get that one run. Most of the 34,000 plus fans took advantage of the traditional seventh inning stretch. Ernie Harwell settled into the TV booth again, having switched with Russ Hodges in the top of the inning.

Now Irvin stood in against Newk. Monte was hitless on the day but had already wrapped up the National League RBI title with 121. The strong left fielder had put together a great year, his best since his belated entry into the majors. He had been a big gun all year and surely didn't want to take the collar in this one. He hung tough against Newk and duplicated what Thomson had done in the fifth, slamming a double to left.

Lockman was next, a left-handed batter facing the righty Newcombe. If big Don was starting to tire, it might be time to have Lockman, a good contact hitter, swing away. But Durocher didn't gamble. He had Lockman bunt. The Dodgers didn't play the ball well. Irvin scooted to third and Lockman was safe at first. Newcombe took a deep breath, as if trying to fight off his growing fatigue. Now Bobby Thomson was at the plate again. Bobby already had two hits on the day and Newk had to be careful.

"When I came up I was thinking how Leo had Whitey bunting," Thomson recalls. "It was Durocher baseball, to play for the tie at home, especially the way Newcombe was pitching. But here I was with a real chance to get the tying run home. Monte was 90 feet away with no one out. I knew it wouldn't be easy. With the tying run on third, Newk was going to pitch me tough.

"I fouled off the first two pitches and suddenly I was in the hole with an 0-2 count. I can't ever remember fighting for my life like I did during that one time at bat. I knew I had to get that run in and I was determined to do it one way or another. The next pitch was nearly under my chin, well off the plate, just a bad ball. And I swung. I was fighting so hard I didn't want to let anything go past me. Somehow, I got a piece of it and fouled it over the Dodger dugout.

"I stepped in again. Newk's next pitch was a hard slider away, which could have been an inch or two off the plate. But I couldn't afford to take anything close in that situation. The fly ball I hit to center was the result of an arm swing with my fanny not really in it. But fortunately, I made enough contact to hit the ball far enough to get the run home."

Snider was playing in medium center field, deep enough to allow Irvin to score with the tying tally. The Duke didn't even bother to try for a play at the plate. He just lobbed the ball back to Reese. Although Newk shut the door after that, the Giants had knotted the game at 1–1. The Giant crowd finally had something to cheer about. Hope was renewed. Like the long, hard-fought season, it looked as if the game was going down to the wire. After 156 games plus seven innings of baseball, the teams were still deadlocked. What Giant fans couldn't know was just how ephemeral their joy would be. It didn't take them long to find out. Sal Maglie had been in such a good groove since the first inning it was hard to envision the Barber losing it now. But in the Dodger eighth something happened.

"I think the Dodger hitters simply decided to dig in," Wes Westrum remembers. "Sal had been keeping them off-balance and really not letting them get set. But they came out in the eighth with a determination to hang in there, to get set and take some good cuts."

Maglie retired Furillo to start the inning. But then Reese singled and Snider followed with a sharp base hit to right, Reese going to third. Now, the dangerous Robinson was up. In the Giant bullpen, Jansen quickly shed his warm-up jacket and began throwing. It would take him a few minutes to get ready, but the Dodgers didn't oblige by waiting. When one of Maglie's curves broke too far, it skittered by the lunging Westrum and rolled back to the screen. Reese scampered home on the wild pitch and the Dodgers had a 2–1 lead.

Durocher quickly went to the mound. With Snider now on second he decided to walk Robby intentionally, setting up a possible double play. Maglie issued the next three pitches wide, and Robinson, who hated to have the bat taken out of his hands, trotted to first. Now Pafko was up. The strong right-handed hitter took a good rip at a Maglie curve, but hit on top of the ball and bounced a tricky hopper toward third.

Bobby went to backhand it, looking to step on third to force Snider. But the ball glanced off his mitt and rolled a few feet off third base. Snider dug home with the third Dodger run as Robinson legged it all the way to third. The official scorer ruled the ball a base hit.

"It was one of those plays where you either do or you don't,"

Thomson remembers. "The ball hit my glove as I tried to grab it between hops and I just didn't come up with it. I tried to grab it in between hops but my timing was just off. Tough spot, but it was one of those things that happens."

Maglie then reached back and whiffed the dangerous Hodges for the second out. Now third baseman Billy Cox was up. Cox hit a bullet toward third, harder than Pafko's. Bobby moved to get in front of the ball but it shot past him into left. Robinson came home with the third run of the inning, making it a 4–1 ball game. Maglie then retired catcher Walker for the third out, but the damage had been done. The three runs put the Brooks in front and the Giants had just two innings to catch them.

"The ball Billy Cox hit at me was the hardest I ever faced at third," Bobby remembers. "When he hit it the thought ran through my head that this ball is probably gonna kill me because I never tried to block a ball like that with my chest before. In fact, I never had a ball come at me that way before or since. It was a blur, a rifle shot that was almost impossible to catch. In my mind I gave it a good try. Still, there were some who figured it was another screwup by Thomson. Either way, I began feeling that the pennant was flying away from us. It didn't take a genius to know this was the wrong thing to happen if we were going to win.

"When we got back to the dugout there was no quit, just a lot of "let 'er rips" and "let's go get 'ems." Guys were hollering for the batter, but Newk was going so well it was hard to see us getting to him."

Newcombe himself said that he didn't expect to lose ball games in the eighth and ninth innings. The varying opinions as to what happened next may well be clouded by the passage of time. Many accounts of this day that have come down through the years have said Don Newcombe began asking out of the game as early as the seventh inning, claiming fatigue. By the eighth, he had thrown more than 20 innings of intense baseball since the previous Saturday. These stories generally have both Robinson and Reese imploring Newk to go back out, with Robinson taking a tough approach, literally screaming at the big guy.

One player who remembers it happening that way is Pee Wee Reese.

"Newk wanted to come out in the eighth," Pee Wee claims. "Jack and I talked him into continuing. I said, 'Newk, damn you. You've been pitching too well to stop now.' So he went back out for the eighth and got them in order."

Duke Snider, however, said he never heard Newk ask out of a game, emphasizing the word *never*. Andy Pafko was another who said he didn't remember it happening that way. "Newk was too much of a competitor to ask out," said Pafko. "He wouldn't do that. He was one of our aces."

Dodger rookie Dick Williams, observing the entire game from the bench, agreed. "I never heard Newk complain that he was tired or Jackie yelling at him to keep pitching," said Williams. "Just look at the way he breezed through the eighth inning."

Then there is Newk himself. When asked today about these stories, he says, emphatically, "I went out there in the eighth inning and never talked to anyone about coming out of the game. In fact, I don't usually read books about '51 and can't recall ever seeing that said before. Those stories just aren't true because I know I was still throwing hard in the eighth inning."

It's not easy to piece together what really happened some 40 years ago when the stories differ so greatly. It seems likely that Dressen and perhaps Reese or Robinson would have asked Newk how he felt. Certainly, after pitching all those innings Saturday, Sunday, and then on Wednesday, Newcombe might have said he was starting to tire. But his performance into the ninth inning doesn't indicate a pitcher who was losing it. Based on that evidence and on Newk's competitiveness, it seems unlikely he would beg out or even ask out. He wasn't that kind of player.

In fact, the Giants would be the first to testify that Newk was still throwing hard in the eighth inning. With Wes Westrum due to lead off, Durocher made a move. He sent up Bill Rigney to pinch-hit for the catcher. Westrum might have more power, but Rig was a contact hitter and Leo was looking for a rally, not a solo home run. Newcombe, good to his word, went to work and seconds later Rigney was walking back to the bench, Newk's second strikeout victim of the game.

"I remember Stanky coming back to the bench about the sixth inning," Bill Rigney says. "He told Maglie then to keep it close because Newk was starting to lose it. So I went up as a pinch hitter in the eighth, figuring I'll take a pitch. Whoosh. Newk threw a rocket right past me. He wasn't losing anything. I remember stepping out of the box and giving a hard look at Stanky, who was on deck. Then I got back in and he finished striking me out."

Bobby remembers that, too. "What impressed me in the eighth was that Newcombe struck Rigney out so easily. I really respected Bill as a contact hitter, but Newk struck him out swinging, blazed the ball right past him, just like that."

Now Durocher sent Henry Thompson up to hit for Maglie. The Barber was done for the day, and maybe for the year. But Thompson couldn't get things going, either. He hit a comebacker and was an easy out at first. When Stanky completed an 0-for-4 collar with an infield pop, the Giants were down to their final three outs.

Larry Jansen came on to pitch the ninth for the Giants. In the Dodger bullpen Carl Erskine and Ralph Branca were starting to throw in earnest. Both had gotten up on the manager's orders in the eighth. Charley Dressen began checking the bullpen situation with coach Clyde Sukeforth, something that struck Sukeforth as odd because the manager had never once done it before.

"Charley never called the bullpen to ask about a pitcher or consult with me," Sukeforth says today, his memory of that final game still clear. "Not once. He would send the pitchers down to the bullpen before the game. Then he would tell me, this guy pitches if we need someone before the fifth, that guy comes in after the fifth, if we get to the eighth we'll use so-and-so. He would always name the relievers, the innings, and the order in which they would pitch before the game. It wasn't until that final game that he started asking questions from the bench."

Once he started, Sukeforth says he didn't stop.

"He started calling in the eighth and kept it up right into the ninth," said Sukeforth. "He must have called half a dozen times. He sounded frantic. 'Who's ready?' he would ask. I'd tell him Branca was ready and then he'd call again. 'Who's ready?' It kept up that way right until he made the change."

Sukeforth began noticing Dressen's behavior in the eighth, when Charley was sitting on a three-run lead. But he wasn't the only one. Dick Williams, watching from the bench, says it was a matter of the manager seeming to lose control in a huge ball game.

"By losing control of himself in the eighth inning," Williams says, "he lost control of the team. Both on the field and on the bench they knew he was getting out of hand. I can remember Robinson shouting in the eighth inning, 'Will someone tell Dressen to sit down. He's making us all nervous.' But Charley kept walking up and down in the dugout, talking up a storm. And he started missing things on the field."

When Jansen came out to pitch the ninth for the Giants, the Dodgers quickly fell into an old habit. Sitting on what looked like a safe lead, already gloating over their apparent forthcoming victory, they resumed kicking sleeping dogs.

"I pretty much tuned people out when I was on the mound," Jansen said, "but I knew they were hollering at me. And to tell the truth, I didn't think we could beat Newcombe once he had that three-run lead. I couldn't let them score again, so I had to bear down. But I certainly remember hearing them yell at me that I should enjoy relieving, because after one more inning I'd be going home."

Jansen did his job. He retired the Dodgers one-two-three, something often overlooked. But for writer Charley Feeney, Larry reacted to the situation like a pro.

"I remember sitting with a writer named Jim McCulley who said to me he felt Jansen was one of the keys to the game," Feeney recalled. "McCulley said a lot of pitchers would have come into that kind of situation really tight, but Jansen just blew them away like a pro. He was right. Another couple of runs and the Giants never would have caught them."

As the Giants came off the field for their final at bat, the wheels were turning in every corner of the ballpark. Bobby Thomson couldn't help thinking about the way the Dodgers had been acting once they got the lead.

"It started with Dressen and Dark the day before," Bobby says. "They were beating us 10–0 in the ninth inning and Dressen began working on Al. 'You'll boot it tomorrow,' Dressen was saying. 'You'll boot the ball and cost your team the game.' He didn't stop. In the ninth inning of that last game Dressen and Dark were swearing at each other. Al was a competitive guy but I had never heard him swear before. He and Dressen were calling each other every name in the book.

"When Jansen came out they started giving it to him. 'Hey, Larry, where you gonna pitch tomorrow?' Stuff like that. They just didn't stop. When I got back to the dugout before the last of the ninth my feeling was one of total dejection, that we just weren't good enough to go beyond this point. I was the fifth scheduled hitter in the inning and the way Newcombe was going the thought crossed my mind that my season might be over."

In the Dodger bullpen Erskine and Branca continued to throw, even while Newcombe took his warm-up tosses for the final frame. Some stories say Labine was warming up, as well. While the rookie might have been the most logical choice, he was simply out in the pen sitting. He never threw a ball until Branca was called into the game.

"Charley had asked me before the game if I could go one or two hitters if necessary and I said yes," Labine explains. "But I was never asked to warm up during the late innings, not once. When Ralph started walking into the game from the pen, that's when the phone rang telling Sukey to get me up."

The Dodger bullpen phone never stopped ringing during the last two innings. Dressen kept asking Sukeforth to evaluate the two pitchers warming up. The veteran coach says even today that it was Ralph Branca who appeared to have the better stuff.

"I was catching Branca and someone else was warming up Carl," Sukeforth recalls. "After I'd catch one of Branca's pitches, I'd look over and watch Erskine throw. Carl wasn't showing me anything. Knowing the importance of the game and knowing Ersk as a competitor, I figured if he felt well he would show me that good curve. I didn't see either the curve or the good fastball.

"Carl had chronic arm trouble during his entire career. Some days he had it and some days he didn't. When he had it he was a fine pitcher. But he wasn't busting the ball in there like Branca. Ralph was really throwing. He was loose and firing. And Charley kept calling. 'Are you ready down there? Are you ready?' "

In the Giant dugout, Durocher tried to light a fire under his troops before going out to coach third base. "Leo was about to head for the coaching lines when he turned back to us," recalls Bill Rigney. "He said, 'Boys, you've come this far. Let's give 'em a finish.' "

Then the manager looked at Al Dark, who would be leading off the inning. Bobby remembers him telling Dark, "It's up to you to get it started." Then the combative manager slapped his hands together and left the dugout. The players watched the number 2 on the back of the uniform shirt as he trotted toward third. He still had a spring in his step and a fire in his heart. But the Giants still had Newcombe to deal with. The big right-hander was already staring in as Al Dark got ready to hit. Dark recalls hearing cries of "Let 'er rip!" coming from the Giant bench.

"Besides saying 'let 'er rip,' we had another saying that helped carry us through those last six weeks," Dark recalls. "It was, 'You never know what's going to happen in the game of baseball.' If we didn't quit the last six weeks, we certainly weren't going to quit the last inning of the last game."

Dark stood in against Newcombe, wigwagging his trademark black bat. But Newk just resumed where he had left off and threw two straight strikes past the Giant captain.

"I still felt Newcombe was throwing the ball awfully well," Al recalls. "It was a dark, overcast day and that didn't help, either. But you've got a job to do and until the pitcher gets you out, he's got a battle on his hands. The next pitch was headed toward the outside corner and I couldn't take a chance letting it go past me. I went with it."

Dark hit a grounder between first and second. Both Hodges and Robinson started moving at the crack of the bat. But, as the players say, the ball had eyes. It ticked off the end of Hodges's mitt, then skipped past the lunging Robinson. Dark had a hit and the Giants had a base runner.

Don Mueller was the next batter. The guy they called Mandrake had had a fine second half of the season, bringing his average from under .200 up into the mid-.270s. Mueller was a hit-em-where-they-ain't type who could really maneuver the bat. Dressen continued pacing in the Dodger dugout, then went over to the bullpen phone again. Newcombe rubbed the ball up and pawed at the rubber. In the Giant dugout, Bobby Thomson began thinking that he might have a chance to hit after all.

"Everything that inning was positive," Bobby says. "I just kept saying, 'Give me a chance to hit.' There was no concern about win or lose at that point, or whether I would get a hit or strike out. After Al's single I was just concentrating on getting up there, on having that chance."

As he stepped into the batter's box, Mueller was planning to hit to his strength, which he felt was right up the middle of the diamond. But that was before he saw where Gil Hodges was playing. The Dodger first sacker, one of the finest fielders of his time, was almost on the bag, holding Dark on. It didn't make sense, because Dark represented a meaningless run. If Hodges played off the bag he'd be in a better position to field a grounder and perhaps start a double play.

"We all knew that Hodges was out of position," Dick Williams recalls, "but we couldn't say anything. Charley ran his own ship and if we told Dressen he would have pinched our heads off."

"There's no way I was about to steal second," Dark says, also remembering that Hodges was too close to the bag. A lot of people say he was on the bag, but I remember him standing a little behind the bag, but still too close to me.

"When something like that happens it always comes from the bench. No one on the bench moved him back. I know if I'd have been managing I would have been making enough noise so he would have moved back where I wanted him. I didn't even have a big lead because I didn't want to take a chance being doubled up if Don hit a line drive."

Mueller also saw the situation at first and quickly changed his mind about trying to hit the ball up the middle. "My stock-in-trade was hitting the ball toward the biggest hole," Mueller said recently. "When I saw Hodges almost holding Dark on I went for the hole between first and second. Charley Dressen later told me he should have had Hodges playing back to cut off the hole between first and second. I told him if Hodges was off the bag I would have looked for another hole to go through."

Mueller often described himself as a "hole shooter," and that's what he did, bouncing a Newcombe offering through the first base hole as Hodges and Robinson again tried in vain to reach the ball. Dark got a good jump and scampered all the way to third before Furillo could get the ball back to the infield. Suddenly the noise in the ballpark began growing and some of the fans who were already inching their way to the exits stopped in their tracks and hustled back to their seats. This one wasn't over yet. Monte Irvin, the Giants' best hitter, was due up.

Dressen again shuffled nervously in the dugout. He then made yet another call to the bullpen, where Sukeforth again confirmed that Ralph Branca was throwing well. But Dressen wasn't ready to make a move. Even though the Giants had a pair of base runners, both hits had just found their way through the Brooklyn infield. It wasn't as if they were hitting shots off Newcombe. He still seemed in command.

As Irvin made his way to the plate the Polo Grounds came alive. Monte represented the tying run and was more than capable of hitting it out. Would there be a miracle finish? That thought had to be on the minds of many. Irvin must have been thinking it, as well.

"When I really wanted just a base hit I almost always used to go to right field," Irvin recalls. "But I came to the plate thinking home run, because that would tie up the ball game. So when I stepped in against Newk I wanted to pull the ball to left."

Newk went to work on Irvin and got the big left fielder to try to pull a slider. The result was a high pop to first. Hodges settled under it and made the catch. Irvin slammed his bat in disgust and walked back to the dugout. Dressen continued to pace. Maybe Newk could still close it out. Now Whitey Lockman was due up and Bobby Thomson moved into the on-deck circle.

As Lockman came up he admitted he had the same feeling as Irvin. "I knew I was the tying run and I went up there looking to hit a home run," Whitey said. "But I wasn't the kind of hitter who would try to pull an outside pitch."

Newcombe knew that Lockman was tough to fool, as well as a guy who would go with the pitch. But he didn't want to give Whitey anything to pull, either. His second pitch was ticketed for the outside corner and Lockman, with his hitting instincts, forgot about pulling the ball and went with the pitch. He hit a solid liner over third.

With every eye in the park following the ball, it hit about a foot or so in fair territory and rolled into the corner. Dark scored the Giants' second run, Mueller rounded second and steamed toward third, and Lockman, his heart fluttering with excitement, headed for second. Pafko fielded the ball in left and whipped it back toward the infield. Mueller picks up the story from there.

"As I was coming around second I was watching the ball to see if the throw to the relay man would be bad or off line," he said. "If it was, I might have a chance to score. Leo was coaching third, but I wasn't watching him. It was my play all the way. I should have slid into the bag, but I didn't. Instead, my foot caught the top of the bag and my ankle twisted as I went down. I ended up with a pulled tendon.

"The funny part is that most reports over the years, and even some in the newspapers the next day, said I got hurt sliding. But I never slid. I should have, but I didn't."

At first, not too many people noticed Mueller lying on the ground in pain. They were too busy rejoicing over the Giant rally that had pulled their team to 4–2 and had the tying runs in scoring position with just one out. But once the excitement died down, everyone focused on third base. Mueller was in obvious agony and almost the entire Giant team ran down to see how bad the injury was. It was a break in the action, an unforeseen event that cut the tension and slowed the rising tide of excitement. But while the injured Mueller was being attended to, then finally removed on a stretcher, Charley Dressen was planning his final strategy.

The Dodger manager had placed one last call to the bullpen, where Clyde Sukeforth told him once again that Branca was ready. The other Dodger infielders gathered around Don Newcombe, who had pitched his heart out. The Giant bats, which until the ninth inning had produced just one run in the last 18 frames, were coming to life, and the Dodger skipper wanted a fresh arm.

"Dressen came out to the mound and Reese, Robinson, and Hodges joined us," Newcombe recalls. "I'll never forget this as long as I live. Charley said, 'Fellas, what do you think? It's your money as much as it's mine. What do you want to do with it?' And Pee Wee said, 'Charley, Newk has given us all he's got. Why don't you get somebody fresh in here.' Charley nodded and said, 'Okay, I'll do it.' "

It was another unusual move for Dressen. He never asked anyone for advice. Once he made up his mind, he acted. But not now, not in the closing innings of the biggest game of his life.

While Dressen signaled for the pitching change, summoning Ralph Branca from the bullpen, the Giants felt that Newcombe still had it. Even Lockman, whose double knocked Newk out of the game, didn't think the big guy had weakened.

"I don't think it was a matter of Newk losing it in the ninth as much as it was us catching up with him," Lockman said. "Remember, Dark and Mueller's hits were just ground ball singles that found the hole. I hit my double solidly, a line drive, but it was a good pitch on the outside that I happened to get."

The Giants were still gathered around Mueller when Branca began walking in from the bullpen in left-center. At the same time, Newcombe started the long walk from the mound to the clubhouse, which was in dead center. The two pitchers passed close to each other midway.

"As he passed me," Newk recalls, "Ralph patted me on the fanny and said, 'Don't worry about it, big fella, I'll take care of everything.' Later, he told me he didn't even remember saying it."

Duke Snider in center field yelled to Branca as he walked by, "Go get 'em, Honk." Honk was short for Honker, a good-natured nickname that referred to the pitcher's rather large nose.

Up in the press box, Irving Rudd was sitting alongside Allen Roth. Roth was the statistician whose pen-and-paper advice was constantly ignored by Dressen. But Rudd knew Roth was the keeper of the numbers on the Branca-Thomson matchup.

"I looked over at Allen as Branca walked toward the mound," Rudd recalls. "He was just staring at the field, so I asked him what he thought. Allen turned slowly toward me and just shook his head in a negative way. He knew Bobby could hit Branca."

The big right-hander says his walk from the bullpen was almost trancelike, as if he were walking someplace alone, isolated. Maybe he was.

"I don't remember anything from the time I left the bullpen until I got to the dirt of the infield," Branca recalls. "It's just a blank. Then I remember seeing Jackie and Pee Wee. They were waiting together on the infield grass. Dressen was waiting at the mound.

"Normally, Charley would be very precise in his instructions to a reliever. He would tell you to remember to pitch this guy one way and that guy another way. This time he just flipped me the ball and said, 'Here, get 'em out.' Maybe he didn't know what to say, but that really struck me as strange."

It struck Duke Snider the same way. "We all knew Dressen always had a conference on the mound with the relief pitcher," said the Duke. "So when I saw Charley flip Ralph the ball from about five feet away I began to worry. I knew Charley wasn't in full control at that point and I believe the rest of the team felt that way, too. It worried me. Managers must be consistent. If they suddenly start to change, you as a ball player start thinking negative thoughts. As a result, you don't win ball games. We all knew about Charley's instructions to his relievers. He would sometimes even stay out on the mound too long. But when he just flipped that ball to Branca I started getting concerned. I'm sure Ralph must have wondered, too."

It may well have been that Dressen was finding the prospect of losing the game and the pennant, especially after having that seemingly insurmountable lead, a very frightening prospect. All the signs pointed to a panicky manager who was losing control.

But that didn't concern Ralph Branca. He began taking his warm-up tosses to Rube Walker as Bobby Thomson came back toward the Giant dugout to get ready to hit. Larry Jansen recalls yelling out to Bobby, "Here comes your boy," a reference to the way Bobby hit Ralph. Bobby didn't hear him.

Clint Hartung had come out to run for the injured Mueller. Durocher grabbed Bobby, put his arm around his shoulder, and said, "Bobby, if you ever hit one, hit one now." Bobby didn't even look at him. He just thought to himself: *Leo, you're out of your mind!*

Up in the press box, reporters were shuffling papers, looking for statistics. Branca was prone to giving up the gopher ball, but was far from the league leader. He had given up 17 homers during the season, but the surprising statistic was that 10 were hit by the Giants. Monte Irvin was the number-one Branca basher with five circuits, while Bobby had hit a pair, including the winning shot in game one.

As Bobby made his way to home plate, the rookie Willie Mays stepped out on deck. Mays hadn't hit well in September and as he came out he thought the Dodgers might decide to walk Bobby intentionally. That would load the bases, set up a force anywhere, and put him up at bat. But Dressen had already dismissed that possibility. He wasn't about to put the winning run on base via a free pass. That wasn't sound baseball.

Mays also felt that if his turn came, Durocher would pinch-hit for him. He almost welcomed the possibility.

"Willie was very nervous when he came out," Monte Irvin recalls. "He told me he thought Leo would pinch-hit for him and I said, 'Heck no. You're his man. No way he would pinch-hit for you.' But he was a rookie and being nervous in that situation was natural."

But none of that mattered to the two main players in the almost private drama that was about to commence. On the mound, Ralph Branca said he was concentrating so hard he didn't even hear the crowd. "I was in a vacuum," was the way he put it.

Bobby admitted later that because of his baserunning rock and his questionable play at third on those two balls he could well have been "goat of the year" had he not come through at the plate. But he wasn't thinking about that in the ninth inning.

"Let's face it, if you think about the possibility of being a goat it's going to take away from your performance," he said. "The only motivating factor for me was the chance to get up to bat."

Like Branca on the mound, Thomson was immersed in a kind of total concentration, his vision focused on Ralph Branca and nowhere else.

"Once I realized Branca was in the game there were no other thoughts in my head," Bobby recalls, quite clearly. "The game situation was no longer on my mind. It wasn't a matter of if I don't get a hit we lose, if I get a hit we stay in the game or maybe win. Men on second and third? I couldn't care less. It was simply hitter versus pitcher. Me against him. Thomson against Branca. Total concentration. I kept telling myself not to get overanxious. *Wait and watch for the ball. Wait and watch.* I repeated it to myself. *Give yourself a chance to hit, you SOB. Wait and watch, you SOB. Give yourself a chance to hit!"*

On the mound, Branca's first concern was getting ahead on the count. Walker signaled fastball and the big guy pumped it right down the middle. Bobby didn't move.

Strike one!

"I nearly fell off the bench when he took that one for a strike," Larry Jansen would say later.

Bobby seemed perturbed, too. He stepped out and grabbed a handful of dirt. On the mound, Branca was satisfied with his first pitch. He knew it was a bit too good and maybe he got away with something because Bobby hadn't swung. Now, though, he could try to set him up. He would come back with another fastball, but this one up and in, off the plate. The Dodger book said Bobby had trouble with a ball up and in. They called it his weakness. Branca looked at it as a waste pitch. The third pitch, then, would be the breaking ball, low and away, the pitch Branca wanted Thomson to hit.

Branca wound and threw again. The ball was headed up and in, maybe just out of the strike zone. But Bobby Thomson wasn't taking. He sprang out of his crouch and lashed out at the baseball, getting out in front of it with his quick hands. The crack of the bat echoed throughout the old ballpark. Every head in the house turned quickly toward the left field fence to follow the flight of the baseball. Hartung and Lockman started running from third and second. Bobby Thomson dropped his bat and began running to first.

High above the field in the radio booth, Russ Hodges was saying, "There's a long fly . . . it's gonna be . . . I believe . . ." He paused for a split second to make sure, then his voice erupted:

"The Giants win the pennant! The Giants win the pennant! The Giants win the pennant! The Giants win the pennant!"

The Giants Win the Pennant

"It was the biggest crowd noise I ever heard, a complete eruption, like the sky was being pulled apart."

This is the way Ernie Harwell remembers the scene at the Polo Grounds moments after Bobby Thomson connected with Ralph Branca's high, inside fastball. Even when talking about it today, Harwell seems in awe of the incredible scenario that unfolded before him. The memory is so clear, so vivid, that although the veteran broadcaster is looking back 40 years, he speaks with an immediacy that makes it seem as if it happened yesterday.

Bobby had hit a sinking line drive to left field that just cleared the high concrete wall at the 315-foot sign and disappeared into the lower stands. With Hartung and Lockman scoring before him, Bobby had not only hit a three-run homer, he had won both the game and pennant with one swing of the bat.

"I knew it was a home run as soon as I hit it," says Bobby. "Home run. Upper deck. That's what went through my mind. Then, all of a sudden, the ball started to sink and for a split second I thought it was gonna hit the wall. Then it disappeared. I had never hit a ball like that before. Apparently I got slightly on top of the ball, which put overspin on it and caused it to sink."

With the Polo Grounds in an uproar, the images came fast and furious.

"When Bobby connected I first had the feeling Pafko would catch it," said Harwell. "Then it went in and I simply said, 'It's gone.' You didn't get as dramatic on the television side as you did on radio."

Andy Pafko's reaction was similar to Harwell's. "When Bobby first hit it I really thought I had a chance to catch it," Pafko said. "I ran back to that concrete wall and when I looked up it was gone. I didn't even see it go in. The ball was really hit hard."

In the Dodger bullpen, Clem Labine was throwing along with Erskine. "Even when you're warming up you always stop and look when someone is making a big pitch," Labine said. "Both of us knew right away. We both felt it was high enough to clear the top of the wall. I sensed immediately that it was destiny. If it wasn't Ralph, it would have been Carl and if it wasn't Carl it would have been me. But the Giants worked very hard for what they did and they got it."

In the Dodger clubhouse, Don Newcombe was taking a shower with the anticipation that he could be out and dressed in time for the Dodger celebration. When he entered the shower room, he said the clubhouse was already a madhouse, crowded with newspaper reporters and television people. That's how he realized something had happened.

"You had to go up a flight of stairs to the showers," Newk recalled. "I was in the middle of my shower when the game resumed and I just *knew* everything would be all right. Then I heard something. It sounded like a stampede, the sound of people and equipment going from our clubhouse to the Giant clubhouse next door.

"I came out and asked John Griffin, our clubhouse custodian, what happened and he just said, 'Thomson, home run!' I turned around and went back into the shower."

On Staten Island, Al Corbin's wife, Buttons, was racing across her lawn to the Thomson house, to tell Bobby's mother the news. Mrs. Thomson couldn't bear to watch the game on television and was doing her housework. As Mrs. Corbin ran toward the Thomson house she shouted over and over again, "Bobby did it! Bobby did it! Bobby did it!"

In Chicago, Ellen Pafko, wife of left fielder Andy, had a cab waiting outside her house to take her to the airport. She was flying to New York for the World Series. When the driver began honking the horn she came out and told him to wait a minute, it was the last inning, there were two outs and she was watching her husband play. Seconds later, Ellen Pafko emerged again and told the driver to leave. She wouldn't be going to New York after all. Instead, her husband would be flying back to Chicago.

For Jackie Robinson, it wasn't quite over yet. A competitor to the end, Jackie watched carefully as Bobby circled the bases. Maybe, just maybe, in his joyous delirium, Bobby would fail to step on one of the bases and Robby could call for the ball, cutting off the last run that would officially make the final score 5–4. But Bobby clearly touched each base and only then did Robinson begin the long, sad walk to the clubhouse.

For the Giants, there was nothing but sheer, uncontrolled emotion. All their hopes and dreams built up over the final six weeks of the season had come true. But not until it had appeared lost. Bobby Thomson had brought them back from the brink of defeat.

"As I circled the bases I started to hyperventilate," Bobby recalls. Then as I rounded third Durocher came toward me and made a grab, almost like he wanted to tackle me. I ran by him and actually pushed off him. When I did that his spike cut my shoe right down the back. I remember my last step to home plate was a jump, actually, into the arms of what seemed like the whole ball club."

"As we headed toward the clubhouse I could feel someone grabbing at my legs. Before I knew it I was riding on my roommate Whitey's shoulders. However, the crowd started to close in and he had to put me down so we could make a beeline for the clubhouse in center field. At that time the only thought going through my mind was: We beat the Dodgers, we won the pennant, we beat the Dodgers, we beat the Dodgers. Over and over again."

The other Giants were as estatic as Bobby. "Bobby hit a ball that was up and in," said Whitey Lockman. "My feeling was it had a chance to go out, but I didn't want to start running toward third until I was sure. So I just kind danced off the base until it went in there.

"My immediate thought right after I crossed the plate was to get Bobby up on my shoulders, because if there was ever a player who deserved to be carried off the field it was him. I got him almost all the way up, but there were so many fans crowding around us that I was starting to strain my neck and I had to put him back down."

Larry Jansen, who got credit for his twenty-third victory of the year after pitching a perfect ninth inning, sought out fellow hurler Sal Maglie.

"I told you I'd win as many games as you," Jansen crooned.

The Barber just grinned from ear to ear. "And I said if you did it we would win the pennant," he answered.

"After coming from 13½ back in August I really believed we were a team of destiny," said Wes Westrum. "Even at the beginning of the last inning, before we came up to hit, I turned to George Spencer and said, 'George, we're going to do it. We're going to win.' "

"I remember groaning on the bench when Bobby took that first pitch," said Monte Irvin. "It was his pitch and he took it. The next one wasn't as good, but he was ready. At first I thought the ball was going to hit the wall, but it went in. It was the greatest thing I had ever been part of."

Al Dark said no one on the team was thinking home run. "I think we were all looking for a base hit to tie it. Then Bobby hit that liner. I couldn't remember ever seeing a ball sneak under the overhang and go into the lower seats like that. It was some kind of bullet."

Dark was right. The facade of the upper deck in the Polo Grounds extended out above the lower stands. So a fly ball home run would always drop into the upper seats or glance off the facade. There was no way the average home run could land in the lower seats. But Bobby hit a topspin liner that dipped in. It was an unlikely place for a game-winning homer, but none of the Giants was arguing. They were all too busy celebrating.

So were the fans. They gathered on the field and wouldn't leave, each one celebrating in his own way. Thousands soon gathered in front of the old clubhouse in center field and wouldn't leave until Thomson and Durocher came out for an encore. They were the two heroes of the day. For Bobby, it was a once-in-a-lifetime thing. For Durocher, it was vindication. He was the guy the fans were reluctant to accept, the guy who had replaced the popular Mel Ott, the guy who was a hated Dodger before his unprecedented one-day conversion. Now, he owned New York. Everyone loved Leo and would always love Leo.

But where there's a winner, there's also a loser. Not only had the Dodgers just lost the pennant in the worst possible way, but it had happened in enemy territory at the Polo Grounds. The ball club felt alone in its devastation. It was a defeat that would be almost impossible to forget.

"Our team took that loss worse than any other," Carl Erskine recalls. "We all felt we had embarrassed the borough of Brooklyn. I know I had a sense of history about my baseball days and when I got to the clubhouse I watched carefully as the other guys came in.

"The first thing Dressen did was take his shirt off. But he didn't unbutton it. He just ripped it off, popping all the buttons in one motion. Jackie looked totally disgusted and he fired his glove down. The rest of the team was quiet. Ralph plopped down on the steps leading up from the locker room to the trainer's room. He sat there leaning over with that number 13 shining on his back.

"With the bedlam so close by on their side, there was almost total silence in our clubhouse. It was almost like death. And while I was on the wrong side of the picture, I knew this was a historic moment in sports. It was the complete picture, starting with the dramatic finish to the way the whole team walked into a locker room in complete devastation. A great team with future Hall of Fame players and nothing but eerie silence. It's a picture that has grown in my mind ever since. It's as vivid to me now as the day it happened.

Pee Wee Reese couldn't believe it was over at first. He thought, somehow, that the game would continue. It *couldn't* be finished. But it was. "It was the toughest thing I ever went through in baseball," the Dodger captain said. "Branca was lying all spread out on the steps and you could see the tears in his eyes. We could hear the people outside yelling and screaming for Bobby and Leo. We all just sat there without a helluva lot to say and we stayed in there a long time. When I finally dressed and walked out and saw my wife, along with two friends of ours from Louisville, I had a few tears in my eyes, too. Then we all went over to Gallagher's Restaurant for a roast beef dinner."

Duke Snider reacted the way any good center fielder would when Bobby hit the ball. He ran over to play a possible carom. "At first I thought it would be off the wall," the Duke said. "Then, suddenly, it was gone. The umpire signaled a home run and I just turned and headed for the clubhouse. One of my first thoughts was how the 1950 season had ended for us on a home run by Dick Sisler. That defeat was bitter, but this one was even crueler.

"I can remember Branca lying on the steps in the clubhouse saying, 'Why me? Why me?' Dressen came in and ripped his shirt off. When I finally left, I met my wife, Bev, then joined my mother and dad for dinner. My mother asked me why I was so quiet and I snapped at her, though I was sorry the minute I did it.

" 'We just lost the National League pennant,' I said. 'That's what's the matter with me.' " The emotion was just so strong I reacted without thinking.

The Duke went on to add that Bobby's homer, in a strange way, eventually made the Dodgers a better team. "We realized we had to work even harder," Snider said. "From there we went on to win the pennant in '52, '53, '55, and '56."

But were those victories ever as sweet as this loss was bitter? Like the other Dodgers, Dick Williams remembers seeing his teammates in absolute devastation and Branca lying on the steps.

"It was a helluva way to break into the majors," Williams said. "I remember Dressen giving a little speech and telling us all to 'Wait till next year.' Maybe he meant it, but at the time it sounded dumb."

Clem Labine called the clubhouse a morgue. "There was poor Ralph laid out on the clubhouse steps," Labine recalls. "No one was saying a word. I couldn't even hear the water flowing in the showers because, like everyone else, I guess I was wrapped up in my own thoughts. At the Polo Grounds, the bullpen guys could duck into the clubhouse to use the facilities and we saw all the TV cameras and cases of champagne waiting for us. And when we walked in after the game it was all gone, moved across to their clubhouse. There was no one to blame for what happened. Clyde Sukeforth was fired after the season, but to blame Sukey for such a thing is idiotic. Ralph had a good overhand curve, just like Carl and myself. Like I said, it was destiny and could have been either one of us."

But it *was* Ralph Branca, not Labine or Erskine. He would forever be remembered for throwing the pitch that Bobby Thomson hit for the most dramatic home run in baseball history and would have to learn to live with it over the years. But on October 3, 1951, it wasn't an easy thing for Branca to accept. Perhaps the most chilling image of that gray October afternoon came from Don Newcombe, who had been in the shower when the game ended.

"When I came back out of the shower I just started drying off in front of my locker," recalls Newk. "I could see the steps where Ralph was. I understand he had been lying face down on the steps when he first came in. When I saw him he was sitting there, with his head down between his legs crying, crying his heart out.

"That image really affected me. I was just 22 years old and at the time it didn't seem that these things should be so important. So you lost the championship. No big deal. You win another one the next year. But as long as I live I'll never forget Ralph Branca sitting there, sitting there and crying like a baby.

"I said to myself, goddamn, is this what baseball does to people?"

 **BOBBY**

Thomson's Finest Hour

Bobby came with me on an overnight trip to do a show for sick
veterans at a hospital near Saranac Lake at Christmastime in
1951. It was a big sacrifice for him to leave his family then, but
we hit the ground running that day, leaving at 6:00 A.M. and not
getting back until after midnight. Bobby went from bed to bed,
autographing balls and talking to the guys. In every room he
went, people would yell out, "Hey, Bobby Thomson! I can't
believe it's Bobby Thomson!" They were really excited about
his being up there. This was just two months after his home run
shot against the Dodgers. He did so much good that day. Those
guys were just so excited and thrilled to see him.

—Irving Rudd

Cloud nine. How else can I describe the feeling? We beat the Dodgers. We won the pennant. I hit a home run. Everybody went nuts.
Storybook stuff, the whole thing. I still don't know why I was hyper-
ventilating as I ran around the bases. It must have been the excitement, the pure joy, all those amazing feelings just coming together.

Somehow, we made it to the empty locker room through a sea of people. No one complained because the fans were great. When you went
through the clubhouse door in the old Polo Grounds you entered
a big main room. There were steps leading down into another room
where the lockers were. There was a table down in the locker area full
of liquor bottles. The first thing that went through my mind was that
Horace had planned to buy us a drink for a good try, some kind of reward for second place. I took one look at the liquor and it gave me a
nauseated feeling. Must have been the excitement catching up to me.

Then the well-wishers began coming in and it seems within seconds it was wall-to-wall people. You couldn't move. Someone was
yelling my name and said I had a phone call. Then there was a telephone in my hand. I can't even recall how it got there. It was Buddy
Kerr, my old teammate, the guy who had been traded to Boston when
Dark and Stanky came over.

"Hey, Hoot Mon. Hey, Hoot. How you feel?" I could barely hear

Buddy through all the noise. He was laughing and so was I. He must have remembered the old clubhouse phone number from his days with the ball club. We talked for a minute, but by then there were so many people in there it was hard to even hear yourself think.

People were sticking microphones in my face and I can't remember half the questions or half the things I said. Someone asked me how I felt running around the bases and I told them I never even touched the ground. I heard that tape some time later and I couldn't believe the way I sounded. I was answering in a high-pitched, Willie Mays voice.

My false modesty surfaced when I described the pitch as being high and inside, claiming a good hitter wouldn't even have swung at it, all that kind of stuff to the point where I was even laughing at myself. But the sheer excitement was still there because it was all in that high-pitched voice.

By then it seemed that everyone in the world was in that club-house. There were the players, families, club officials, their families, newspaper reporters, TV people, friends of the ball players, and probably even some fans. You couldn't move. Someone gave me a bottle of beer and I even had trouble lifting it to my mouth. That's how crowded it was.

The tumult continued. At one point I was aware that someone was working his way toward me. Turns out it was Red Barber, the popular Dodger broadcaster. Red wasn't a big guy and he really had to battle to get over to me. When he finally made it he stuck the microphone right under my nose.

"Bobby—" That was the only word that came out of his mouth. Before he could say another word someone yanked the microphone right out of his hand. It was Stanky, still being the Brat. Eddie had the mike and shouted into it, "And this is Red Barber signing off for 1951." That was it. Either they never turned it back on or Red couldn't get hold of it again. No more interview.

I felt badly for Red. You know, to us the Dodger broadcasters were no different from the players. They were all the enemy. I never really got a chance to talk to Red over the years, but interestingly enough, I was asked to receive an award for him when he became the first sportscaster voted into the radio hall of fame. Red wasn't able to attend and I felt it a great honor to fill in for him.

A few of the Dodgers came in. Robinson was the first. Let's face it,

Jackie had to have real character to do that, the way he always played against us, his feud with Leo. Yet he was the first guy to come in and congratulate us. Bill Rigney told me that Jackie came over to him and said, "I just want you to know one thing. We didn't lose. You won." I probably didn't appreciate that until I got out of baseball. Eventually you do grow up a little and get over that stuff you were into when you were competitors.

Pee Wee came in for a few minutes, so did Duke and Preacher Roe. There might have been more, but I don't recall. Besides congratulating us, they also told us not to screw things up in the World Series. But I don't think any of us were thinking of the Series then, even though we had to play the next day.

Monte Irvin tells a story that Pee Wee came up to him and kept saying he couldn't believe it. "I was planning to be at Yankee Stadium tomorrow," Pee Wee said, "I can't believe you guys have done this to us." Monte told him, "Pee Wee, don't go to the Stadium tomorrow. You'll be the only Dodger there."

At some point in the middle of the locker room celebration some guy came up and said, "Bob, we'd love you to go on the "Perry Como Show" tonight. We'll give you $500 for appearing."

Perry had a 15-minute live program then. I said, "Hey, that sounds great and so does the $500, but I really want to get home and share everything that happened with my family. No thanks."

It was true. None of my family had been at the game. Only Al Corbin, our neighbor, was there and I really wanted to get home. But this guy kept trying to convince me and I kept turning him down. Until he upped the ante.

"I'll tell you what, Bobby, we'll give you $1,000," he said.

I said to myself, well, for $1,000 the family can wait. My Scottish heritage won out.

It wasn't a wild party, nothing compared to the celebrations you see today on TV. Nobody drank that much because there were so many people crowded in there. And the Yankees were waiting for us. The World Series would start on schedule. We had a game the next day. But we must have stayed a couple of hours because it was already getting dark when I left the clubhouse. One thing I'll never forget happened after I showered and was shaving. Henry Thompson, of all people, came up and kissed me.

When I finally agreed to go on the Como show I asked my friend,

Al Corbin, to drive my car home for me. That left me on my own after the show. I took a cab and then the Staten Island ferry home, by myself. It was a strange feeling after being inundated with people all day long. But now I was anxious to see my family.

The first person I saw was my brother, Jim. He was a battalion chief with the fire department on Staten Island and was working that night. I felt bad he couldn't have been at the ball game, so I stopped at the firehouse on the way home. Jim came out and the two of us just stared at each other for a minute. I didn't know what to say.

"Jim, it's crazy," was all I could finally manage. Then I pointed up to the sky to indicate that the Good Lord must have had something to do with it. Jim just looked at me.

"Bobby," he said, shaking his head. "Do you realize what you did today?"

What a silly question, I thought. Of course I knew. I was there. I was the guy who hit the ball. And I said something to that effect to him.

"No," he said. "Do you realize something like this may never happen again?"

Up to that point, all I could think was: We beat the Dodgers; we won the pennant; we play the Yankees. But Jim made me stop for a moment and then it started to sink in. Maybe it was something pretty special after all.

Jim was given a few hours to celebrate with us and we drove home in his car. The house was dark and I realized my mom was next door at the Corbins. We walked across the lawn and could see them in the living room. Instead of going to the door I just tapped on the window. The biggest hero in all of New York and all they could see was a face in the window, tapping on the glass like a lost soul.

We went to the Tavern on the Green, the number-one eating place on Staten Island, where we often ate. The whole family joined us, as well as many of our friends. Even the press found us and the next morning there were pictures of the celebration in the New York and Staten Island papers.

I had a few drinks anyway, but with a game the next day I didn't want my picture taken with a glass in my hand. So each time one of the newspaper photographers cranked it up, I'd hand my glass to Al Corbin. Al ended up taking a good ribbing. All the photos showed me empty-handed and Al with a glass in each hand.

We had a great time. I was still on that cloud, but at about 11:00 I knew I had to call time. "Hey, folks," I said. "We better end this because we have a ball game with the Yankees tomorrow."

So that was it. The end of the most eventful and wonderful day in my life. I had been given a chance few people ever have and made the most of it. I feel the most important part was that I gave myself a chance to hit. I was able to wait and watch. It was a matter of total concentration and determination. This is what I was proud of. After that, only the Lord knows. Call it blind luck, fate, or destiny, whatever you wish.

When I looked at the films I was proud of my swing. I jumped on the pitch, lashed out at it, hit it hard. Some say it would have been an out at Ebbets Field. Who cares? I hit it at the Polo Grounds over a 25-foot wall at the 315-foot mark and we beat the Dodgers. No need to say any more than that.

Great storybook ending you might say. But there was still an unfinished chapter. We had to play the Yankees, a team with the likes of DiMaggio, Berra, Rizzuto, Bauer, Woodling, McDougald, our old friend Johnny Mize, and a rookie named Mickey Mantle. The pitching staff starred Reynolds, Raschi, and Lopat, as good a trio of starters as you could find. It was the Yanks' third straight American League pennant and they were heavy favorites to beat us in the World Series.

I went into the Series with a good feeling which carried over from the day before. My troubles at the plate during the first half of the season had disappeared. I ended the year hitting .293 with 32 homers and 101 runs batted in. And most of that came after people said moving to third would make my hitting suffer.

There were a lot of people who thought the Series was an anticlimax for us, that our personal "World Series" was beating the Dodgers. I never looked at it that way because it sounds as if winning the Series wasn't important to us. That isn't true. Sure, you can't win the Series if you don't get there, so winning the pennant was certainly important. I'd certainly rather lose the Series than the pennant for the same reason. But you've got to remember we'd played three tension-filled player games without a rest and started against the Yanks the very next day. We didn't even have time to savor our victory. On Thursday, the playoff was behind us. That was yesterday. Now we're playing in a World Series and we were a hot team, a team on a roll. Why couldn't we beat the Yankees? To a man, the Giants expected to win.

I'll never forget arriving at Yankee Stadium for the first game. I was walking toward the players' entrance when a guy came up to me and said he had the baseball I'd hit into the seats at the Polo Grounds. He showed me a ball and swore it was the one. All he wanted in exchange were two tickets to the game.

I told him to wait and went into our clubhouse. Eddie Logan, the clubhouse man, was there, and I explained what had happened. Eddie started laughing. I said, "Eddie, the guy is waiting outside. What's so funny?" He just pointed to the chair in front of my locker. It was covered with baseballs and all of them were supposed to be *the one.* That winter I received several letters from fans saying they had the ball. Some even included their ticket stubs to indicate where they were sitting. But I'd already given up. It would be great having it, but it wasn't meant to be.

There were no clubhouse speeches before the Series. But speeches weren't necessary. We were loose and relaxed. In fact, it was the most relaxing game I ever played in my life and it was in front of 65,000 people. The year before, the Phillies had been blown away in four straight by the Yanks and the writers all said they were overawed by the Yankee Stadium crowds. But with all that had happened to me so far, I never felt more relaxed in my life or enjoyed playing a ball game more.

We surprised the hell out of everyone in the first game. Leo had to pitch Dave Koslo and he was great. We beat the Yankees 5–1. Monte had four hits and stole home, the first time that had happened in a Series game since 1928. You can't say enough about Monte Irvin.

They evened it up in the second behind Eddie Lopat, but we won the third one on a strong game from Jim Hearn. Mueller, of course, missed the Series with that ankle injury and Leo played Henry Thompson in right. I didn't realize it at the time, but apparently it was the first all-black outfield—Irvin, Mays, and Thompson—in major league history. But we did miss Don's bat. He might have made a difference.

That third game was the one in which Eddie Stanky kicked the ball out of Phil Rizzuto's glove on a play at second. We went on to score four more runs in the inning. Good old Eddie. Always the Brat. I remember Rizzuto complaining to the umpire and acting as if Eddie shouldn't have been allowed to do that sort of thing. The funny part was that it had happened before. In the 1934 World Series Jo-Jo White of the Detroit Tigers kicked the ball out of the glove of the St. Louis shortstop. Who was the shortstop? Leo Durocher. The one and only. Leo always seemed to be in the middle of something.

We were leading 2–1 in games and one of the Yankees' second-line pitchers was due to start. But the game was rained out. I know both Rigney and Dark felt that the rainout broke our momentum, and I've got to agree with them. It gave Allie Reynolds an extra day's rest and Allie was a great pressure pitcher. After the rainout they took three straight and closed us out.

Maybe the pennant race had taken something out of us. I know Al Dark has said that. He feels we were drained by that last month and a half, playing nearly every day as hard as we could, then having the playoffs and going right from there to meet a well-rested New York Yankee team. But we tried. Al thinks the Giants were readier to win the Series in '54. Maybe he's right. But I can't say because I was in Milwaukee by then.

The 1951 World Series marked the changing of the guard for the Yankees. It was the last World Series for Joe DiMaggio. Joe D retired before the 1952 season and we were all sorry to see him go. Joe was in a class by himself. But the Yanks had his replacement ready and waiting. Mickey Mantle was a rookie in 1951 and started in right field at the beginning of the Series. Unfortunately, Mickey stepped in that drain hole in the second game and hurt his knee. But like Willie, he would quickly become a great, great player.

Surprisingly, I had a very quiet off-season. Let's face it, if I hit that kind of a home run today I would probably have agents banging down the door, endorsement opportunities, my choice of appearances. But it was a different world in 1951. I still lived with my mother and there were no player agents or attorneys to speak of in baseball. Sure, I got phone calls for interviews. But at that time I wasn't into making speeches and guest appearances. I was uneasy in those situations. I remember one offer to go on a four- or five-day speaking trip to New England for something like $700, but it didn't seem worth it. So outside of little things like newspaper and magazine interviews, it was an uneventful winter. The home run had passed.

I thought the home run would help to get me a nice salary increase for 1952. It wasn't easy getting raises out of management back then and Horace Stoneham was no exception. The new contract arrived in early January, with a $2,000 raise. I couldn't believe it. I was in the $23,000 to $25,000 range in 1951 and besides hitting the home run I'd had a darned good all-around season. I felt I deserved more. So I didn't sign.

A short time later I went to Boston for a writers' dinner and ended up sitting next to Leo on the dais. He asked me if I signed and I told him no and the reason why. Leo wanted to know what I wanted and I gave him a figure. He patted me on the leg and said, "You're okay, stay there." That's all he said. The next day he went back to New York and the day after that the Giants called me to come in and sign. They were giving me the raise I wanted, bumping me up into the $35,000 to $40,000 range.

That was Leo. He would back his players to the hilt if he thought they deserved it. Every once in a while when the team seemed to be letting down a bit he would hold a meeting. And he'd say, "Fellas, you better start thinking about next year. Don't wait until it's too late because if you come around looking for something and I don't think you're worth it, I'll let you know. But if I think you're worth it I'll be right there in your corner." And he was. Thanks to Leo, I felt the Giants had played fair with me.

There's one subject that I've saved until last. Ralph Branca. It wasn't always easy for the two of us in the first years after the play-offs. But I'll say this about Ralph—he didn't run away and hide. He was at the opening game of the World Series the very next day and posed for pictures with me. The most famous one shows him chok-ing me, me in my Giant uniform, Ralph in a coat and tie. We both attended the New York Sport Writers dinner in January of 1952 and as it turned out the two of us were the hit of the show. They put on a skit in which the writers played the parts of Durocher, Dressen, Stoneham, and O'Malley. Ralph and I played ourselves. It was a mu-sical spoof of my home run and I had to sing something about an inky dinky fly ball.

When I was going over the lyrics with Ed Efret, a sportswriter with *The New York Times,* I asked him what he meant by an "inky dinky fly."

He said, "You hit the home run and it rhymes, so what do you care?" The lyrics were sung to the melody of an old song, "Because of You." Mine were:

> Because of you, there's a song in my heart.
> Because of you, my technique is an art.
> Because of you, a fastball high
> Became an inky, dinky fly
> Now Leo and me-o won't part.
> My fame is sure, thanks to your Sunday pitch.
> Up high or low, I don't know which is which.
> But come next spring, keep throwing me that thing,
> And I will swing, because of you.

Then Ralph came on and sang his song. It must have been tougher for him. I can't recall all of his lyrics, but they had to do with the Dodger fans being forlorn and yelling drop dead and wanting his head. I'm not sure I could have sung those words, even in fun, and I admire him for going along with it. So did the writers. They gave him a rousing cheer for being such a good sport and, more than likely, for being a much better singer than I was.

It's odd, but for a while I was sometimes embarrassed by the home run. Maybe the embarrassment was because of Ralph. The first time I faced him the following year, the *last* thing I wanted to do was hit a home run. And I've often felt uneasy when I'd hear the Russ Hodges call of the homer at old-timers' games and other events.

People often ask me if the home run put pressure on me, whether I felt that expectations for Thomson were much higher after 1951. That's a tough one. If anything, the home run made me concentrate harder and gave me a feeling of confidence. I remember talking with Al Corbin about it. Al went to every game of the '51 World Series and he remembered a spot in the sixth game when the Giants had two on and I was up. He said he looked at his watch and it was almost four o'clock, almost the exact time I hit the homer off Branca. All admitted his first thought was: Wouldn't it be great if Bob could do it again?

Of course, I didn't. But when Al told me about this I realized there were probably a lot of other people thinking the same thing, waiting for lightning to strike again, and maybe again after that. And then Al said something that pretty much sums up what happened on October 3, 1951. He said it was a moment you can never repeat. And he's right. Once in a lifetime. Cloud nine. Maybe you can never repeat it, but baby, you can't take it away, either.

Epilogue

Shortly after the playoffs ended, Clyde Sukeforth was fired as a Dodger coach. Dodger watchers quickly pointed out that a year earlier, when the Dodgers were beaten by the Phils in the final game, coach Milt Stock was fired after waving Cal Abrams around third with the potential winning run only to have the slow-footed Abrams cut down at the plate.

Why did the Dodgers always seem to need a scapegoat? Several players already said that Sukeforth couldn't be blamed for tabbing Branca over Erskine. The evidence also would seem to indicate that Charley Dressen wasn't a pillar of strength during the last two innings of the final game.

Following the playoffs, there were many calls for Dressen's scalp. Charley wasn't exactly Mr. Popularity in the borough of Brooklyn. In fact, several hours after Thomson's blast had changed the course of baseball history, the Dodger manager was being hanged in effigy from a lamppost at 75th Street and Third Avenue in Flatbush. Yet while many of his late-season moves were being questioned, Walter O'Malley rehired Dressen to manage in 1952.

Before long, the recipient of *The Dressen Book of I* was up to his old tricks. In an article appearing in the *Saturday Evening Post* prior to the 1952 season, the once and future manager explained why the Dodgers wouldn't blow it again. But the first order of business was for Charley Dressen to take himself off the hook.

"[Just] ten minutes after the roof fell in on us, Walter O'Malley ... had told the players the defeat wasn't my fault and that I'd be back as manager," Charley wrote.

Dressen then went on to say that his ball club "was overrated last year. They weren't good enough to be out in front by thirteen and one-half games in August." Was he trying to say his managing had brought these underrated players their big lead? Duke Snider had said the Dodgers of 1951 were one of the great teams ever.

Statistically, the Brooks dominated the National League. They led the league in runs scored, doubles, home runs, team batting average, and slugging average. They were also tops in stolen bases, double plays, and in strikeouts by their pitching staff. Despite some late-season slumps, the ball club was still an offensive powerhouse.

Jackie Robinson explained the season's outcome by saying the "Giants caught lightning in a bottle." Ralph Branca explains it as a matter of "Dressen's mismanagement and the hitters not hitting." Others point to a tired pitching staff and a mediocre bench. Still others, such as Labine and Newcombe, simply say it was destined to happen and nothing could stop it. Who can really say?

It is generally agreed that, man-for-man, the Dodgers had a better team than the Giants in 1951. But that statement has to be qualified, too. Maybe Whitey Lockman explained it best.

"Over the long haul," said Lockman, "the record shows that the Dodgers had the best team of the entire era. But from August 12 to the end of the season in 1951, we were better than they were."

Dressen received some measure of vindication the next two years when his ball club won the National League pennant. Though they were beaten both times by the omnipresent Yanks in the World Series, Charley did have the satisfaction of piloting a winner. The 1952 Giants finished second, just 4½ games behind, despite losing Monte Irvin to a severely fractured ankle and Willie Mays to the army. Both were gone almost the entire year. Many baseball people feel Durocher did his greatest managing job to keep the club close that season. By 1953, however, the team had started to fade and changes were made. One result of those changes was Bobby Thomson's trade to Milwaukee for pitcher Johnny Antonelli. The final by-product was a pennant and World Series win for Durocher and the Giants in 1954 as Antonelli won 21 games.

By that time, Charley Dressen was gone. This complex man once again fell victim to his own stubbornness. Walter O'Malley had a tradition of giving his managers one-year contracts. Prior to the '54 season, Dressen suddenly insisted on a two-year pact. Some say that his wife was pushing him. She wasn't well at the time and wanted some additional security. But Carl Erskine, for one, has another.

"Charley left the Dodgers after a very successful three-year-run," Erskine says, "and the reason was his insistence on a two-year contract. The *only* reason he wanted a two-year deal was because Leo had just gotten one. He was still competing with Durocher and was staunch in his demand. He said he had a better year than Leo in 1953. When O'Malley was equally staunch in his refusal, it was Dressen who had to go."

Harold Parrott, the Dodger's longtime traveling secretary, had said that O'Malley wanted to replace Dressen all along and when Charley asked for the two-year deal, it gave the Big O the excuse he wanted. Parrott said O'Malley wouldn't return Dressen's phone calls, even when Charley finally relented and was willing to accept a one-year deal. By then, O'Malley had closed the door. Dressen was gone. O'Malley wasted no time in hiring a manager from the Dodgers' minor league organization. Walter Alston would pilot the Dodgers for the next 24 years . . . all of them on one-year contracts.

As for Charley Dressen, he was too good a baseball man to go quietly. He resurfaced as the manager of the Washington Senators in 1955 and promptly lost 101 games with an awful ball club. He couldn't turn the team around and was fired early in the 1957 season. He had a second-place finish with Milwaukee in 1960, then left after 1961, and took over the Detroit Tigers during the first third of the 1963 season. Charley guided the Tigers to a pair of fourth-place finishes the next two years, bringing them in above .500 each time. In 1966, in failing health, he left the team after just 26 games.

Charley Dressen finished his managerial career with 1,037 victories and 993 losses in 16 seasons, a winning percentage of .511. He died of a heart attack on August 10, 1966, a little over a month before his sixty-eighth birthday.

Leo Durocher continued to pilot the Giants through the 1955 season. The club won the pennant and World Series in 1954, then finished third the next year. However, all was not well within the Giant family. There had been rumors that Stoneham felt Leo was getting too much credit for the team's success as far back as 1951. When another rumor surfaced in 1954, claiming Leo had signed to be a broadcaster at NBC, Stoneham asked if Leo was walking out on his contract, which had one more year to run. Leo said no, but the relationship between manager and owner continued to sour.

The Giants finished a distant third to the Dodgers in 1955, and after the season ended Stoneham told Durocher the Giants were going to make a change, naming Bill Rigney the new manager. The Durocher era, which had begun so dramatically with the one-day switch from the Dodgers to the Giants in 1948, ended quietly and without fanfare in 1955.

The Lip would return to manage the Chicago Cubs from 1966 to midway through 1972, and finally the Houston Astros from late 1972 through 1973. By then the game was changing and so were the players. Never one to give an inch, Leon had more than his share of troubles with the modern, often pampered major leaguer. The players couldn't handle Leo's old-fashioned style of discipline and conversely, the manager couldn't handle the players' newfound feeling of independence.

As a manager, Leo Durocher won 2,010 games, losing 1,710 for a winning percentage of .540. Yet despite his success and longevity, he has never been voted into the Hall of Fame. Most of his former players and many of his opponents feel he belongs. Leo insists his exclusion from the Hall doesn't bother him. He lives in retirement in sunny California, as feisty and sharp-tongued as ever. In July of 1990, he celebrated his eighty-fifth birthday.

There was one final irony, a postscript to 1951, that involved Leo Durocher. After leaving the Giants in 1955, Leo returned to baseball as a coach with the Los Angeles Dodgers in the early 1960s. In 1962, the Dodgers under Walter Alston had another powerful team and were leading the San Francisco Giants for most of the season. Then, like 1951, the Giants caught them at the wire, necessitating another play-off.

It was a case of deja vu without the Thomson homer. The Dodgers led by two runs in the ninth inning of the third and final game, only to lose it once more. There were rumors afloat several times during the season that Leo was going to replace Alston, but it never happened. Finally, late in the year, Leo rebelled against Alston's conservative approach and as the third base coach began ignoring the

Dodger manager and flashing his own signs. He knew he would be fired for what he was doing, but he still had to do it his way.

Though Leo claims he never second-guessed Alston publicly, he also felt the 1962 Dodgers were a team that should not have lost. During the stretch run, Leo said, there were too many team meetings, too much criticism, too much dissecting and picking apart. Instead, the ball club—featuring the likes of Maury Wills, Tommy and Willie Davis, Frank Howard, Don Drysdale, and Sandy Koufax—should have been praised, built up, and allowed to play to the level of their natural talents. Sound familiar?

Willie Mays and Duke Snider were the only two leftovers from '51 still remaining on the 1962 teams. Unlike '51, Mays was itching to hit with the game on the line. He had become a full-fledged superstar, one of the greatest the game had ever seen.

A number of players performed for both the Dodgers and Giants during their careers. Durocher, of course, managed both teams. One player, however, refused to make such an ignominious change. When the Dodgers announced they had traded Jackie Robinson to the Giants prior to the 1957 season, Robby said no way. Instead of donning the enemy uniform, he simply retired. That's how strong Jackie's feelings ran.

One who did make the change was Sal Maglie. The Barber was picked up by the Brooks from the Cleveland Indians early in the 1956 season. At the age of 39, Maglie was close to brilliant. His 13–5 record helped bring Brooklyn another flag and he was the losing pitcher when Don Larsen of the Yanks threw his perfect game in the '56 Series. Larsen had to be perfect, because the Barber gave up just two runs.

Carl Erskine has never forgotten the first time he saw Maglie in a Brooklyn uniform. When I saw Sal standing in the clubhouse in a Dodger uniform," he recalls, "I said to myself there was nothing in this world that could ever surprise me again. That was such a fantastic turnaround, seeing Campy walk out to the mound with him, his arm around Sal's shoulder. Wow! Sal turned out to be a real gentleman. But whenever he pitched he was in charge. He was a hard-nosed professional who didn't give the opposition anything."

Years later, Maglie ran into Ralph Branca at a sports dinner and the two former pitchers wound up sitting together. Invariably, the conversation came around to 1951. Ralph told the Barber why he had come inside with the second pitch, the one Thomson hit. He was trying to set Bobby up for the curveball, low and away.

"Maglie and I had become friends when he joined the Dodgers in 1956," Branca says. "But Sal had never talked about '51 with me before. And when I told him what I was trying to do that day, he looked at me and said, 'If you wanted him to hit the curve, why didn't you just throw him the damned curve?' It was something to think about."

Of course, any great event is second-guessed, and this one is no exception. There are still those who feel Dressen should have walked Thomson to load the bases, even if it meant putting the potential winning run on base. After all, Willie Mays, a nervous rookie, was on deck and none of Durocher's pinch hitters was wielding the same kind of hot bat that Bobby Thomson was.

Both Durocher and Monte Irvin have commented that Campanella might have been the difference behind the plate. "Campy would have called time and told Ralph to keep the ball down and away, not to give Bobby anything inside," Irvin has said. "Ralph was an outstanding competitor. He just threw the wrong pitch."

"Campy was a great catcher," said Durocher. "He knew the hitters and was very smart back there. I was very happy when they never brought Roy into the game."

Yet Branca refuses to place any blame on Rube Walker. "Rube was a helluva receiver, at least the equal of Campanella as a defensive catcher," Branca said. "I pitched three shutouts in August and Rube caught all three. Almost all the games he caught were low-run games. Remember that game against Pittsburgh when I was going for a no-hitter and I lost it on a Baltimore chop in the ninth? The only base hit came after I shook off Rube and threw the pitch I wanted."

Wes Westrum, the Giant catcher, knows exactly what he would have done if he had been behind the plate with Bobby batting. "If I was catching Branca I would figure it this way," said Wes. "Branca didn't have the best curveball in the world. He was a notorious fast-ball pitcher. What I would have done is set up on the outside and dared the hitter to try to pull the outside fastball. I would not allow my pitcher to fool around with the inside part of the plate, not at the Polo Grounds with that short porch and not when I had first base open."

It goes on and on. What if? It's fun, but it won't change history. By the same token, the so-called miracle ending to the 1951 National League pennant race cannot be broken down to the simplest terms— hero and goat. Things don't work that way. It's safe to say that Ralph Branca got a lot of other people off the hook when he served up the most famous gopher ball in the history of the game. He made it easy for everyone. You threw the ball, Ralph. You did it! Sure, Ralph Branca threw the pitch and has had to live with it ever since. But he was just a small part of a much larger story.

The Dodger team of the 1950s *was* the best National League team of its era and maybe of any era. The nucleus of the team stayed together for a decade and they were always winners. As of 1991, four members of the 1951 Brooklyn Dodgers—Jackie Robinson, Roy Campanella, Duke Snider, and Pee Wee Reese—have been enshrined in the Base-ball Hall of Fame. That's half the starting lineup. Two other starters, Gil Hodges and Carl Furillo, were close to Hall of Fame caliber as well.

By the same token, the 1951 Giants have just two players in the Hall—Willie Mays and Monte Irvin. Irvin's induction was as much for his play in the Negro Leagues as in the majors. There were surely other outstanding players on that Giant team, but most didn't have the successful and lengthy careers of their Dodger counterparts.

To win the way they did, the Giant team had to have as much character as it did talent. Qualities of character and leadership stem from the manager. For the men who toiled under Leo Durocher, these qualities were communicable. The result was described by Wes Westrum.

"The 1951 Giants were probably the greatest ball club on which I ever played. Leo was a strict disciplinarian. When he put the uniform on he was all business. He knew baseball. He was always one or two plays ahead of every situation. He made sure he had good coaches and listened to them.

"We must have all learned something from him. Think about it. Five players from that team went on to become major league managers, and two more were pitching coaches. Jansen and Maglie were the coaches, while Dark, Rigney, Lockman, Stanky, and myself all managed in the big leagues at one time or another. I think it's pretty amazing that so many of us coached and managed. We had to have some good teaching, and it was Leo who taught us. I know I took a page out of Leo's book when I managed. I think we all did."

Though a number of the players from the 1951 Giants and Dodgers are gone now, those who remain still think about those closing weeks of the pennant race. They can't help it. Bobby Thomson's Shot Heard Round the World is one of baseball's most memorable events, especially in the nostalgia-filled climate of the 1990s. Whenever one of these men attends a dinner, a card show, or an old-timer's game, he's invariably asked about the home run, about Bobby and Ralph, Leo and Charley, the New York Giants and Brooklyn Dodgers. Why was it all so special?

"I think there are a number of reasons the 1951 season is remembered so well," Pee Wee Reese said. "To begin with, the Dodgers and Giants had a great rivalry. And blowing a 13½ game lead isn't something that happens every day. I also think there was a certain mystique about the Dodgers. Jackie was the first black, we had the Sym-Phony band, fans like Hilda Chester that everyone knew, and Ebbets Field. There was just something special about it.

"And I don't think there can ever be two clubs with our kind of rivalry again. It can't happen. It's gone forever."

Whitey Lockman sees nostalgia as a big reason 1951 has never been forgotten. "It's the nature of the sport," he explained. "People are very nostalgic about records, about the big events in the game, and it's at a fever pitch right now. Even younger people bring Bobby's home run up wherever I go. In fact, they remember pretty much the entire inning. I never start the discussions about it, but invariably someone else will."

Don Newcombe says, "When the Giants and Dodgers moved to the West Coast in 1958, the rivalry immediately became a watered-down version of the real thing. There wasn't the closeness anymore. That was something germane to New York and Brooklyn, something that will remain there forever and, if necessary, be buried there. It's only in our memories now and that's one reason 1951 is remembered so clearly."

Duke Snider is another who feels it was the uniqueness of the Dodgers that has helped preserve not only the rivalry, but Bobby Thomson's homer. "People are always talking about where they were and what they were doing when Bobby hit the home run," says the Duke. "Brooklyn fans still love the memories of their Brooklyn Dodgers and their children seem to cherish those memories, as well. Many

Mets fans were frustrated Dodger fans looking for a new team. The true Dodger fan could simply not become a Yankee fan."

But perhaps it was Clem Labine, more than any other player, who really caught the essence of 1951. A Rhode Island native, Labine has always held a special place in his heart for Brooklyn. He even made it a point to return when Ebbets Field fell victim to the wrecking ball. Since then, he has always thought long and hard about the 1950s, about Brooklyn, and about the Dodgers.

"The borough of Brooklyn has suffered like no other because of their big league team leaving," Labine says. "In a sense, I've always felt that 1951 was a kind of last hurrah, even moreso than the World Series victory in 1955. The reason is the relationship not just between the two ball clubs but between the two boroughs themselves, Brooklyn and Manhattan. I've gone back to Brooklyn a number of times after the Dodgers left for California. Those people lost something that was irreplaceable. The ball club was part of their badge of honor, something they practically wore. Then they lost it and can never get it back.

"For that reason, I've always felt that 1951 was remembered more by Brooklyn fans than by Giant fans, and the memory of the Dodgers has helped to keep it alive. Even today the Brooklyn Dodgers have what you might call a cult following. So all big events are remembered and Bobby's home run has to rank very high."

Interestingly enough, it is the former Dodger players who speak of the special qualities of Brooklyn, the only borough ever to have a big league team named for it. Giant players and others talk of the rivalry, nostalgia, card shows, memorabilia, and the continued interest in baseball history and tradition. When told about Labine's comment, Bobby Thomson said he felt there were still enough former New York Giant fans around to say the old club has a kind of cult following of its own. But Thomson acknowledged once more that the closeness of Brooklyn, the community feeling that permeated the entire borough back in the 1950s, did set the Dodgers apart. Even Bob's wife, Winkie, acknowledged it.

"There is something about living in Brooklyn, about being born and raised there, that never leaves a person," Mrs. Thomson said. "I came to realize that during the years the Giants played the Dodgers. There must have been something very special about being a kid in Brooklyn back then. Having been a ball player's wife and traveling all around the league, I really don't think there could be any other situation in baseball that can compare to this special group of people who grew up in Brooklyn.

"Back in 1951 I had no understanding of this, didn't really think about it. But as the years passed and people began talking about the home run again, and Bob began seeing Ralph more often and going to more events, I slowly began to realize that the Dodgers were a special ball club. You can really see why the finish to the 1951 season was such a terrible thing for the team and for Brooklyn."

Spanish writer Miguel de Cervantes, author of *Don Quixote,* once wrote, "There's a time for some things, and a time for all things; a time for great things, and a time for small things."

The 1951 National League pennant race was just such a time. It provided some things, like the great individual battles between the likes of Maglie and Robinson, Durocher and Dressen. It also gave the baseball world all things, an unparalleled pennant race that involved two boroughs in the same city and two teams that aroused the passions in each other in a way that has never happened again.

Then there were the small things, such as Thomson taking over at third base or Labine going into Dressen's doghouse, that ultimately influenced the outcome of the race. And finally there were great things, especially at the end, such as Robinson's diving catch and clutch home run to save it, then Bobby Thomson's epic home run to win it. A time for everything.

As Clem Labine said, it was a last hurrah. Time has healed many of the old wounds. Though the Dodgers will forever remain in the hearts of many Brooklyn residents, they can now forgive some of their old adversaries. Bobby Thomson dealt Brooklyn a blow still vivid, still remembered. Yet today, Bobby is a proud member of the Brooklyn Dodger Hall of Fame, ensconced alongside Stan Musial and others in a recently added category labeled "Friendly Enemies."

But, forgiveness goes only so far. Irving Rudd recently made mention of the Dodger Hall of Fame, saying that Bobby Thomson was such a super nice guy he deserved the recognition. But Rudd noted there was someone not yet in the Dodger Hall, someone conspicuous by his absence.

"It always kind of surprised me," Rudd said, "but Durocher isn't there. They never voted Leo in."

 **BOBBY**

Closing the Book

I remember reading that Bill Russell, the great basketball star with the Boston Celtics, once said that all professional athletes have been on scholarship since the third grade. In many ways he's right. We have so many things done for us that we can become spoiled and pampered. It keeps us from facing reality, the kind that hits you when you retire.

—Bobby Thomson

I don't think I truly appreciated the work ethic until I retired from baseball. But work after baseball gave me a different kind of satisfaction than I got from playing the game. It was like moving into a new world and a much broader life. After tests indicated an aptitude for sales, I interviewed various companies for three months before finally taking a job with a paper company in New York called Westvaco.

It wasn't easy at the beginning, because I had to do things I had never done before. I had to face up to responsibilities such as speaking in front of groups. As a ball player, I generally shied away from anything I found difficult.

I worked for Westvaco for over 25 years, from 1960 through 1986, and was always very proud of this fine company and the qualities it stood for. Then Stone Container, a Chicago-based integrated paper company, bought the Westvaco division in which I worked. With Stone, it became a whole new ball game. Though I was still a salesman, they decided to treat me more like Bobby Thomson than Robert Thomson—as the former ball player who hit the "Shot Heard Round the World."

Recent years have brought about a changing climate for former ball players, with the increasing interest in baseball nostalgia, in card shows and memorabilia, in athletes used as commercial spokesmen and celebrities. I have to admit I feel good about the way my role with Stone has refocused my life. It's fun being Bobby Thomson again.

Looking back, I often wonder what makes the years pass so quickly. I was once the youngest of six children; we are now only four after the passing of my brother, Jim, and more recently my sister, Marion. The family, however, is not getting any smaller. I have two wonderful grandchildren. Nieces and nephews keep popping up and it's not always easy to keep track of them all.

I often think of my parents and the chance they took when they came to America, the land of opportunity. My one regret is that Dad did not live to see me play for the Giants. Even though he was a great Dodger fan, I'm sure he would have forgiven me for the October 3 home run.

Looking back now, I can remember the night after the game, after I had gone on the "Perry Como Show" and returned to Staten Island alone. I walked into the firehouse to see my brother. His words mean so much more now than they did even then.

"Bobby, do you realize what you did today?" Jim said to me so long ago. "Do you realize something like this may never happen again!"

No, I didn't realize it then. It has taken me a long time, all of 40 years. But Jim, you were right. It was special and it can never happen just that way again.

Afterword
by Ralph Branca

It's hard to believe that 40 years have passed since that October day when I stood on the mound at the Polo Grounds facing Bobby Thomson. With everything that's happened since, there's one thing that still amazes me. I can be at a sports dinner, a card show, or a golf tournament with Bobby, having a good time, and someone will invariably come up to me and say: "You talk to him!"

Funny how some people think we should be mortal enemies for life. Yet, in truth, Bobby Thomson is not only a friend, he's one of my best friends. We spend a great deal of time together, both with baseball matters and socially. In fact, I talk to him more often than I do any other former player from my big league days. But I have to admit it wasn't always this way and it wasn't always easy.

It was tougher in the earlier years, especially when I was still playing. I was an intense competitor who always wanted the ball. That's why I was in the bullpen that day, even though I had pitched eight tough innings on Monday and two innings of relief the day before that in Philadelphia. It was my competitiveness that made the whole thing difficult to live with. There were always people ready to say, "Branca lost the pennant."

I was in a situation where I was taking the blame for losing the pennant when in truth we shouldn't have even been in a playoff. We had a 13½-game lead and I certainly didn't lose all the games from that point on. Maybe Rocky Bridges, who was the Dodgers' backup shortstop in 1951, put it best when he said we lost the pennant because we lost on opening day. It's a very simple statement but it happens to be true. Games in April count. One loss then is the same as one loss in September. And one less loss and there wouldn't have been a playoff.

I'm far from a Shakespeare buff, but I remembered reading a quotation from *Julius Caesar.* "The evil that men do lives after them, the good is oft interred with their bones." So be it with Caesar; so be it with Branca. How many people remember that I was the youngest guy in the National League to win 20 games in a season until Dwight Gooden did it 38 years later? I was 21 years old when I won 21 in 1947. In fact, I won 48 games in three years despite missing parts of both the 1948 and 1949 seasons with an arm problem. Yet I still made the All-Star team in 1947, 1948, and 1949, as well as the *Sporting News* All-Star team, along with Bob Feller, in 1947.

But I gave up the homer to Bobby and that's what people remember. Not too long ago a sportswriter compared my situation to that of an alcoholic. He said, "An alcoholic is an alcoholic until the day they put him in the ground." He's probably right. In the same sense, I'm going to hear about Bobby's homer until the day they put me in the grave.

People read about what happened and say Branca lost the pennant. Baseball records say the Dodger hitters didn't hit the last seven weeks. No one credits the Giants, who were 37–7 in the last 44 games. That's one heck of a stretch run. They weren't a bunch of lollipops over there. Durocher had a fine ball club and the Giants, in turn, had the best manager in baseball then.

Leo was my guy, my first manager, and the best I ever played for. Had he stayed in Brooklyn I'm convinced we would have won in 1948, 1949, 1950, 1951, 1952, and 1953. What I'm really saying is that had Leo not moved from the Dodgers to the Giants in 1948, the Dodgers would have won without a playoff in '51, and I wouldn't be doing an afterword to Bobby Thomson's book. Perhaps in a strange kind of way then, it was good for baseball that Leo changed teams. Because the '51 season—the way it unfolded and ended—has become maybe the most memorable pennant race and single most dramatic moment in baseball history.

As the years passed, the home run kept coming up again and again. I remember in 1976, I went to old-timers' days in Texas and San Diego. It was the twenty-fifth anniversary of Bobby's home run that year and in both places they played Russ Hodges's famous call: *"The Giants win the pennant! The Giants win the pennant!"* They didn't tell me ahead of time because they probably figured I would veto it. I remember Pee Wee Reese coming over to me after they played it and saying, "Man, you must be awful sick of that stuff," And, in truth, I was.

It seemed to ease off somewhat after that. There are still some painful moments now and then. I have to admit I still get annoyed when I'm introduced to some guy and the first thing he says is, "Oh, yeah, Bobby Thomson."

Of course, right after the game I was devastated by what had happened. But so were the rest of the Dodgers. After all, we had gone from a 13½-game lead in mid-August to losing the pennant in the last inning of the last game. But once that initial emotion passed and I came to accept the defeat and the way it happened, I was okay.

What also helped was meeting my wife's cousin, who was waiting with her after the game. He was a priest, Father Frank "Pat" Rowley, and I guess I asked the question that had to be asked sooner or later: Why me? I told him I didn't drink or smoke, and was always in shape ready to play. So why me? And he simply said, "Maybe God chose you because *He* knew your faith would be enough to bear this cross." That helped me immensely. Then Ann and I joined Rube Walker and his wife for dinner at a steak restaurant, Paul Daube's, up in the Bronx.

I can't recall much of the conversation, but I remember the restaurant, the sawdust on the floor and the steaks hanging in a glass case. I still had the feeling that, hey, it's over. We lost. But that initial pain I felt in the locker room was already gone, thanks to Father Rowley.

Another reason I think the pain left so quickly was because I truly felt I had done my best and Bobby just hit a home run. He was the better man that day. The one thing all professional athletes know is that no one goes undefeated. You win some and you lose some. One of the toughest things you've got to learn is not to take the game home with you, to leave it behind. It's over and done with, but if you are overly competitive, which I was, and probably still am, it's a very hard thing to do.

Yet it wasn't even that bad the next few years. I had a back injury in 1952 and my main concern after that was trying to prove to myself and to others that I could still pitch. Psychologically and mentally I was ready, but unfortunately, I couldn't do it physically. Because I struggled, I was more concerned with my own being, my own preservation, to see if I could still pitch competitively. But after I retired, those first few years were rough, especially with Bobby.

Maybe it was all still too close because the memory became painful again. I guess I hadn't proven to others that the home run had not affected me adversely. During that time I didn't want to be around Bobby and I believe he felt uncomfortable around me. Then, maybe 10 or 12 years after it happened, we began to see each other more often and started becoming friends.

On my part, I think the friendship began growing out of a gradual respect for the way Bobby handled the whole thing. At first, we were both a little reluctant, a little hesitant. But as we got to know each other, something just began growing between us and I think it became a kind of mutual respect. It wasn't any one incident. We just kept running into each other more often, doing baseball-related things together, and we got to be friends.

Now, I can honestly say that if somebody had to hit that home run, I'm glad it was Bobby Thomson. I'm not so sure how some other guys would have handled it. Bobby has never bragged or gloated over his achievement. He's carried himself with grace and class all the way. In fact, even today Bobby tells people he was lucky to hit a home run and lucky to hit it in that spot. And he means it. That's how he sincerely feels.

About that fateful pitch. I was not then, or ever, ashamed that I threw it. Disappointed? Yes. Ashamed? No. I took my best shot; so did Bobby. I'm sorry it happened to me, but since it did, I'm glad it was Bobby who did it.

Of course I've said many times over the years that if I had it to do all over again, I'd gladly give everything back to just strike Bobby out. I wouldn't be human if I didn't feel that way.

So what was it? Fate? Destiny? Who knows? There are so many things that had to be just right. And if you want to play "What if?" here's something that may surprise you.

I grew up in Mt. Vernon, just north of New York City. To get to Brooklyn from there . . . forget it. So I was a big Giant fan all the while I was growing up. When I was 16, my brother, John, who was the star pitcher for A. B. Davis High, was chosen as the pitcher for the *New York Journal American* High School All-Star Team. He went for a tryout with the Giants and I went along with him, hoping to show my stuff, just like any other 16-year-old kid. But there were 300 to 400 guys there and I never got the chance. A year later, it was the Dodgers who signed me.

Yes, there have been painful moments. But knowing Bobby Thomson and being his friend have helped ease the pain over the years. Just recently, Bobby and I were invited to the same golf tournament. It was the kind of setup where you could sit with anybody, but Bobby and I sat together. Neither one of us thought twice about it. That should really tell you the kind of relationship we have today.

A Note About the Controversy

Through the years, Bobby Thomson's Shot-Heard-Round-the-World home run has continued to be one of baseball's most legendary moments, an achievement revisited and replayed time and again. Since I first began writing *The Giants Win the Pennant! The Giants Win the Pennant!* more than ten years ago, Bobby's pennant-winning homer seems to have gained even more mythical proportions. In the eyes of many, it now ranks as the single most dramatic moment in all of baseball history.

That's why many longtime baseball fans, as well as the surviving participants from the 1951 pennant race, looked forward to the events of 2001. After all, this would be the fiftieth anniversary of a season never to be forgotten, and one, because of the demographics of the game back then, that could never again be duplicated. Before moving to the West Coast in 1957, the *Brooklyn* Dodgers and *New York* Giants were the only two teams in the same league playing in the same city at the same time. Over the years, that made for the most intense rivalry in all of sports.

Thus 2001 promised to be a gala celebration. With a half century having passed, the legend was larger than ever. Bobby Thomson and Ralph Branca, forever linked in baseball lore, had also become good friends and fully anticipated sitting on the podium at more than one dinner, sharing the microphone during countless numbers of interviews, and being on the dais together as the testimonials to that remarkable season of long ago continued.

The celebration was slated to begin on Sunday, February 4, when Thomson and Branca would appear together at two separate events, the New Jersey Sports Writers Association Banquet at Edison, and later that night at the seventy-eighth dinner of the New York chapter of the Baseball Writers Association of America, at the Sheraton Hotel in Manhattan. Then, just three days before the dual fetes, a story came out in the *Wall Street Journal* that, while not exactly surprising those who knew the game of the 1940s and 1950s, sent the writers scrambling for the telephones and racing to their computers. This was hot copy, a story that would open the entire pennant drive in 1951, as well as the Thomson home run, to a whole new series of conjectures and speculations.

The *Journal* story said, flat out, that the Giants were stealing signs at home games during the second half of the season, when they overcame the Dodgers apparently insurmountable thirteen and a half game lead. Only they weren't doing it the old-fashioned way, with runners reaching second trying to pick off the catcher's signals to the pitcher, then relaying them to the hitter. No, the story said that the Giants went high-tech for their time, stationing someone in the distant centerfield clubhouse at the Polo Grounds with a high-powered telescope, then buzzing the signals to the Giants bullpen, where they were relayed to the hitter. So, in effect, the Giants hitters knew whether to expect a fastball or an offspeed pitch, in those days usually a curve.

The scheme was hatched by none other than manager Leo Durocher, a guy who admittedly always looked for the edge, for new ways to win baseball games. The story also said that several people, including coach Herman Franks, relayed signals from the Giants clubhouse to the bullpen with a buzzer system created by an electrician named Abraham Chadwick. Second-string catcher Sal Yvars then relayed the signals to the batter, a scenario that Yvars readily confirms.

"Everything is true," the seventy-seven-year-old Yvars said, when asked about the story. "I'm the villain. I'm surprised it didn't come out sooner. People didn't want to believe it. . . . Between you and me, we had every damn sign."

When the next pitch was buzzed to the bullpen from the clubhouse, Yvars took it from there. He said that he told his teammates, "Watch me in the bullpen. I'll have a baseball in my hand. If I do nothing, it's a fastball. If I toss the ball in the air, it's a breaking ball."

Monte Irvin, the Giants star left fielder in 1951, also confirmed the *Journal* story. "Leo asked me if I wanted the signs," Irvin, now eighty-two, said. 'Wouldn't you want to know when a big fat fastball was coming?' was the way he put it. I said, 'Yeah, if I was one-hundred-percent sure; nobody is.' "

Apparently, there were some who were shocked and surprised by the revelation, perhaps more so because the story broke in such a normally staid publication as the *Wall Street Journal*. However, nearly everyone involved with the game back then knew that sign stealing was almost expected, the norm as opposed to the exception. In fact, it wasn't even illegal. Players on second base were stealing signs for years; still do. Using a telescope from the clubhouse might have raised the bar, but while it was considered by many to be unethical, it broke no rules. Baseball didn't outlaw stealing signs by mechanical means until 1961.

When researching this book more than a decade ago, I had no trouble finding people willing to talk about the stealing of signs. Dick Williams, a rookie with the Dodgers in 1951, told me that "Leo definitely had a guy in a clubhouse stealing signs with a spyglass. He'd beep it to one of their guys in the bullpen, who would then relay it in." (See p. 178.)

Walker Cooper, who was with the Giants from 1947 to 1949 said he recalled a game when the Giants were playing the Cubs. "We were calling their signs from our clubhouse and they were stealing our signs from their clubhouse," Coop said. Then he added, "In Comiskey Park (home of the American League White Sox) they used to have a guy out in the scoreboard stealing signs. The guy would use a towel to signal his team. Believe me, Leo wasn't the only manager in the league with a spotter."

Most of the old-timers agree that even with the signs, the batters couldn't hit a hot pitcher. As one scribe pointed out, you don't win sixteen straight (as the Giants did) because somebody is relaying signs via a telescope. That doesn't help the pitchers to get outs and the fielders to make plays. It was also pointed out that the Giants won fourteen of their final eighteen road games that year, where there was no telescope, just the conventional means of runners on second trying to pilfer signs.

Yet the story quickly became front-page during the hot-stove days of early February, just as the first forays of celebration and remembrance were beginning to mark the fiftieth anniversay of Bobby Thomson's home run. How then, did the story affect the two main protagonists, Bobby and Ralph Branca?

At first glance, it would seem that Bobby had more to lose. As the hero who hit a home run for the ages, a natural question suddenly arose: "Did he know what pitch was coming?" For Ralph Branca, who had a half century of wearing perhaps the largest pair of goat horns ever given a baseball player, the specter of a stolen sign could definitely take some of the length from those horns. Now these two men, inexorably linked in diamond history would have to deal with the issue of stolen signs. Some wondered if it would put a strain on their relationship.

"I've known [about the sign stealing] since 1954," Branca admitted, "but I never said anything. When I was traded to Detroit that year, a guy on the Tigers who had a friend who played on the nineteen fifty-one Giants told me about the sign stealing. But until now, Sal Yvars . . . was the only other guy who ever mentioned it to me.

"When I was told, I knew I would never say anything," Branca continued. "I would sound like a sore loser. For one thing, as time went on, [the home run] became one of the legendary moments in sports, and I didn't want to tarnish it. Two, Bobby became a good friend, and he's a humble guy with good values; I don't want to tarnish what he did; I think he hit a tough pitch."

At the same time, however, Branca admits that the story provides him enough of a crack in the door to put a foot through. "I'm ambivalent," he said. "I don't think it ruins the number-one moment in baseball history, but it opens it up for me to talk. I'm glad to talk. I get tired of being introduced as a good pitcher who's known for throwing one pitch."

Because of the way Branca has handled the albatross he has always had to wear, no one can blame him for taking even an ounce of satisfaction from the furor surrounding the story. As for Bobby, he suddenly found himself caught between the proverbial rock and a hard place. He knew he would be asked about it, and he answered in his usual honest, somewhat humble manner.

"Sure, I've taken signs," he admitted quickly, "obviously, in the not-very-nice way the Giants did it. Stealing signs is nothing to be proud of."

At the New Jersey Sports Writers banquet the two met for the first time since the story broke. They greeted each other immediately, then walked away to speak privately for a few minutes.

"It was like getting something off my chest after all these years," Bobby said. "I'm not a criminal, although I may have felt like one at first."

"It's been a cleansing for both of us," Branca said. "He knew that I knew. It's better this way."

Yet Thomson maintains that he didn't have the signs in that last at bat, the one that produced the Shot Heard Round the World.

"It would take a little away from me in my mind if I got help on the pitch," Bobby said. "My answer is no. I was too busy concentrating on what I had to do when I got to the plate. I told myself, 'Give yourself a chance to hit, you son of a bitch.' I got back to fundamentals. I waited and watched for my pitch, and I was always proud of that swing."

Will the story take some of the gloss from this magical baseball moment? Probably not. If anything, it might make Ralph Branca a little less of a goat, but it shouldn't diminish Bobby Thomson's stature as a cult hero. The Shot Heard Round the World will continue to be ranked as one of baseball's most dramatic moments. In addition, the entire story leading up to and including the 1951 pennant race remains a totally fascinating one, its genesis going back some twenty years with a myriad of subplots and a whole cast of interesting and multi-layered characters. Stealing signs was a small and accepted part of the tale, just a piece of the puzzle that would lead to the final moment, with Ralph Branca getting ready to pitch and Bobby Thomson standing at the plate.

Bill Gutman
Dover Plains, New York